Bodoland

A Study of NDFB's Struggle for Bodo Autonomy

Dr. Nabin Hakhrari (1982-) is presently an Assistant Professor in the Department of Political Science at Bodofa U.N. Brahma College, Kokrajhar, Assam. He obtained his Ph.D. from North-Eastern Hill University, Shillong, Meghalaya. He has to his credit a good number of research papers published in various journals and magazines of repute. Also he has presented papers in many national and international seminars. His area of study includes "Ethno based-insurgency in India's Northeast region."

Bodoland

A Study of NDFB's Struggle for Bodo Autonomy

Nabin Hakhrari
Ph.D.

AVI Publishers

Second Impression 2022

Cataloging in Publication Data--DK
Courtesy: D.K. Agencies (P) Ltd. <docinfo@dkagencies.com>

Hakhrari, Nabin, 1982- **author.**
Bodoland : a study of NDFB's struggle for Bodo autonomy / Nabin Hakhrari.
pages cm
Includes bibliographical references and index.
Includes bibliographical references (p.) and index.
ISBN 13: 978-81-927021-3-1 (HBD)

1. Bodo (Indic people)--India--Assam--Politics and government. 2. Assam (India)--History--Autonomy and independence movements. 3. National Democratic Front of Bodoland. I. Title.

DS432.B63H35 DDC 305.800954162 23

Published by:
Avi Publishers
A-18, Mohan Garden
Near Nawada Metro Station
New Delhi–110 059
Phone: +91-98100-89095

Email: info@avipublishers.com
Web: www.avipublishers.com

Printed at: D.K. Fine Art Press Pvt. Ltd., New Delhi

Dedicated to

my parents

Mr.Chandra Hakhrari

Mrs. Padmeswari Thakuria

who provided my rights to see this world

Contents

Abbreviations

AAGSP	All Assam GanaSangramParishad
AAPTL	All Assam Plains Tribal League
AASU	All Assam Students' Union
ABPF	All Bodo Peace Forum
ABSU	All Bodo Students' Union
ABWJF	All Bodo Women's Justice Forum
ABWWF	All Bodo Women's' Welfare Federation
AFSPA	Armed Forces Special Powers Act
AGP	Assam GanaParishad
ATWWF	All Tribal Women's Welfare Federation
BAC	Bodo Autonomous Council
BDLP	Bodoland Demand Legislative Party
BdSF	Bodo Security Force
BLTF	Bodo Liberation Tigers Force
BNC	Bodo National Convention
BNPCC	Bodo National Peace and Co-ordination Committee
BPAC	Bodo People's Action Committee
BPP	Bodo People's Party
BSMC	Bodoland Statehood Movement Council
BSS	Bodo Sahitya Sabha
BTC	Bodoland Territorial Council
BVF	Bodo Volunteer Force
NDFB	National Democratic Front of Bodoland
NDFB-P	National Democratic Front of Bodoland-Progressive
NDFB-R	National Democratic Front of Bodoland-Ranjan
NDFB-S	National Democratic Front of Bodoland-Sangbijit
NSCN	National Socialist Council of Nagaland
PDF	People's Democratic Front
PJACBM	Peoples Joint Action Committee for Bodoland Movement
PLAM	People's Liberation Army of Manipur

PTCA	Plains Tribal Council of Assam
PTCA-P	Plains Tribal Council of Assam-Progressive
SJSS	Sanmilita Janagosthiya Sangram Samittee
UBNLF	United Bodo Nationalist Liberation Front
ULFA	United Liberation Front of Assam
UPDF	United People's Democratic Front
UTNLF	United Tribal Nationalists Liberation Front
YBNA	Youth Bodo Nationalist Association
YPTCA	Young Plains Tribal Council of Assam

List of Tables

List of Figures

1

Introduction: Concepts and Issues

The Bodos are the most numerous and widely spread plains tribe in the north-eastern region of India. According to E. A. Gait, they are "the aborigines or the earliest known inhabitants of the Brahmaputra Valley".[1] Their original home is believed to have existed somewhere between the 'Yang-Tse-Kiang' and the 'Hwang-Ho' rivers in China. It is believed that several hundred years ago, they had migrated to Assam, North Bengal and to 'Tipperah' in the West.[2] The Bodos are a part of the Kachari race and they are referred to as 'Bodo' or 'Bodo-fisa' in the Brahmaputra Valley and 'Dimasa' or 'Dima-fisa' or sons of the great river in the North Cachar Hills.[3] It is known from history that just before the advent of the Ahoms into Assam i.e. in the beginning of the 13th century A.D., the Kachari reigned over the western part of Sibsagar district, the present Nagaon district and the northern part of the Cachar district, with their capital at Dimapur. Later, unable to resist the Ahom invasions, they shifted their capital to Maibong in North-Cachar hills, but even Maibong was not spared by the Ahoms and finally the Kacharis were driven to the plains of Cachar where they established their new capital at Khaspur. That line of the Kachari race, which settled in North Cachar hills,is called 'Dimasa' and the other line, which settled in the Valley of Brahmaputra,is referred to as 'Bodos'.[4] S.K. Chatterjee places them in the 'Indo-Mongoloid' group in his '*Kirata-Jana-Kriti*' to connote "at once their Indian connection and their place within the cultural milieu in which they found themselves as well as their racial affinity."[5]

Who is Called Bodo

The word 'Bodo' is also called 'Boro'. In Bodo language, the letter 'd' or 't' is (in some cases) also pronounced as 'r' e.g. gidid (big) as 'gidir', 'khat' (to run) as 'khar', 'thalit' (banana) as 'thalir', 'lid' (washing of house by mud) as 'lir' etc.[6] G.A. Grierson used the term 'Bodo' in his *Linguistic Survey of India 1903*. He included Meches, Sonowals, Boros, Tripuris, Deuris and Koches within the term Bodo. Some scholars use the term 'Bodo' to refer to only those people who are known as Boros. Others use the term to include all the Tibeto-Burman speaking people of Sino-Tibetan origin, except Kuki-Chin. To them, the Boros, Koches, Rabhas, Lalungs, Hajongs, Chutiyas, Meches, Dhimals and Sonowals of Brahmaputra Valley and North-Bengal, the Dimasas of North Cachar Hills, the Tripuris of Tripura and the Garos of Meghalaya belong to the Bodo race.[7]

Over the years, there have been many controversies about the clan and sub-clan, origin and about the status of the Bodos. However, for the purpose of the present study, the term 'Bodo' is used to mean the Boro speaking people of Brahmaputra Valley, particularly the area that the NDFB has been demanding as Bodoland. Other Bodo speaking people like Garo, Rabha, Dimasa, Tripuris, Hajong and Deurisare not covered by the term "Bodo" in the present study.

It is important to point out that although the term 'ethnic' is commonly used in the northeast region to refer to the groups of people with distinct cultural characteristics, such a use does not reflect the reality that these groups are in different stages of nationality formation.[8] In the first stage of ethnicity, a cultural group differentiates itself from other groups, but remains politically insignificant. In the second stage, political consciousness of cultural identity evolves leading to the pursuit and protection of community interests. In the ultimate stage of nationality formation, right to self-determination sought to be asserted through political action and political mobilization.[9] Baruah argues in this connection that the Asomiyas, the Bengalis, the Khasis, the Bodos, the Mizos, the Nagas and even the Karbis appear to have become nationalities demanding the political right to control their own affairs.[10]

Demographic Profile of Bodos in Assam

A large number of ethnic groups are residing in the state of Assam. According to the Census of India, 1991, Bodos have the largest population among the total Scheduled Tribes Population of Assam (as shown in Figure 1.1). Bodos cover nearly 41.12% of the total Scheduled Tribes population and Deori covers only 1.14%.

Fig. 1.1 Percentage-wise distribution of Scheduled Tribes, 1991

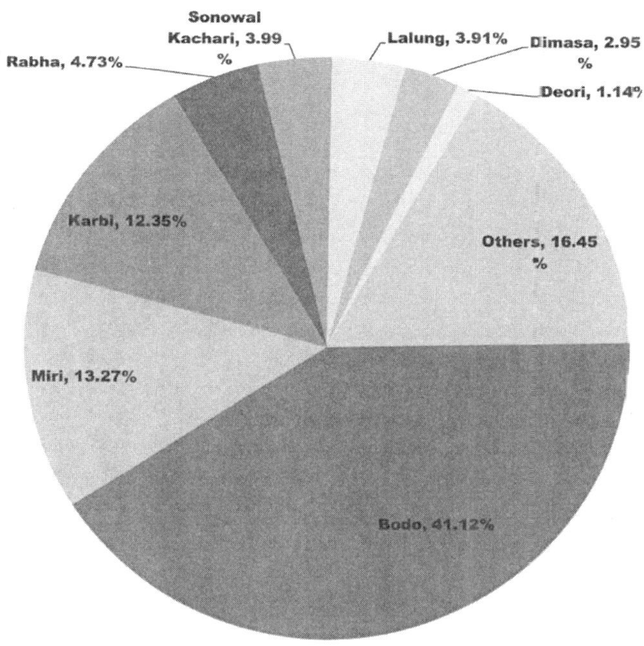

Source: Census Report 1991[11]

The Census of India 2001 has recorded as 33,08,570 accounting for 12.41% of total Assam's population. The decadal growth rate of tribal population in the state is estimated as 15.15% as compared to 18.92% of total state population growth. Among the main tribes of Assam, Bodos and Miris together account for roughly half of the total tribal population of the state.[12] Bodos alone constitute about 40.90% of the total tribal population, followed by Miris with 17.80%, Karbis with 10.70%, Rabhas with 8.40% and Sonowal Kacharis with 7.10%. The spread of tribal population across the districts of Assam is, however, not even (as shown in Figure 1.2).[13]

Fig. 1.2 Percentage-wise distribution of Scheduled Tribes, 2001

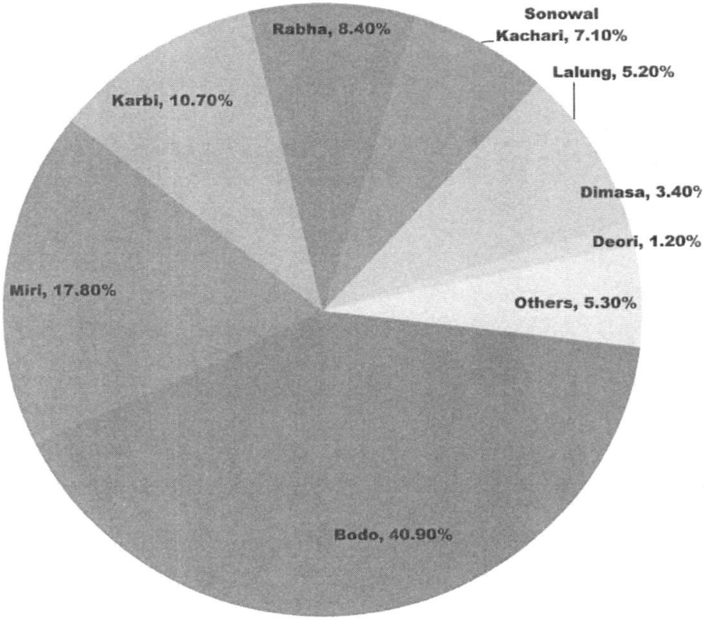

Source: Census Report 2001

However, according to the Census of India, 2001, Bodos have marginal negative growth. There is 41.12% of Bodo population amongst the Scheduled Tribes in 1991 and that percentage decreased to 40.90 in 2001, while other Scheduled Tribes increased their percentage considerably. Total Bodo population increased but Bodo population decadal growth is less than the other Scheduled Tribes population in Assam.[14]

Thus over the years, there have been some changes in the population distribution of Bodos in Assam. Bodos constituted about 43.19 per cent of tribal population of the state in 1951. The figure has been fluctuating from one Census year to another. In 1971, it was reduced to 40.11 per cent and then increased to 41.12 per cent in 1991.[16] Again in 2001, it marginally decreased to 40.90 per cent.

The Bodos, the tribe of our concern, are mostly concentrated in five districts of Assam, namely, Barpeta, Bongaigaon, Darrang, Kokrajhar and Nalbari (as shown in Figure 1.3). In these five districts, total Bodo population in 1991 was 7.15 lakhs, which accounted for about 13.43 per cent of the total population of these districts. After a decade in 2001, the Bodo population increased to 8.42 lakhs, accounting for 13.73 per cent of the total population.

It appears that a section of the Bodo educated youth was getting thoroughly disillusioned with the constitutional safeguards like autonomy arrangements and resorted to a secessionist struggle by floating extremist outfits like the National Democratic Front of Bodoland (NDFB), which has not only radically transformed the character and substance of the Bodo movement from autonomy to secession in terms of goals, but also the methods of achieving it, by showing preference for extortion, murders, kidnappings, and ambushes over strikes, road blockades, etc. This shows a departure from mass movement to armed struggle.

A politically significant phase of the assertion of Bodos actually started when Bodofa Upendra Nath Brahma, the leader of the All Bodo Students' Union, announced, on March 2, 1987, that they had started a massive movement for the creation of a separate state for Bodos. They claimed the north bank of Brahmaputra River as the geographical area of the proposed state. The Bodo People's Action Committee (BPAC) spearheaded the movement, which witnessed an outburst of violence by militants targeting those whom they perceived as the "enemies of the Bodos". The ABSU leadership denied the acts of violence, but agreed that police atrocities provoked some Bodo youths to take arms. Bodo Volunteer Force emerged as the military wing of the ABSU to wage an armed struggle.[17]

Meanwhile, Bodo Security Force (BdSF), now known as National Democratic Front of Bodoland, was formed on October 3, 1986, demanding the creation of a sovereign Bodo nation. It believed that it was the British, and not India, who invaded and conquered the Bodo Kingdom. Therefore, Bodos have the right to freedom after the British left India.[18] After the failure of the "Bodoland Autonomous Council" accord, a section of the Bodo Volunteer Force (BVF) declined to lay down their arms as they formed the Bodo Liberation Tiger Force (BLTF) on June 18, 1996, and continued to fight for greater autonomy.[19] There have been some fundamental differences between the NDFB and the BLTF. The NDFB is struggling to establish a sovereign Bodo nation, while BLTF is demanding the creation of a Bodo state within the Indian Union. The NDFB and the BLTF had been at loggerheads leading to fratricidal clashes.[20]

On February 10, 2003, the Assam Government, the Union Government and the BLTF signed the Memorandum of Settlement on Bodoland

Fig. 1.3 Districts-wise Bodo population in 1991 and 2001

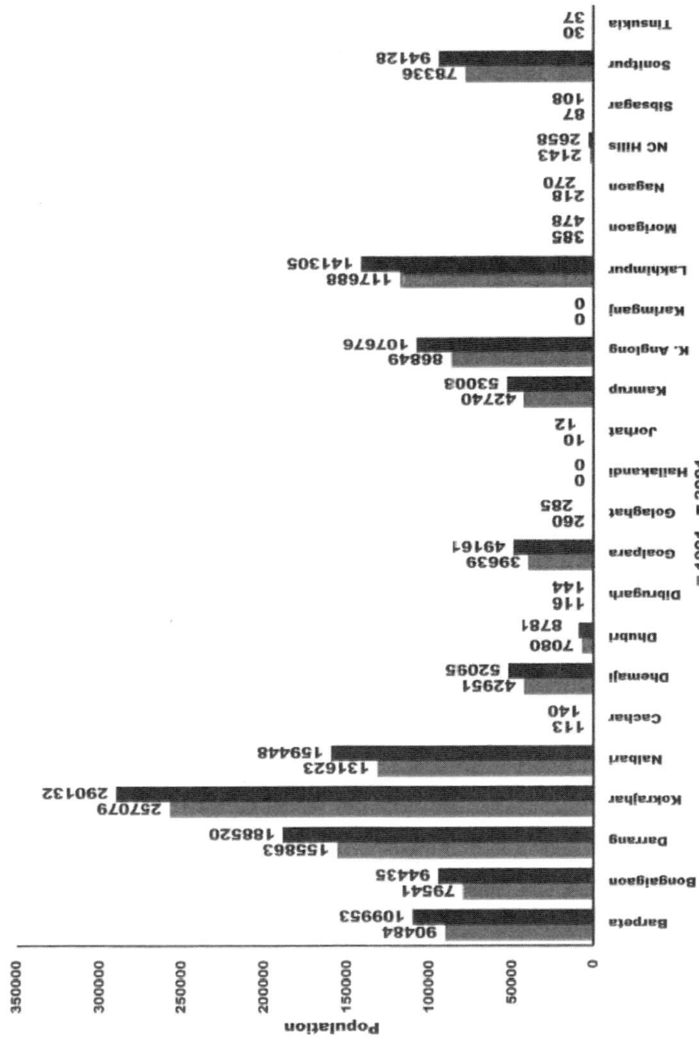

Source: Census Report 2001[15]

Territorial Council in New Delhi.[21] It appears that the creation of BTC was an attempt at fulfilling some of the genuine aspirations of the Bodo people, even if to a partial extent, in the sense that the demand of Bodoland raised by ABSU, BPAC and BLTF was partially achieved by the BTC. After the BTC accord, BLTF has joined the national mainstream. However, the demand for a sovereign Bodoland voiced by the NDFB remained elusive. The NDFB was also not satisfied with the geographical area that covers only four districts (Kokrajhar, Baksa, Chirang and Udalguri) as per the BTC Accord. It may be noted that NDFB is also not satisfied with the declaration of Kokrajhar as the capital of Bodoland. It is because the main base of NDFB has been at Udalguri. It is alleged that the NDFB now uses "ethnic cleansing" as its *modus operandi*.[22] This has led to the displacement of huge population belonging to other communities.

It appears that the relations between NDFB and other Bodo organisations are sometimes close. In the BTC election held on April 8, 2010, Bodoland People's Front had alleged that the United Progressive Democratic Front (UPDF) was contesting and campaigning in the elections with the help of the NDFB.[23] Therefore, it is important to examine the links between the NDFB and other Bodo organisations.

In view of the above,kthis work seeks to examine the major demands and strategies of the NDFB for an understanding of its role in Bodo politics. An attempt is also made to analyze the responses of Bodoland Territorial Council (BTC), the Union and the State Governments to the demands raised by the NDFB. The work also explores the relationship of the NDFB with the other Bodo organisations.

Concepts

It may be noted that several terminologies have been used by scholars to describe the violent course of action followed by certain organisations for the fulfillment of their political objectives, viz., , Terrorism, Extremism, Militancy, Separatism and Secessionism. Hence, these terms constitute the key concepts of the study in order to understand the politics of the NDFB. The key concepts of the study are as follows:

Insurgency

"Insurgency" can be defined as an armed uprising against the state. V.K. Anand defines insurgency "as an extra constitutional completely progressive and variegated struggle launched against incumbent authority by a consciously mobilized section of indigenous masses for the fulfillment of certain goals manifesting emancipation".[24] Noted insurgent theorist, Bard O'Neill, defines insurgency as, "a struggle between a non-ruling group and the ruling authorities in which the non-ruling group consciously uses political resources and violence to destroy, reformulate, or sustain the basis of legitimacy of one or more aspects of politics."[25]

Insurgency may be said to represent a people's movement with a political cause, usually aiming for independence and often settling at some stage for political autonomy. O'Neill observes that the most important aspect in understanding an insurgency is the nature of the conflict.[26] In essence, identifying the insurgents' goals allows for an understanding of the nature of the conflict. Insurgent goals cover various aspects of change such as anarchy, secession, return to traditional ways, or reform of government.[27] The challenge is to determine the insurgents' aims and to understand that these objectives may transform during the conflict. Once those goals are determined, identifying the means to achieve those ends allows greater depth of understanding into the severity of the conflict. Insurgents may employ a combination of terrorism, guerrilla warfare, and conventional warfare. The enduring nature of insurgency includes three core functions: an insurgency must survive, it must strengthen itself, and it must weaken the power structure or state. An insurgency accomplishes these three objectives constitutes the changing character of the phenomenon.[28]

An insurgency is a less overt, classic military struggle. It is more of a social, political and economic struggle for the support of the indigenous population over a prolonged period. Basic causes of insurgencies include: population pressures for government change, a deep perception of inequality, or unresolved religious or ethnic problems.[29] Other causes may include a weak national administration, lack of political infrastructure, disenfranchisement, corruption and mismanagement, difficult civil-military relationships, the mal-distribution of resources, or social divisions. Discontent elite that can organize antigovernment movements and some measure of popular support may be the preconditions of an insurgent movement.[30] Additionally, insurgencies must have charismatic leaders, attainable goals, motivating ideology, and access to internal or external resources.[31]

Insurgency uses violence against the state equipment and particularly the security forces. Normally, insurgents do not carry out terrorist attacks against civilians. However, sometimes they do, when it is believed to be favourable to their armed struggle. Legitimacy is sought through popular support; it therefore attempts to create an alternate state structure. Even though violence may be intense, it is neither random nor meant purely for effect. The battle is for the hearts and minds of the people, based on a perceived cause, with the insurgents likely to have an initial advantage.

Insurgency, like a war, has an enduring nature and a changing character. It remains a strategy entailing violence used by the weak and desperate against a power system.[32] Out of weakness, the organisation using a strategy of insurgency attempts to shift the focus of conflict away from domains where the state or other power structure is particularly strong, particularly the conventional military. Insurgents seek to make domains decisive where morale and other psychological characteristics matter more than tangible power, recognizing these characteristics even the odds to a certain extent.

Insurgency is a violent political struggle for control of people and resources. Insurgent groups often pursue some common objectives to undermine the legitimacy of the government and bolster their own standing with the population. They seek to undercut the ability of the government to provide the population security and public services, including utilities, education, and justice. An insurgent group may attempt to supplant the government by providing alternative services to the people, or it may be content to portray the government as impotent to obtain the active or passive support of the population. Not all support has to be or is likely to be gained from true sympathizers; fear and intimidation can gain the acquiescence of many people. Insurgents try to provoke the government into committing abuses that drive neutral civilians towards the insurgents and solidify the loyalty of insurgent supporters. They seek to undermine international support for the government and, if possible, gain international recognition or assistance for the insurgency.

Insurgency is primarily a political competition for legitimacy, violent aspect of the struggle most often alerts observers to the insurgency's existence. Insurgent warfare is characterized by the lack of front lines, sequenced battles, or campaigns; a protracted strategy, often lasting more than a decade; and unconventional military tactics, including guerrilla warfare, terrorism, or ethnic cleansing. The distinction between civilians and combatants is blurred in insurgency, often resulting in proportionally higher casualties than suffered in conventional conflicts.[33]

Throughout the long history of insurgency, there have been multiple types or models. Today, three exist in various parts of the world. One is the *proto-state*. Derived from the Maoist movements of the twentieth century, this is often considered the gold standard for any insurgency. In this model, an insurgency weakens the state through guerrilla attacks, terrorism, subversion, and psychological operations, while it simultaneously serves the functions of the state in the areas it controls. By demonstrating that it can provide better services than the existing state, it hopes to win support and eventually replace the existing government. This type of insurgency was particularly effective in peasant societies where active popular support mattered greatly; hence, the insurgents and the state competed for that support. In the classic Maoist method, final victory comes when the insurgency equals the state politically, militarily, and economically.

The second model, which is more controversial among insurgency theorists, is *non-political*. Rather than seeking to replace the state, this type of insurgent simply wants to weaken the state sufficiently to be free of its control. Normally, it is the insurgent's intent to practise some form of organized criminal activity. Like organized crime everywhere, these insurgents seek passivity more than active popular support. The methods of such insurgents, though, are quite similar to the politically focused insurgent.[34]

The third model consists of insurgencies that hope to replace the state but, because they are unable to control significant territory, approach the goal of destroying the state and replacing it in a sequential rather than simultaneous manner. Their initial focus is destruction. Again, active support is less important than passivity. They use a dispersed, networked organisation and rely on the swarming method of attacks dominated by terrorism, rather than guerrilla or conventional military operations. To augment their ability to survive and increase their own strength, they develop an important transnational dimension.[35] However, traditional Maoist style insurgencies seek to carve out, administer, and govern "liberated areas," they are intimately connected to specific locales and populations in those locales. According to Metz, networked insurgencies do not seek or are unable to develop liberated areas which they administer and govern; they are less intimately linked to specific locales and populations. They can shift their area of operations to different parts of a country or even to other countries with little effort.[36]

Mao Tse Tung, a noted revolutionary and military analyst, creates a three-phase model that emphasizes the political mobilization of the people and army to create a protracted popular war. First, organisation of the party and preservation of what little combat power exists.[37] Second, transition to combat is initiated when conditions are met that allow progressive expansion of the influence of the party by achieving the support of the population. These second-phase operations include minor skirmishes against government forces when the guerrillas possess an overwhelming advantage. Upon completion of assured victory, the guerrilla quickly fades into the population to swarm at a later time. During the third and final phase, the guerrilla forces make transition into conventional military operations against government forces. Mao's model emphasizes that the element of time is on the insurgent's side in order to build resources and support. There is no rush to meet the government forces in fixed battle. The primary emphasis is to live amongst the population, convince the people that the guerrillas offer a better alternative, and win their trust and support. In summary, the guerrillas must exist like "fish" in the people's "water."

However, it is observed that the NDFB lacks some elements which are associated with an insurgent outfit viz., (1) the outfit never made a distinction between combatants and non-combatants which insurgent groups often do; (2) the insurgent groups attempt to replace the government by providing alternative services to the people or its intent to show the government as impotent to obtain the active or passive support of the population. But, the activities of the NDFB do not reflect the above elements.

Terrorism

The term 'Terrorism' is derived from the Latin word *terrere*, which means 'to frighten'. The U.S. Department of Defense's *Dictionary of Military Terms* defines terrorism as "the calculated use of unlawful violence or threat of unlawful violence to inculcate fear; intended to coerce or to intimidate governments or societies in the pursuit of goals that are generally political, religious, or ideological."[38] According to William Blum, the term 'terrorism' means "the use of violent actions in order to achieve political aims or to force a government to act." He observes that the word 'terrorism' is now commonly used simply to stigmatize any individual or group one does not like for almost any kind of behaviour involving force. In addition, to him, terrorism is a methodology aimed at forcing a superior power to concede demands, usually withdrawal of forces, or the granting of independence, homeland, autonomy or some other goals. It is a tactic and not an entity in itself, with a life of its own. In brief, 'terrorism' is an organized violence against civilians in pursuit of certain objectives; the fact that violence is organized with political objective is what distinguishes terrorism from common crime. Occasionally, terrorist movements also engage with government security forces, but their primary operational target is the civilians.[39]

Violent actions inflicted upon secondary targets may be conducted by an individual, group, or government with the wider purpose of attracting attention, gaining support, or forcing concessions from the primary target on personal or political issues. Perpetrators of terrorism normally select, either purposefully or indiscriminately, illegitimate secondary targets—that is, non-combatants and civilians—and target them with bombings, hijackings, and other violently coercive methods. These targets are 'intermediaries' used by terrorists to manipulate the primary target and subsequently to achieve an objective; and such actions are employed in expectation that a harsher reaction by the primary target will in turn generate support for the issues espoused by the terrorists. Although states continue to employ terrorism, the concept of state terrorism is generally understood as a nation-state that supports or condones activities as described above, not one that conducts such operations. The term 'international terrorism' denotes actions conducted by groups outside the country of their origin, residence, or the location from which their activities are co-ordinated. Terrorism primarily involves semi-clandestine groups opposed to their home government or an external one.[40]

Terrorists have adopted numerous organisational structures, from single or two person operations to durable, identifiable groups or clandestine, solvent cells. Al-Qai'da, or The Base, has developed a modern structure often described as a 'network', with the dispersion of affiliated but autonomous individuals over vast expanses of territory organised as 'sleeper cells'. Operating with minimal communications, the well-trained members of these cells are afforded the opportunity to rehearse, and then they disperse after completing their missions. Such factors necessitate greater time and effort in planning, but also make possible larger operations with higher mortalities. Some groups that employ acts of terrorism reject the stigma attached to this method of conflict engagement that is widely considered illegitimate and egregious. This is especially true in cases where terrorism is one of the several employed and the overall objectives are widely believed to be legitimate and worthwhile. Nonetheless, the method usually overshadows the issues.[41]

Though, at present, there is no universally agreed definition of 'terrorism', it generally refers to those acts which are intended to create fear (terror), are perpetrated far an ideological goal (as opposed to lone attack), and deliberately target or disregard the safety of non-combatants. Since 1994, the United Nations General Assembly has repeatedly condemned terrorist acts using the following description of terrorism, "Criminal acts intended or calculated to provoke a state of terror in the general public, a group of persons or particular persons for political purposes are in any circumstance unjustifiable, whatever the considerations of a political, philosophical, ideological, racial, ethnic, religious or any other nature that may be invoked to justify them."[42]

Terrorism relies on the strength of arms. But terrorists know that direct military victory against the establishment is not possible and that is why they often engage in guerrilla warfare. This has led some social scientists like Walter Laqueur referred to guerrilla warfare as the "weapon of the weak" and terrorism as the weapon of the weakest".[43] In order to get media attention, the terrorists feel the need to generate widespread fear and therefore engage in increasingly dramatic, violent, and high-profile attacks. These have included hijackings, hostage takings, kidnappings, car bombings, and frequently, suicide bombings. Although apparently random, the victims and locations of terrorist attacks often are carefully selected for their shock value. They have been targeting schools, shopping centres, bus and railway stations, restaurants, night clubs and such other crowded places.

The goal of terrorism is generally to destroy the peace and increase the sense of insecurity in most familiar places. Major targets sometimes also include buildings or other locations that are important economic or political symbols, such as embassies or military bases. The terrorist presumes that the sense of terror these acts engender will induce the population to pressurize political leaders towards a specific political end.[44]

It may be noted that although the NDFB has resorted to terror tactics for achievements of its goal, it has extensively made use of peaceful methods like *bandhs* etc. Hence, it will not be appropriate to describe the NDFB as an out and out terrorist organisation.

Extremism

Another related concept is 'Extremism'. The term 'extremism' is often used to label a political ideology that is far outside the political centre of a society. In terms of actions, the term 'extremism' is often used to identify aggressive or violent methodologies used in an attempt to cause political or social change. According to Roger Scruton, 'extremism' may mean:

> *(i) 'taking a political idea to its limits, regardless of 'unfortunate' repercussions, impracticalities, arguments and feeling to the contrary, and with intention not only to confront, but also to eliminate opposition'; (ii) 'intolerance towards all views other than one's own'; (iii) 'adoption of means to political ends which show disregard for the life, liberty and human rights of others.'*[45]

It may be noted that someone's 'extremist' might be a 'freedom fighter' for another. It is seen that extremists are completely intolerant towards others' views and reject democratic ways of solving problems as well as the existing social order. An 'extremist' would not generally accept that what they practise or advocate constitutes violence and would rather speak in terms of 'acts of resistance' or 'militant action or the use of force.'

Militancy

The word 'militant' usually means vigorously active, combative and aggressive, especially in support of a cause, as in militant reformers. It comes from the 15th century Latin word '*militare*' meaning "to serve as a soldier". However, the current meaning of militant does not have to refer to a registered soldier; it can be anyone at all who subscribes, either in whole or in part, to the idea of using violence to achieve some larger objective, usually political. For example, when one is referred to as a "militant political activist", the term 'militant' is meant there to contrast with a pacifist political activist whose political principles do not allow him or her to use violence to achieve any end.[46] A militant in fact usually uses a range of tactics, including peaceful or semi-peaceful ones, when trying to achieve an end. The main difference between a militant and non-militant is the militant's willingness to actively use violence when he or she considers it necessary.

Separatism and Secessionism

Some scholars have used the terms "separatism" and "secessionism" interchangeably. Others define separatism rather broadly to include "all alliances of political alienation which feature a desire for reduction of control by a central authority in a specific area, and of the subsequent achievements independence and sovereignty, to the concept of secession. 'Secession' is described as "the action of withdrawing formally from membership of a federation or body, especially a political state."[47] In the context of North-East India, the secessionist movements are, therefore, those movements, which advocate the withdrawal of a particular state from the Indian Union.[48]

In the light of the above discussion, it may be observed that each of these phenomena is associated with a kind of protest movement against the prevailing political regime, although the means for achievement of goals may vary from one phenomenon to the other. It may also be argued that the terms 'extremism' and 'extremist politics', which do not figure often in the available literature on the northeast, are fairly comprehensive and encompass each of these phenomena with their different connotations. In view of this, the two aforesaid terms are found appropriate for an analysis of the role of the NDFB in Bodo politics.

Within the broad framework of our conceptual analysis, it seems pertinent to examine some important issues, viz., the factors that persuaded the NDFB to adopt extremist methods for achievement of its goals, the nature and extent of support for the NDFB's demand for a Sovereign Bodoland, the relationship of NDFB with the other Bodo organisations and responses of the BTC, as well as Union and State Governments to the demands of the NDFB. An attempt has been made in the following chapters to address some of these issues.

References

1 Gait,E.A. (1967).*A History of Assam*, Guwahati: Lawyer's Book Stall.

2 Barkataki,S.(1969).*Tribes of Assam*, New Delhi: N.B.T.

3 Gazetteer of India (1969).Assam State, U.M. & N.C. Dist, Dispur: Gazetteer of India.

4 Barkataki. *op. cit.,* pp.63-66.

5 Chatterjee, S. K.(1974).*Kirata- Jana- Kriti*, Calcutta: Asiatic Society.

6 Machahary,P. (2004).*Socio-Political Life of Boros in Karbi Anglong District of Assam*, Nagaon: Maulana Offset Press.

7 Barpujari, H.K. (1990).*The Comprehensive History of Assam*, Vol-I, Guwahati: Publication Board Assam.

8 Baruah, A.K. (2007). 'Communities and Democracy: A Northeast Indian Perspective'. *North East India Studies*, Vol.1, No.1.

9 Brass,P. R. (1991). *Ethnicity and Nationalism: Theory and Comparison*, New Delhi: Sage Publications.

10 Baruah,A. K. (1991).*Social Tensions in Assam-Middle Class Politics*, Guwahati: Purbanchal Prakashan.

11 Census Report 1991, Govt. of India, as cited in *The Bodos*, Souvenir, Bodo Sahitya Sabha, 40th (1993) Issue, also cited in *Statistical Hand Book*- 2007 Assam.

12 *Census Report 2001*, Govt. of India, as cited in *The Bodos*, Souvenir, Bodo Sahitya Sabha, 45th (2005) Issue, also cited in *Statistical Hand Book*- 2007 Assam.

13 *Census Report 1991,op.cit.*

14 *Census Report2001,op.cit.*

15 Census Report 1991 and 2001, *op.cit.*

16 In 1981, in Assam, due to Assam Agitation population Census was not held.

17 Bhuyan, A. (2005).*The Socio-Political Movement for Bodoland and Beyond: A Gendered Paradigm*, Guwahati: Peace Studies.

18 *A Brief History of the Boro People (2002).*Publicity Wing: National Democratic Front of Bodoland. It may be noted that the NDFB always uses the term 'Boroland' in all its documents and literature including its Constitution. On the other hand, other Bodo organisations like All Bodo Students' Union, Bodo Sahitya Sabha and Bodo Liberation Tiger Force etc. used the terms 'Bodos' 'Bodoland' etc.

19 *Manifesto of Bodo Liberation Tigers Force* (1996).Publicity Wing: Bodo Liberation Tiger Force.

20 Pegu,J. (2004). *Reclaiming Identity: A Discourse on Bodo History*, Kokrajhar: Jwngsar Publications.

21 Lt Col Chadha,V.(2005). *Low Intensity Conflicts in India: An Analysis*, New Delhi: Sage Publications.

22 Baruah, S. (1999). *India Against Itself: Assam and the Politics of Nationality*, New Delhi: Oxford University Press.

23 UPDF Contesting in BTC Elections for the NDFB.(2010, April 5). *Bodosa,* p.1. The United Progressive Democratic Front (UPDF) was a political party formed by the members of the All Bodo Peace Forum (ABPF). It was alleged that NDFB-P had formed the UPDF to capture the political power in Bodo politics.

24 Anand, V.K. (1981).*Insurgency and Counter Insurgency: A Study of Modern Guerrilla Warfare*, New Delhi: Deep and Deep Publications.

25 O'Neill, B. (1990).*Insurgency and Counterinsurgency: Inside Modern Revolutionary Warfare*, Virginia:1990, Brassey's Inc. Dulles.

26 *Ibid.,* p.27.

27 *Ibid,* pp. 22-23.

28 Metz, S. (2012).'Rethinking Insurgency'. In Paul Rich and Isabelle Duyvesteyn (eds.) *The Routledge Companion to Insurgency and Counter Insurgency*, London: Routledge.

29 Galula, D. (1964).*Counter-Insurgency Warfare, Theory and Practice*, New York, 1964:Frederick A. Praeger, pp.36-39.

30 O'Neill,B. E. (1977). Insurgency: A Framework for Analysis. In John F. Endicott and Roy W. Stafford, Jr. (eds.), *American Defense Policy*(164-172*)*. Baltimore and London: The Johns Hopkins University Press.

31 Lansdale,E. G. (1972). *In the Midst of Wars: An American's Mission to Southeast Asia*, New York: Harper and Row.

32 O'Neill, B. E. (1990).*Insurgency & Terrorism: Inside Modern Revolutionary Warfare*, New York: Brassey's.

33 US Government (2012).*Guide to the Analysis of Insurgency*. Retrieved November 12, 2013 from *www.mccdc.marines.mil/*.../Guide%20to%20the%20 Analysis%20of%20...

34 Metz,S. (2012).*The Future of Insurgency,* Carlisle Barracks, Autumn: United States Army War College Strategic Studies Institute.

35 Metz, S. (2012). *The Internet, New Media, and the Evolution of Insurgency*, Carlisle Barracks, Autumn: United States Army War College Strategic Studies Institute. Retrieved September 13, 2015 from http://www.dtic.mil/cgi-bin/GetTRDoc?AD=ADA598619

36 Major Molinari,R. J. (2004). *Winning the Minds in 'Hearts and Minds": A Systems Approach to Information Operations as Part of Counterinsurgency Warfare,* School of Advanced Military Studies. Retrieved September 12, 2013 from http://www.au.af.mil/au/awc/awcgate/sam/winning_minds_molinari.pdf

37 Tung, M. T.(1966).*Selected Military Writings of Mao Tse-Tung*, Peking: Foreign Language Press.

38 United States Department of Defense (2004). *Dictionary of Military Terms.* Retrieved February 16, 2009, from http://www.asafm.army.mil/pubs/jp1-02/jp1-02.pdf

39 Gunaratna,R. (2007).'Ideology in Terrorism and Counter Terrorism: Lessons from Combating al Qaeda and al Jemaah Islamiyah in Southeast Asia'. In Anne Aldis & Graeme Herd (Eds.), *The Ideological War on Terror: Worldwide Strategies for Counterterrorism* (21-34).New York: Routledge.

40 Hoffman, B. (2006). *Inside terrorism* (2nd Ed.).Columbia: Columbia University Press.

41 Thackrah,J. R. (2004).*Dictionary of Terrorism* (2nd Edition).London: Routledge Publication.

42 United Nations, 1994 United Nations Declaration on Measures to Eliminate International Terrorism annex to UN General Assembly resolution 49/60, "*Measures to Eliminate International Terrorism*", of December 9, 1994, 84th plenary meeting, A/RES/49/60,

43 Laqueur, W. (1999). *The New Terrorism: Fanaticism and the Arms of Mass Destruction*, London: Oxford University Press.

44 Juergensmeyer,M. (2000).*Terror in the Mind of God*, California:University of California Press.

45 Scruton,R. (1982).*A Dictionary of Political Thought*, New York:Hill & Wang.

46 Mannan,Md. A. (2006). Militant Islamism in Bangladesh – Global Jihadist Connection Perceptions. Retrieved from http://sam.gov.tr/wp-content/uploads/2012/01/Abdul-Mannan.pdf.

47 Lyon,P. (1981).'Separatism and Secessionism in the Malaysian Realm, 1948- 65'. In Collected Seminar Papers, No. 19, Institute of Commonwealth Studies,*The Politics of Separatism*(67-88). London: University of London.

48 Sen,A. (2011).*Marginal on the Map: Hidden Wars and Hidden Media in Northeast India*, Reuters Institute Fellowship Paper. London: University of Oxford.

*****

2

Emergence of NDFB: Organisation and Leadership

During the British rule, the Bodos became backward educationally, socially, economically and even politically. The limited job opportunities offered by the colonial job market led to an intense race for grabbing of jobs by the middle classes among both tribals and caste Hindus. It was a difficult pursuit and, moreover, the aspirations of the Bodo middle class did not find expression in the mainstream Assamese polity.[1] Being thus excluded, Bodo regional identity was articulated by its middle class through political discontent and political exclusionism.[2] It may be noted that the term 'middle class' was in common use in some parts of the world by the 1840s when it came to be viewed as basically consisting of various social groups which occupy an intermediary position between the proletariat and the bourgeoisie.[3] The term 'petty bourgeoisie' was more familiar than 'middle class' in Marxist literature. Non-Marxist scholars have been using the term in the Weberian sense. Marxists have been arguing that the term 'middle class' as used by bourgeoisie social scientists was unscientific because it was based on an unscientific concept of class in the sense that it was not defined in terms of the position occupied in the system of production. Rather it looks at class as an economic position in a society, based on individual achievement and birth. Though these two different approaches to the use of the term 'middle class' has important distinguishable consequences for social and political analysis, yet the term is commonly used in social science literature to refer to social forces.[4]

During the British period, the Bodos failed to occupy any prominent place in the British administration. Important positions were held either by the Bengalis or the Assamese caste-Hindu elite.[5] Therefore, it appeared to the Bodos that they were neglected and deprived of their legitimate share of administrative jobs and other privileges under the British rule. The educated middle class among the Bodos felt the need for an organisation for the assertion of Bodo identity which, in course of time, culminated in the formation of different organisations, viz., Haoraghat Bodo Sanmilan, Boro Kachari Jubok Sanmilan, Boro Jubak Chatra Sanmilan, Assam Tribes and Races Federations,Assam Bodo Chatra Sanmilan(1918), All Assam Plains Tribal League (1932), Bodo Sahitya Sabha (1952), All Bodo Students' Union (1967), Plains Tribal Council of Assam(1967), Boro Security Force (1986), Bodo People's Action Committee (1988), Bodo People's Party (1993), Bodo Liberation Tiger Force (1996), People's Democratic Front (1996), Bodoland Statehood Movement Council (1996), Bodoland Demand Legislative Party (2001) and so on.

Development of Bodo Politics

Those above stated organisations had adopted various modes of operation and even varied in their demands in different phases of Bodo identity assertion. In terms of the nature of their demands or goals, social background of the leadership, mode of mobilization, etc. these phases may be discussed under the following heads:

The Initial Phase

Though formation of Assam Bodo Chhatra Sanmilan, in 1918, at Dhubri was regarded as the first students' union and first organisation of the Bodos; yet Tribal League in 1932 marked the beginning of the Bodo identity assertion in the political sphere. However, Chhatra Sanmilan played a leading role in the socio-cultural and educational development of the community. It adopted a number of chosen measures along with the Bodo Maha Sabha (formed in 1924), to bring about a number of reforms in the age-old beliefs and practices prevailing in the society. They also tried to generate mass awakening for improvement of the dejected plight of the Bodos. The Chhatra Sanmilan began to publish a periodical magazine called the *Bibar*[6] which gave impulsion to upcoming Bodo writers. These two organisations fancied to reform and develop the Bodo society. As such they took various measures in this direction. Through these organisations, Gurudev Kalicharan Brahma, a reformist, craved for general enhancement in the language, culture and educational facilities and also a solution for some of the smoldering political and economic issues like employment facilities of the Bodos.[7]

The Chhatra Sanmilan took up a few issues related to the Bodo students in the perspective of their special cultural and ethnic environment. The activities of this organisation brought in for the first time a sense of harmony among the Bodo students all over Assam and taught how to fight for some genuine grievances and rectify them. As a consequence, a few more Bodo youth organisations like the Assam Kachari Youth Association and Goalpara District Bodo Association were soon formed to voice grievances on issues which were not strictly fallen under students' activities. However, in later period, these two organisations also joined hands in some political activities. In India, the demand for separate electorate was raised by the Muslim League, and the British availed separate electorate to Muslims through Morley-Minto Reforms Act 1909. That act virtually paved the way to raise demand for separate electorate for other religious or linguistics minorities. Thus Bodos also met Simon Commission in 1928, when the Commission visited Shillong, the then capital of Assam. The Assam Kachari Youth Association and the Goalpara District Bodo Association had taken initiative and met the Commission at Shillong. They submitted a memorandum demanding separate electorate status for the Bodo community and formation of a separate Bodo Regiment in the British Indian Army. It is noteworthy that the British at that time confined recruitment for the army mostly to the Punjabis, Gorkhas and Marathas and portrayed the people of eastern India not suitable for army service. In order to remove this uncharitable dishonour as well as to find more possibilities for employment, particularly for the less educated and even uneducated youths, many communities in eastern India started demanding for separate regiments on communal or regional basis. It was in this context that the demand was made, however, the demand for Bodo Regiment was never fulfilled.[8]

In 1932, another prominent organisation All Assam Plains Tribal League was formed. It was undeniably a big step. This organisation was formed under the initiative of Rupnath Brahma, Bhimbar Deuri, Jadav Chandra Khaklary, Satish Chandra Basumatary, Rabi Chandra Kachari, Karka Chandra Doley, Kharsing Terong, Dhirsing Deuri and so on. It was an effort to form a purely political front of all the plains tribal communities of Assam under one umbrella organisation. It is observed that at the beginning of the twentieth century, various tribal communities of Assam felt disgruntled with the role of national political parties. It seems that classification in the Hindu society was the root cause of such a feeling. This feeling of discrimination towards these communities encouraged the growth of a number of organisations, for example, Assam Bodo Chatra Sanmilan, Damgari Kachari Youth Sanmilan, Bodo Maha Sabha, Assam Kachari Youth Sanmilan, Chutiya Sanmilan, Koch-Rajbonshi Sanmilan, Muttack Association and so on throughout Assam. Initially these organisations worked independently and limited their activities within their respective communities; however, in the 1930s, they joined hands. As an upshot, in the session of the Assam Kachari Youth Sanmilan held at Raha of Nowgaon District, on April 17, 1932, the organisations together formed the all Assam Plains Tribal League. Jadav Chandra Khaklary was the President and Heramba Nath Borah was the Secretary of the League.[9]

The formation of the League was a beginning to bring all the t and communities into a common political platform. League's basic aim was to fight for the solution of the socio-economic problems of the tribes. They worked constantly for spread of primary education among the tribals and for the eradication of the opium consumption habits from their society. They clamoured for the preservation of the Line System, without which they felt that the entire tribal economy and culture would be jeopardized by the unrestrained influx of the immigrants. However, the demand for a separate electorate with reservation of five seats in Legislature and retaining of the Line System were the prime objectives of the Tribal League.

As per the demand of the League, in the Government of India Act of 1935, provisions were made for reservation of five seats for the plains tribes in the Legislature. Thus, in the Legislative Council elections held in 1937, five persons were elected from the League against the reserved seats. They were Dhirsingh Deori, Rupanth Brahma, Kharsing Terong, Rabi Chandra Kachari and Karka Chandra Doley.[10] The Tribal League became a determinant factor in the formation of ministries since 1937 and till independence of the country. In fact, both Gopinath Bordoloi and Sir Mohammad Sadullah needed support from the Tribal League to form ministries.

However, dubious ideological position of the League was cleared in the fact that the League leaders served in each and every ministry, either of the Congress or of the Muslim League, without any hitch, till the Independence. They, however, justified this act by asserting that their main objective was to ensure the well-being of their community, and their being a part of the government was prompted by this consideration. It is not hard to realize that it was an excuse used by the League leaders for being enduringly stay in power. Thus it realized that Tribal League was a passive spectator to the growing poverty of the Bodo peasantry. Such pauperization was due to rising of illegal migrants' infiltration under the auspices of the Sadullah-led Muslim League Ministry. Later on, consequent to the internal feud, some leaders like Jadav Chandra Khaklary, Rupnath Brahma and Jogendranath Hazarika joined the Indian National Congress and some others joined the Socialist Party. As a result, Tribal League lost its strength as a political platform of the tribals of Assam. In its tenth and the last annual session held at Baropujia, Nowgaon in 1953, the Tribal League was converted into a social welfare organisation and its name was changed to the All Assam Tribal Sangha. The All Assam Tribal Sangha had been recognised by the Assam Government as a competent body to scrutinize and issue Scheduled Tribe Certificates to the genuine tribal claimants.[11]

From the above discussion, it appears that before the Independence of the country, the Bodos had no specific strong organisation; they struggled like other tribal communities for some socio-economic demands. Only in 1932, all the tribal communities of the plains united and formed the Tribal League, the first political organisation of the Assam plains tribes. However, after the independence of the country, various Bodo organisations emerged. The activities and the agitational programmes of these post-independent organisations have national attention from time to time.

Second Phase: Movement for Recognition of Bodo Language (1952-1967)

This phase is marked by aggressive mass movements on questions solely relating to Bodo identity for the first time in Bodo political history. In addition, this phase also witnessed radicalization of the Bodo political scenario compared to the phase led by the Tribal League. Hence, the Bodo Sahitya Sabha (BSS), a most important literary organisation of the Bodos, was instrumental in the assertion of Bodo identity and issues of language and script were integral to such assertion. The origin of the BSS is perceptible to a very infinitesimal organisation known as the Boro Literary Club, founded by a handful of elites working in the Government offices in Dhubri. This organisation was to attempt for the perfection of the Bodo language and literature. Its objective was also to urge emerging Bodo litterateurs to write books and bring out journals written in Bodo language. To implement this policy, Boroni Onsai Aphat, an organisation akin to a students' union launched by the Bodo students studying at Dhubri,assisted Boro Literary Club to a considerable extent. These two organisations, working unitedly for a common cause,soon realized that the basic objectives set before them could not materialise without the support and active participation of the entire Bodo community in Assam and the adjoining areas of Bengal, Tripura and even Nepal. With this end in view, the Bodo Literary Body met on September 26, 1952, at Kokrajhar High School, under the Presidentship of Bandhuram Kachari. In that meeting, a decision was taken to hold a general convention of Bodo language speakers throughout the northeastern region. Consequently, a convention was held at Basugaon on November 16, 1952, under the Presidentship of Dharanidhar Basumatary, an MP from Kokrajhar constituency. In the convention, the BSS was founded and it elected Joy Bhadra Hagjer as President and Sonaram Thaosen as the General Secretary.[12] Other noteworthy founder members of the Bodo Sahitya Sabha (BSS) were Satish Chandra Basumatary, Jogendra Kumar Basumatary, Pramod Brahma Patgiri and Madaram Brahma. This period was marked by a preponderance of issues related to language and script as the driving force of the Bodo identity assertion. The principal demands of this phase were the introduction of Bodo language in schools in the Bodo dominated areas and the recognition of Roman script for it in place of Assamese.[13] The BSS published an annual mouthpiece, named *The Bodo*, and Satish Ch. Basumatary was the editor of the first issue. *The Bodo* had contributions in all three languages that an educated Bodo is expected to know, namely Bodo, Assamese and English. Initially, BSS had avoided all kinds of linguistic chauvinism. One of the aims of the BSS was to bring all the Bodo groups of languages currently spoken in the north-eastern region under one umbrella organisation.

Though the main activities of the BSS were to develop and promote Bodo language and literature, later on, it participated in agitational politics also. In October 1960, the Assam Legislative Assembly at Shillong passed the Assam State Language Bill making Assamese as the only state language of Assam. It received tumultuous reactions throughout the undivided Assam comprising of present Nagaland, Arunachal Pradesh, Meghalaya and Mizoram. The Act gave a blow to the unique sense of unity in Assam setting a process of disintegration and resulting in the creation of separate states like Meghalaya, Arunachal Pradesh and Nagaland. This Act also set in a process of alienation of the Bodos from the so-called mainstream Assamese society. The BSS lodged a strong protest against the Bill and demanded the recognition of Bodo language as the medium of instruction at primary level of education in the Bodo dominated areas of Assam. After prolonged agitation and as a result of its untiring efforts, the Assam Government introduced Bodo language as the medium of instruction. It was promulgated at different levels of education in Assam in successive stages such as, at elementary stage in 1963, at secondary stage in 1968 and as MIL, at college level, in 1977.

The BSS also protested against the policy of the Government of Assam to abolish English as the medium of instruction in college and university levels and introduce Assamese in its place in 1972. Joining other linguistic minorities, the BSS pleaded for the retention of the English language along with the Assamese language in the said levels of the education system of Assam. It may be mentioned that the Bodos inherited no script of their own. Bishnu Prasad Rabha, the noted writer, singer and revolutionist of Bodo origin, claims that in ancient times there was a kind of Deodhai script among the Bodos.[14] However,perhaps, in course of time, they lost their script with the fall of the kingdom. Therefore, in the absence of their script, the people used their language and literature in various scripts. Towards the end of the nineteenth century, the Christian missionaries tried to write a language in Roman script, but it remained a limited practice. Later on, they adopted Assamese script to write the Bodo language.

Since its beginning, the BSS faced the problem of using multiple scripts for writing the Bodo language and literature, and felt the need of a common one. With the introduction of the Bodo language in primary education, the script problem became acuter than ever before, because the textbooks in Bodo language had to be produced in one script only. The question of having a common script was discussed inside the forum of the BSS. The suitability of Roman, Assamese, Bengali or Devanagari script in the context of Bodo language was examined at various levels over the years and the idea of adopting the Roman script commanded the widest support. Finally, on the recommendation of the Saisingra Sub-committee, which was appointed by the BSS to examine the issue, the BSS in its 11th session at Mahakalguri, West Bengal, held on February 24-26, 1970, accepted the Roman script by a formal resolution. The BSS appointed an implementation committee headed by Thaneswar Boro. The implementation committee decided to implement the Roman script for the Bodo language with effect from the academic session of 1974-75.[15] The release of a book, entitled "*Bithorai*", written in Roman script on April 22, 1974, marked the formal inauguration of the Roman script as the script for writing the Bodo language and literature. On that very day, the BSS declared the "*Bithorai*" being adopted as textbook for class I students and called upon all teachers of the Bodo-medium schools to introduce it accordingly.

The Government of Assam, perhaps, sensed a separatist tendency in the move and refused the demand of the BSS. The dominant Assamese elite and the Asom Sahitya Sabha, the prominent literary organisation of Assam, also opposed the move having seen anti-Assamese feeling in it. The unilateral move of implementation of the Roman script by the BSS and the compliance of the Bodo-medium teachers to the BSS direction regarding *Bithorai* provoked the Government of Assam to withhold the salaries of the teachers concerned. In view of this, the BSS launched a full-scale movement demanding Government's recognition of the Roman script for the Bodo language and literature and withdrawal of Government's action against the teachers of the Bodo-medium schools. It was a mass movement which included the participation of organisations like the Plains Tribal Council of Assam (PTCA) and the All Bodo Students' Union (ABSU). There were continuous *bandhs* and boycott of schools and colleges for several months in the Bodo-dominated areas. Later on, the movement turned violent and 16 young Bodos died in police firing.[16] Finally, the Government of Assam referred the matter to the Central Government in New Delhi. Meanwhile, the state of emergency was proclaimed throughout the country by Indira Gandhi Government in 1975. The Central Government utilised the threat of emergency provisions of arrest and detention to force the Bodo leaders to accept Devanagari script for the Bodo language. The Devanagari script for the Bodo language was, thus, adopted, since then for all official works as well as for college textbooks, the Bodo language is being written in Devanagari script. The replacement fuelled the anti-Assamese attitude of the Bodo educated youths.[17] A small section of the Bodo elite is still advocating for the Roman script.

However, the prolonged use of the Devanagari script in all the matters of communication became, gradually, convenient for the Bodo people to accept the script in their language. In the 39th Session of the BSS, held at Simbargaon, Kokrajhar, on 25th to 28th February, 2000, it was resolved unanimously to take Devanagari script for the Bodo language and to permanently retain it, otherwise they would have to retreat back to old times negating the progress made so far with it.[18] More so, to take in Roman script afresh would entail a copious work for large bulk of their literature which is already beset in the Devanagari script. Above all, the BSS felt that in the interest of the integration of the nation, it would be more pertinent to include Devanagari script as the unifying force. It is observed that the phase of Bodo identity assertion, which was led by BSS, was different from the earlier phase in the sense that active involvement of the masses which was virtually absent in the former was predominant in the latter period.

Third Phase: Transformation of Ethnic Identity Assertion to Political Autonomy Assertion

The year 1967 marked the beginning of a new transformation phase in the history of Bodo ethnic assertion. On 13 January 1967, the then Prime Minister, Indira Gandhi, announced that Assam would be reorganised on a federal basis. The ABSU, formed on 15 January 1967,welcomed the move.[19] This declaration gave a new fillip to the political aspirations of the Bodo middle class and it found expression in their demand for a separate Union Territory for the plains tribes of Assam.[20] Till then, Bodos tried to improve their community by demanding reservation of seats in the Parliament and the Legislative Assembly. It was in fact with the active support of ABSU that the PTCA was formed on 27 February, 1967 under the Presidentship of Modaram Brahma, to formulate a suitable response to Mrs. Gandhi's proposal.[21] Subsequently, the Bodos started demanding an autonomous region under the banner of Plains Tribal Council of Assam (PTCA) for the plains tribes of Assam. The PTCA was, in essence, a Bodo political party despite the fact that its name suggested a common platform for all plains tribes of Assam. In this context, Sharma points out that the initiative to construct a pan-tribal identity always came from the Bodo leadership.[22] The PTCA submitted a memorandum to the President of India on May 20, 1967. In the memorandum the PTCA demanded:

> *'Full autonomy in the predominantly plains tribal areas of the northern tract of Goalpara, Kamrup, Darrang, Lakhimpur and Sibsagar districts including all the Tribal Belts and the Blocks of those areas, so that the tribals can-(a) adequately protect their land, (b) give effective check to economic exploitation of tribals by non-tribals, (c) conserve their language , culture, customs and what best in them, (d) prevent political domination by non-tribal over tribals and imposition of anything which would disrupt their traditions and customs and (e) grow according to their own genius and traditions.'*[23]

Their second demand for autonomy got a solid fillip by passage of the Assam Reorganisation Act 1969 with a view to reorganising Assam in federal lines. As per the provisions of this Act, the state of Meghalaya was formed on 2 April, 1970. By 1972, Mizoram was also carved out of Assam. This gave an impetus to intensify the Bodo Movement for a separate Union Territory.

In 1972, the PTCA presented another memorandum to the Prime Minister demanding a separate Union Territory to be named as Udayachal, comprising the Bodo and other plains tribes dominated areas all along the northern bank of the Brahmaputra extending from the western border of Kokrajhar sub-division (now district) right up to the eastern border of North-Lakhimpur sub-division (now district).Besides the Bodo dominated areas, the Mising (another plains tribe community) dominated areas in North-Lakhimpur sub-division were also to be included in this proposed Udayachal territory. The intensity of their movement increased when Assamese was adopted as the sole medium of instruction in the universities of Assam in 1972. However, their demand for "Udayachal" was slightly dampened as they had to work for the Roman script movement in 1974-75. During the period of Emergency also the PTCA did not organise any movement.

Subsequently, in the post emergency general election the Janata Party came into power. A top leader of the PTCA, Samar Brahma Choudhury, joined the Janata Party Government in Assam as a Cabinet Minister and the Secretary of the PTCA, Charan Narzary, was elected as a member of the Lok Sabha. As the PTCA deviated from its professed ideological stance, it lost its influence over the Bodo masses. More so, their vested interests deflected their original demand of Udayachal. As a result, a new era of political polarization came about amongst the Bodos. Dissatisfied with the leadership, one dissident group left the original organisation and formed a splinter organisation named PTCA (Progressive). This splinter group reflected its more progressive views by demanding the creation of a separate state named Mising-Bodoland as the homeland of the two plains tribes.[24] This proposed state was envisaged to comprise of more or less the same areas as earlier proposed for the Union Territory Udayachal. Thus, gradually the mass base of the party declined after a decade of its domination in the identity politics of the Bodos, primarily because of its deviation from its own declared goals and principles.[25] It is observed that another factor responsible for its decline was severe infighting due to political differences among its leaders.

However, the ABSU had been taking keen interest for the unification of PTCA and PTCA (P) since 1979, but did not succeed. ABSU organised a convention of all tribal organisations from April 17 to 19, 1984 at Harisinga in Darrang district, Assam. It was then the PTCA (P) was dissolved and a new political party, United Tribal National Liberation Front (UTNLF), was formed on April 19, 1984 under the Chairmanship of Binai Khungur Basumatary. The UTNLF first submitted a memorandum for a separate Union Territory to the Prime Minister of India on May 2, 1984 in New

Delhi giving the nomenclature of 'Tribal Land' to the proposed Union Territory. Since then, the UTNLF had also been submitting memorandum from time to time demanding separate homeland for the plain tribes of Assam. For example, the UTNLF submitted another memorandum to the President of India, on May 29, 1984, demanding a separate state for the plain tribes of Assam along the foothills of Arunachal Pradesh and Bhutan. The jurisdiction would extend to the predominantly tribal inhabited areas of Assam, comprising the districts of Dibrugarh, Lakhimpur, Sonitpur, Darrang, Kamrup, Barpeta, Kokrajhar and Dhubri of Assam. It also demanded the creation of Sixth Schedule Areas in the predominantly tribal inhabited areas of Nowgong, Kamrup and Goalpara districts adjoining the Karbi-Anglong district of Assam and the state of Meghalaya.[26] It also put forward a demand to the Election Commission of India for registration of it as a political party under the Election Symbols (Reservation and Allotment) Order, 1968.[27] Moreover, another memorandum was submitted to the Prime Minister of India, on July 10, 1985, in which it stated:

> *"We desire a separate political identity recognising our age-old political and geographical areas in the form of a separate state (Union Territory status) to be carved out of the present artificial political arrangement called Assam, within the Union of India."*

It is noteworthy that, during the period of anti-foreigners movement of AASU, the Bodo movement kept a low profile. In the initial years of AASU agitation, both ABSU as well as other Bodo political leaders extended full support to the AASU leaders in their anti-foreigners' movement, because the ABSU was equally interested in driving out the Bangladeshi and Nepali immigrants of Assam. But during the later years of the movement, the Bodo leaders apprehended that the real aim of the movement was to establish the hegemony of the dominant section of the caste-Hindu Assamese speaking people over all other communities of Assam. Gradually, the Bodo leaders, particularly the ABSU leaders, started dissociating from the AASU movement. The final rift came when the Assam Accord was signed and no specific provision was made in the Accord to protect the tribal interests, in general, and the Bodo interests, in particular.

The ABSU took particular exemption to two specific provisions of the Assam Accord. Clause 6 of the Assam Accord solicits the legislative and administrative safeguards "to protect, preserve and promote the cultural, social, linguistic identity and heritage of the Assamese people."[28] The ABSU leaders took it as complete negation of the composite and diverse cultural and linguistic milieu of Assam in the context of the most indigenous section of the population of Assam i.e., the Bodos. Another clause i.e. Clause 10 of the Accord, provided that "Strict enforcement of all relevant laws would be made for prevention of encroachment of all Government lands and lands in the Tribal Belts and Blocks." The ABSU leaders apprehended that while the first part of the clause would be enthusiastically implemented by the AGP Government, the second part of the clause would be conveniently ignored. This apprehension was not altogether devoid of reasoning. Implementation of the first part would not adversely affect the Assamese people, whereas it would do so to the Bodos. Most of the Government lands were Reserved Forest lands where hardly any Assamese people had encroached, but the landless Bodos had made massive encroachment there when they were deprived of their own cultivable lands by the Assamese people as well as the immigrants. The Bodo leaders asserted that if the second part of the clause is implemented, it would benefit the Bodos and other tribal people but hurt the interest of many Assamese people. It appeared to them that, the AGP Government would implement the second part of this clause.[29]

Fourth Phase: Movement for Right to Self-Determination

After the virtual departure of the PTCA, a new phase began. This phase of identity assertion of the Bodos was also marked by territoriality and this period saw the consolidation of the Bodo regional identity which manifested itself in the demand for a separate state of Bodoland. The reigns of leadership during this turbulent phase of Bodo political history were assumed by a student organisation, viz., All Bodo Students' Union (ABSU). led by Bodofa Upendra Nath Brahma.[30] What demarcates this phase from the earlier phases is the recourse to violence let loose by the armed wing of the ABSU, especially on those who were perceived as pro-PTCA or those who did not endorse the organisation's policies and actions. For this purpose, the ABSU armed wing, Bodo Volunteer Force (BVF), was formed in November, 1987.[31] Meanwhile, an umbrella organisation, named Bodo People's Action Committee (BPAC), was formed on 8 November, 1988, to unite all sections of Bodo people irrespective of age and political affiliation.[32] S.K.Bwismuthiary was the Chief Convener, Karendra Basumatary was the Chairman and Subhas Basumatary was the Vice-Chairman of the BPAC.[33] The ABSU and BPAC jointly launched an agitation for the redressal of the Bodo grievances. Further, some of the action programmes undertaken by the AGP Government provided immediate provocation to the ABSU and the BPAC leaders.

The AGP Government launched a large-scale operation for the eviction of unauthorised encroachers from forests and other Government lands all over Assam. Naturally, a very large number of Bodos was evicted from these lands. The ABSU and BPAC leaders made vociferous protests against these operations, but these protestations fell on deaf ears. No alternative arrangement for the rehabilitation of these evicted Bodos was made by the Government. On the other hand, when the ABSU and the BPAC leaders demanded the demarcation of a separate Bodo area comprising the north bank districts of Assam for the creation of an autonomous Bodo region, the AGP Government strongly opposed it and started redrawing district boundaries by creating new districts and sub-divisions, allegedly to make them appear as non-Bodo majority areas.

In 1986, immediately after assuming power, the AGP Government issued a circular through the Secondary Education Board of Assam (SEBA) making the Assamese language as the third compulsory language in educational institutions of Assam. The Bodos vehemently opposed the circular and announced some agitational programmes for the withdrawal of the SEBA circular.

Under these state of affairs, the ABSU decided to launch a massive movement with effect from March 2, 1987 by holding mass rallies at all District Headquarters. It stressed the demand of a separate Union Territory for the tribal people on the north bank area of Assam and also the formation of separate Autonomous District Councils in the south bank areas with compact concentration of the plains tribes. On November 10, 1987, ABSU submitted a memorandum to the Central Government demanding the creation of a separate Union Territory of Bodoland, the creation of Autonomous District Councils named Nilachal in Kamrup-Boko Area and Lalung in Nowgong district as well as inclusion of the Bodos of Karbi Anglong district in the Hill Scheduled Tribe category. It appears that the language policy of the AGP Government was perceived as linguistic chauvinism by the Bodo leadership and it persuaded them to raise territorial demands as well as demands for more autonomy.

> *"The arguments of the Assamese people and Assam Government are like that the Assamese language is the official as well as regional language of Assam, a link language among different communities of Assam, language for the integrity of Assam and that is why everyone must read Assamese, must speak Assamese, must know Assamese. Those who*

live in Assam must speak Assamese and those who do not speak Assamese they are non-Assamese or indigenous people of Assam. Assam is only for the Assamese, they think."[34]

This period of the ABSU movement experienced violence and bloodshed on an unprecedented scale. Though the movement under ABSU was professedly non-violent, but BVF was involved in the persecution and even killing of non-Bodos as well as Bodos who were sympathetic to PTCA or opposed to the ABSU-led movement. As Sharma points out, the causes for losing initial heat of the ABSU-led movement was due to the monotonous, static and one-dimensional agenda of the movement (especially, without any worthwhile socio-economic programme for the Bodo peasantry who formed the bulk of the rank of active participants in the movement) extinguished the fire of emotion off its participants. Meanwhile, there were certain parallel developments during this period, the most spectacular one being the demand for sovereignty voiced by an underground militant outfit, viz., Bodo Security Force (BdSF). To forestall the possibility of seizing of the Bodo movement in the hands of the BdSF, the ABSU leadership was keen to grip an opportunity for the solution of the Bodo problem and this desire materialized in the form of the Bodo Accord, which was signed on February 20, 1993. The Accord paved the way for the formation of the Bodoland Council (BAC). Meanwhile, the ABSU formed the Bodo People's Party (BPP) to capture political power in the BAC. This was followed by an intense struggle for power and internal squabbling among the Bodo leadership for primacy within the BAC, so much so that the Bodo Accord, once hailed by some, was reduced to a political farce.[35] This shows that the common people's interests figured nowhere in their scheme of things and that their sole interest was usurpation of political power for their own sake. On 18 June, 1996, a meeting was held at Dotma, in Kokrajhar district, by a section of the Bodos who dissatisfied with the BAC and formed the Bodo Liberation Tigers Force (BLTF). The BLTF was constituted by a group of BVF members who declined to lay down their arms after the BAC Memorandum of Settlement.[36]

After the failure of the BAC Accord, On February 10, 2003, the Central Government, the State Government and the Bodo Liberation Tigers Force (BLTF) signed a new Bodo Accord for creation of a 'Bodoland Territorial Council' (BTC) under modified provisions of the Sixth Schedule of the Constitution. Under the Sixth Schedule, the BTC will have control over 10 major socio-political areas. These include land, any forests other than reserved forests, any canal or water course for purposes of agriculture, any form of shifting cultivation, establishment of village and town committees, all matters relating to village and town administration, appointment of headmen for villages and towns, inheritance of property, conducting marriages and divorces and other social customs.[37] However, the laws made by the Council in all the areas under its control must have the assent of the Governor of Assam. The Governor can dissolve a council on the recommendation of a committee appointed by him for the purpose of reporting on its functioning.[38]

This brings us to the present, contemporary phase of identity assertion by the Bodos. This phase distinguishes itself by the near marginalisation of the Bodo regional identity by secessionist overtones of a number of militant outfits which has not only radically transformed the character and substance of goal, but also the methods to achieve it. The emergence of the Bodo Security Force (BdSF) was an offshoot of this trend.

Bodos in Electoral Politics

Since 1937, all the plains tribes including the Bodos participated in the electoral politics under a common banner i.e. the Assam Plains Tribal League that used to provide them the required leadership. Rupnath Brahma defeated Rabin Basumatary with the margin of 1373 votes for his historical win and became the first Bodo MLA.[39] In 1957 Assembly election, Brahma was re-elected as MLA from the same constituency.[40] In 1962 Assembly election, Rupnath Brahma and Bahadur Basumatary (Panery ST Constituency) won election.[41] Although the PTCA was a political organisation, it did not participate in the by-elections to the Kokrajhar Lok Sabha constituency held in 1967 and May 1968. To press for its demand, it, rather, gave a call to boycott the election. Yet, there were nine Bodo candidates who contested in the 1967 elections among them four candidates won the election.[42] Meanwhile, as a part of the protest, thousands of volunteers of the PTCA picketed polling booths during these elections and a large number of leaders of the party were arrested and detained for long time. After their return from jail, the leaders organised a conference of the PTCA at Tezpur from January 12 to 14, 1969. In this conference, they firmly demanded "to ensure peace and better and more efficient administration in the northern tracts of Goalpara, Kamrup, Darrang and Lakhimpur up to the foothills of Bhutan and Arunachal, autonomy has to be granted to the above tracts."[43]

Till this demand was made, the PTCA had some relationship with the plains tribal MLAs and the ruling Congress party. After raising these demands, the PTCA was completely alienated from the ruling Congress party. The PTCA decided to contest the midterm poll of 1971 to the Legislative Assembly of Assam and none of its candidates won. But in the General Elections held in 1972 for the Assam Legislative Assembly, the PTCA succeeded in returning its General Secretary, Charan Narzary, by defeating a Congress candidate, Ranendra Narzary. But, in this election, Charan Narzary contested from two constituencies viz., Sidli and Kokrajhar (west) and in Sidli he was defeated by Uttam Brahma (INC).[44]

In 1977 Elections to the Lok Sabha, the PTCA fielded its lone sitting MLA Charan Narzary as candidate from the Kokrajhar constituency. He won by a huge margin by defeating Dharanidhar Basumatary, the veteran sitting M.P. of Congress Party. This election result qualified the PTCA to secure recognition as a regional political party and the election symbol 'cultivator cutting crops' was allotted to it by the Election Commission.[45]

In the general elections to Assam Legislative Assembly held in 1978, the PTCA contested in seven constituencies out of which they secured four seats in the Assam Assembly.[46] The rest of Bodo inhabited constituencies were left to the Janata Party as part of the electoral alliance.[47] After the election, the Janata Party and its alliance formed the first ever non-Congress government in Assam. The Vice-President of the PTCA, Samar Brahma Chaudhury joined the Assam Cabinet as Minister of Forest, Vetenary and Animal Husbandry. But a sizeable section of the Bodos criticised this move of the PTCA and accused the PTCA leadership of compromising Bodo people's demand for Udayachal for their narrow personal gain.[48] The youth wing of the PTCA, the Young Plains Tribal Council of Assam (YPTCA), vehemently opposed the PTCA's hobnobbing with the national political parties to remain in power. The accusations were not without ground when the PTCA did not hesitate to join the Congress-led government formed after the fall of the Janata Government in 1979. Dissatisfied with the PTCA, the YPTCA severed its ties from the parent body and formed another political party, named PTCA (Progressive), under the Presidentship of Padma Lochan Boro, independent Bodo MLA from Bijni constituency. Thus, the PTCA (Progressive) made its presence at the Legislative Assembly.

In 1983 Assembly elections, out of 15 constituencies contested PTCA won the Barama, Sapaguri and Udalguri constituncies.[49] Altogether 17 independent Bodo candidates contested the election, but failed to win any seat. Binoy Khungur Basumatary, who was elected from the Udalguri Legislative constituency, became the leader of PTCA Legislative Party in the Legislative Assembly. So far the PTCA had occupied the centre stage of the Bodo Autonomy movement. But the vacillation on the part of the PTCA leaders and their hobnobbing with the mainstream political parties in power began to alienate them from the common Bodo people. Beginning with the formation of PTCA (P), the dissidence in the PTCA leadership began to grow. Because of its deviation from the declared objectives, the PTCA started losing the centre stage that provided the leadership to the political articulation of the Bodo people. The PTCA (P) was dissolved and a new political party, United Tribal National Liberation Front (UTNLF), was formed on April 19, 1984 under the Chairmanship of Binai Khungur Basumatary.[50]

In terms of the Assam Accord, Assam Legislative Assembly was dissolved and the Eighth General Elections to the Lok Sabha and the State Legislative Assembly were held simultaneously in December 1985. Both the PTCA and UTNLF participated in the election.[51] The candidates of the regional political parties' viz., Asom Gana Parishad (AGP), the United Minorities Front (UMF) and UTNLF contested as the independent candidates because those parties were not yet recognised by the Election Commission. The PTCA won the Kokrajhar Parliamentary seat out of the three seats it contested. The UTNLF failed to win any Parliamentary seat. In respect of the Legislative Assembly Election, the PTCA bagged three seats, while the UTNLF won the lone Udalguri constituency by returning its party president, Binoy Khungur Basumatary. The PTCA's better electoral performance in 1985 election was, perhaps, due to the electoral alliance it made with the AGP. By making the alliance it could draw the non-Bodos' votes also. On the other hand, in comparison with the PTCA, the UTNLF was new and it had less organisational strength at the grassroot level.[52]

Meanwhile, it is observed that the plans and policies of other Bodo organisations had changed recurrently; after achieving the political power many Bodo leaders changed their attitude towards the Bodo society. The above discussion shows that after Independence in every Assembly/ Parliamentary elections, Bodos were able to get political representation (as shown in Figure 2.1). In spite of that, Bodo leaders failed to promote the issues like economic underdevelopment, unemployment, illiteracy, etc. Bodo leaders' self-centred political hobnobbing and unstable political principles caused the growth of dissatisfaction towards them and their ideologies. Bodos were expecting more from their political leaders who were supposed to represent the interest of the community. But, the ratio between expectation and achieving have had huge gap. For this reason, the feeling of deprivation has grown in the minds of the youths. Over the time, many Bodo political groups have undergone the short of fission and fragmentation. In fact, the

Fig. 2.1 Election-wise distribution of Bodo representatives in Assam Legislative Assembly

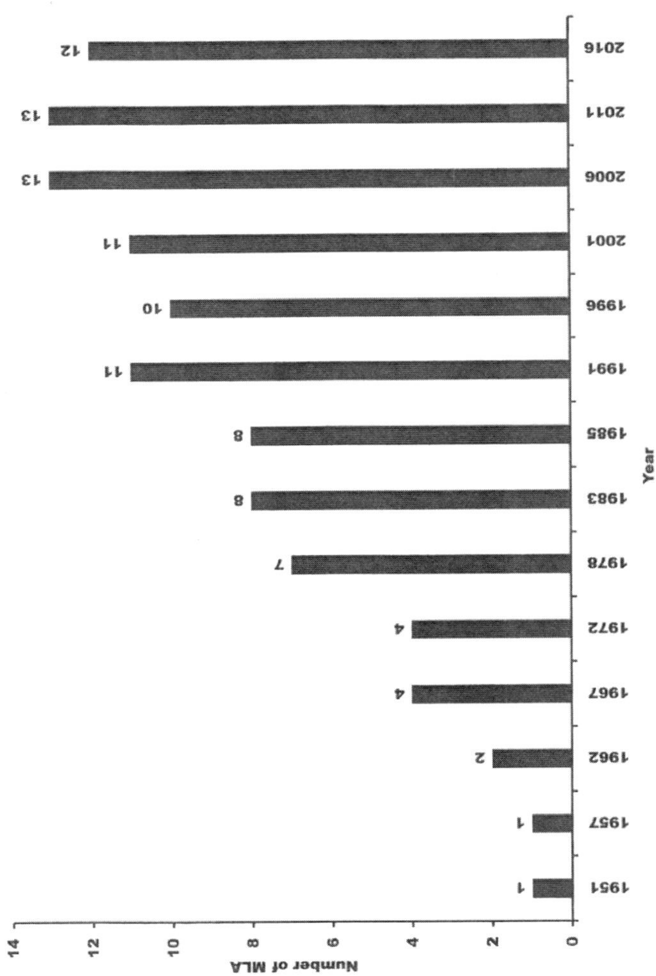

Source http://www.elections.in/assam

phenomenon of fragmentation and factionalism has become so rampant in various other Bodo organisations that it has resulted in utter obfuscation of their basic demands.[53] Hence some youths tried to rectify the incorrect policy that the Bodo organisations and their leaders had adopted.

Formation of the NDFB

The National Democratic Front of Bodoland (NDFB) was formerly known as Bodo Security Force (BdSF).The origin of BdSF can be traced back to another organisation called Youth Bodo Nationalist Association (YBNA), which was formed in a meeting held on 17 and 18 January, 1983, at Udalguri, Darrang district. A group of nationalist-minded Bodo youths had taken initiative to form the YBNA with the objective to fight for the freedom of Bodos, equal rights and freedom from all aspects. Ranjan Daimary joined the YBNA in 1983. The YBNA embarked on a mission to install "nationalism and socio-economic and political consciousness among the illiterate, ignorant and uneducated Bodo people".[54] Apart from the aforesaid objectives of the association, its main objective was to enhance the people's love for Boro nation and to realize this aim, a weekly news magazine by the name '*Bibungsar*' used to be published regularly.[55] The YBNA tried to establish contact with other armed revolutionary organisations of the North-East region and asked for help in order to have mutual arms and manpower.[56] It is important to note here that the YBNA activists often met in Shillong since the majority of the YBNA members were North Eastern Hill University students. The YBNA set up contact with the NSCN, the People's Liberation Army (PLA) of Manipur and other militant outfits of the region. It was also drawn to the idea of liberating the Mongoloid dominated Indo-Burma region. Meanwhile, NSCN played an important role in the formation of the Bodo Security Force. Finally, the BdSF was formed at Odla L.P. School at village Odla Khashibari on 3rd October, 1986 with 77 youths who met for the purpose. After night long confabulation, committed Bodo youths decided to go underground and take up arms.[57] Ranjan Daimary alias D.R. Nabla was elected as Chairman and B. Erakdao was elected as Information and Publicity Secretary of the BdSF. It was resolved that in the course of revolutionary struggle, the BdSF shall form and establish the People's Revolutionary Government known as the Government of the People's Republic of Bodoland. To carry out the armed struggle for national liberation, the BdSF should have its own army known as the Bodoland Army. The Bodoland Army should be regulated through Bodoland Army Formation.[58]

In a meeting of the Standing Council of the BdSF, held on 18 April, 1993, a resolution was unanimously adopted to change the nomenclature of the organisation as the National Democratic Front of Bodoland and its Army as the Bodoland Army.[59] The same resolution was approved to be enforced with immediate effect in the National Council's meeting from 22 to 25 November, 1994. Hence, the National Democratic Front of Bodoland, an armed revolutionary organisation, had rechristened forthwith as having the same principles and views of the Bodo Security Force.[60]

The Constitution of the National Democratic Front of Bodoland was adopted on 10 March, 1998. The First Edition of the constitution was published in June, 1998 and the Second and an updated and amended (1st Amendment) version was published in February, 2002.

The NDFB has a Flag of its own which is green in colour of 3:2 (Length is to Breadth) in size and in the left top corner there shall be red circle of one fourth of the length of the Flag and shall be yellow in colour within the red circle. The Green symbolizes Dynamism and Revolution. The star symbolizes Truth, Peace and the guiding Light of the Bodo Nation.[61] The Sijau (Cactus or Euphorbia Splenden) branch and the Flaming Fire within a green circle (which signifies the ever green Bodoland) constitute the Emblem of the NDFB and it shall be used in any purpose where insignia of the Party is required. The Emblem shall signify Truth, Prosperity and Continuity.

Training of the NDFB

In 1984, Ranjan Daimary first wrote to the leaders of the NSCN seeking their help. But, before that in 1982, Daimary tried to go to the NSCN Headquarters but failed to do so. Eventually,he reached the NSCN Headquarters in July, 1987 and after a long discussion finally NSCN agreed to help the NDFB. The NDFB first started a training camp in the forests north of Rangapara in Sonitpur District in 1989 and in October, 1989, the NSCN sent three trainers to train the NDFB and they were "2nd Lieutenant" Thamraipam, "Sergeant" Wampam and "Lance Corporal" Stone. The 1st Batch training of the NDFB had started on 26 October, 1989 and the training was completed on the 14 November, 1989. After 15 days of training, on the last day, the NDFB observed Closing Day Ceremony and decided to observe 14 November as the 'Bodoland Army Day'. However, in a pamphlet, the date designated for the formal establishment of Bodoland Army was given as 10 February 1995.[62]

The NDFB is divided into four regional commands, viz., Eastern, Western, Central and Southern, directly under a General Headquarter. It is based on the formulating order of the Bodoland Army Number 1/1995 NDFB (spelled as Bodoland Army in the pamphlet) dated 7 February 1995. The pamphlet throws a great deal of light on the organisation and functioning of the Bodoland Army. While stating the criteria for recruitment, it says: Recruitment of the Bodoland Army is on strict observance of all essential prerequisites of a good soldier.

The Bodoland Army has a three month training period for recruits after they take an oath of allegiance as specified by the Constitution of the NDFB. Their term of service is 12 years compulsory service to the nation and the unmarried Bodoland Army recruit shall marry after minimum five years of service but he/she must complete 28 years of his/her age.' The 'Bodoland Army' is organised in a manner similar to most regular armies with a Chief and Deputy Chief of Army Staff heading it. They have divisions, brigades, battalions, companies, platoons and sections just like a regular army. The personnel are liable to be transferred at the discretion of the Chief and Deputy Chief of Army Staff. The cadres are authorised to have 30 days of leave in a year. Long leave to officers and others is granted in special or exceptional cases. Similarly, a clear hierarchy has been laid down for promotions, discharge/resignation, and honours and awards.

There is a lot of emphasis on discipline, with stress on personal example, laid out at the very beginning of their booklet. It states, 'Each and every senior officer in the Bodoland Army should be exemplary for learning of good discipline and be the institution imparting national responsibility to the juniors.' Commenting on equality, it says, 'Propagation and practice of "ism" such as "groupism", "nepotism", "sectarianism", "regionalism" that are detrimental to integrity of the army personnel in the Bodoland Army is strictly prohibited and is subject to severe punishment.' Desertion is seriously dealt with, and those found guilty of it may be given a death sentence. Any cases of surrender are similarly dealt with.[63]

Organisational Structure of the NDFB

In terms of power and functions, the NDFB is a hierarchical organisation. Its organisational activities are focused on the group's central headquarters and the orders of the Chairman who is also the Chief of the Bodoland Army. General Assembly is the largest body in the organisation, followed by National Council which consists of 15 members.[64]

The members of National Council are elected by the General Assembly. The Constitution of the NDFB mentions that Dwimu is the Head Quarter of the NDFB and have no jurisdiction as far as the operation is concerned.[65] Below the central headquarters are territorial directorates, which are responsible for certain geographic zones. Group leaders are organized according to military designations.[66]

The organisational structure shall be of three tiers and each one of them is enumerated under separate clause. Clause I mentions Unit as the body at the lowest rung of the structure. Clause 2 mentions Regional Unit as the second body in the organisational structure and clause 3 mentions Central Council as the next higher body in the organisational structure of the NDFB.[67]

Fig. 2.2 Organisational structure of the NDFB

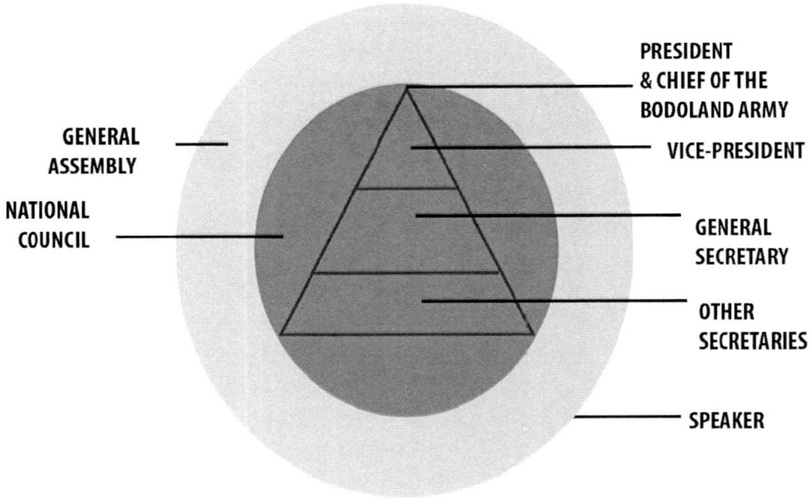

NDFB and its Principles

The NDFB and their revolutionary patriots have own principle to wage a revolutionary struggle backed by arms. Over-estimation of the enemy's strength tends to cause fear psychosis that leads to adopt unfounded and feeble policy which enables the enemy to take offensive action in all fronts forcing the opponent waft away towards expediency at the cost of principle.

The NDFB believes that underestimation of enemy's strength either leads one to adopt haphazard decision, consequences of which would definitely be disastrous The outfit accused that most of the Bodo organisations that upheld the cause of the Bodo nation had to sacrifice their principle just because of their wrong assessment of the enemy's strength. Thus, NDFB tried to know the enemy—his strength, weakness and the nature accurately. The principle enshrined in the Party's Constitution is the general truth and very foundation of the NDFB on which it has germinated and strengthened for their national cause and the patriots of the NDFB shall stick to it at any cost. Hence, NDFB tried to rectify the incorrect policy that other Bodo organisations had adopted. NDFB believes in the freedom of religion. To them, the term religion connotes faith, belief and conscience. The citizens of Bodoland shall have the right to choose or practise their choice. But while practising it, the social harmony and the national existence shall not be threatened. However, the NDFB believes in secularism. People of any community or religion shall live in sovereign Bodoland but their living in Bodoland should not be at the cost of their land and identity.[68]

NDFB's Membership Criteria

For acquiring the membership of the NDFB, every son and daughter with revolutionary and nationalist spirit who declares allegiance to the Constitution of the NDFB shall be eligible to become a member of the NDFB. He/she shall have to submit an application addressed to the President of the NDFB for membership. After thorough scrutiny of his/her revolutionary character, his/her membership shall be granted. He/she shall have to serve and sacrifice for the nation for a minimum of 12 and 8 years.

Legislative and Executive Body

The members of the NDFB who complete three years of service after military training shall constitute the General Assembly and it shall meet once in a year or at any given time the members shall constitute its General Assembly. The General Assembly elects the National Council, the highest legislative and the executive body of the outfit every three years. The Assembly scrutinizes and approves the Financial Statement of the year and shall appoint the auditors. It amends any provision of the Constitution of the party and shall make omission and commission of the Bodoland Army Formation by a support of two-third majority of the members present in the Assembly. Besides, the National Council may call a special General Assembly session as and when required. The General Assembly may also be held by requisition of 50 or more members of the NDFB.

The General Assembly may, from time to time, by a support of two-third majority of the members present and single majority of the total members, repeal any provision of the Constitution, without however impairing the basic objective and the spirit both implicit and explicit in the preamble and the article. Any member can bring up the motion of amendment or any other suggestion therein in writing.

The General Assembly elects its own Speaker who presides over its sessions. He maintains order and decorum in the Assembly. He decides points of order put up by the members and permits them to speak. He puts questions to the vote of the house and declares the result thereof. He maintains order in the premises of the Assembly and protects privileges of the members.

The National Council of the NDFB

There is a National Council constituted by the General Assembly every three years. It shall consist of 15 members. The Members of the National Council elect the President, Vice-President and General Secretary. The President, in consultation with the Vice-President and the General Secretary, appoints the other secretaries and office bearers. The National Council can impeach any official for violation of the Constitution and the party line and discipline and can remove them from the office. The term of National Council is ordinarily for three years. However, under special circumstances, the term of the National Council can be extended to an indefinite period exceeding one year.

The National Council is responsible for the general administration, charting of programmes consonant with the objectives and financial management. It executes all the decisions and policies adopted by the General Assembly. It may appoint sub-committees for any of the purposes. Two-third members present in the meeting or a single majority of the total members of the party shall form the quorum of both the General Assembly and the National Council.

Powers and Functions of Office-bearers

The NDFB President is the topmost official of the outfit and the Supreme Commander of the Bodoland Army. He presides over the sittings of the National Council of the party. In passing any resolution or in any decision making, his approval is required. He suggests and supervises all the office bearers of the National Council in respect of their functions. His resignation letter is to be addressed to the Vice-President.[69] Each and every member of the NDFB has to swear the oath. The swearing-in-ceremony is administered under the President of the NDFB. In the absence of the President, any of the officials of the National Council may be authorized to administer the swearing. The Vice-President assists the President in his activities and assumes all the powers and functions of the President during his absence, illness and in his resignation or demise succeeds the President till new President is elected.

The General Secretary is the main executive office bearer of the party. His responsibility is to execute the functions of the National Council and to execute decisions and resolutions. He notes down the minutes of sittings of both the General Assembly and the National Council and submits the report of over all activities of the party. He suggests and distributes his functions to other secretaries in consultation with the President and Vice-President. He convenes both the General Assembly and the National Council.

Rules and regulations of the NDFB

The NDFB has set up certain rules and regulations for its each and every member who has to abide by the Code of Conduct. According to Article 15, a member of the revolutionary patriot it is desirable that they should obey orders; should not smoke/drink/use intoxicating drugs; should be polite and gentle in behaviour; should not take liberty with men or women; and unmarried member should marry after minimum five years of service but male must complete 28 years and female must attain 25 years of age. Each and every member of the NDFB is subject to disciplinary action as per the rules and regulations of the Bodoland Army Formation for any misconduct or offence or violation of the Code of Conduct and the Constitution of the NDFB. The NDFB has a Judiciary known as the People's Revolutionary Court for free and fair trial of conviction.

Thus, the NDFB has laid some Code of Conduct in order to maintain discipline among the cadres of the outfit. It is important to note here that

Bodos have the tradition of drinking rice-beer. In the subsequent period, many social reformers as well as Bodo educated people tried to reform the society. The NDFB also realized the bad effects of consuming liquor and made strict prohibition of smoking, drinking and use of intoxicating drugs. Besides this, the NDFB also set minimum age for its male and female members to curb the practice of under-aged marriage prevailing in Bodo society.

Leadership

The President is the top most official and the supreme commander of the NDFB. Ranjan Daimary was elected as the first President and Commander-in-Chief of the NDFB. On March 28, 1998, the NDFB constituted full-fledged National Council by dissolving the Standing Council, which was formed in 1994. The 15 members of National Council included the Chairman, General Secretary and a Speaker. Ranjan Daimary and Govinda Basumatary were re-elected as the President and the General Secretary, while former military and judicial secretary B. Sungthagra alias Dhiren Boro was elected as the Vice-President of the NDFB.[70] On December 5, 2002, the NDFB 'Secretary General' Govinda Basumatary was taken to Delhi after he was arrested on an unspecified date while on board the Kamrup Express, at Rangiya railway station.[71] Though he was arrested, yet he remained as General Secretary till the split in the NDFB which had occurred on January 1, 2009.[72]

Meanwhile, another prominent leader of the NDFB, Dhiren Boro, Vice-President, was arrested on January 1, 2003, from Tadung in Gangtok, Sikkim's capital, along with his wife, two children and two other NDFB cadres. [73] The arrest of two front ranking leaders within a short period of time was a major setback for the NDFB. The NDFB got another major blow when the police arrested the NDFB 'Speaker', Sunil Brahma alias B. Simong alias B. Benga in Kolkata, on April 30, 2003.[74] The arrest or surrender of top ranking leaders gradually led to a change in the strategies of the NDFB which culminated in the signing of ceasefire agreement with the Union Government. Moreover, mutual distrust among the leaders of the NDFB resulted in its split into two factions, viz., the Anti-Talk faction led by Ranjan Daimary and the Pro-Talk faction led by Dhiren Boro.

It is observed that most of the top leaders of the NDFB, engaged in negotiations with the Union Government, teamed up and expelled Ranjan Daimary from the organisation. They regained faith in negotiations with the

Indian Government and have agreed to abstain from any violent activities. Therefore, the pro-talk faction tried to abide by the ground rule of the ceasefire agreement.[75] Meanwhile, those leaders of the NDFB who were in peace talks with the government perceived the serial bomb blasts as a propaganda to derail the ongoing peace-process. On December 15, 2008, the NDFB held its General Assembly meeting at Serfanguri designated camp in Kokrajhar District and elected Dhiren Boro as the new 'President' of the outfit. Meanwhile, there were reports that the October 30 serial bomb blasts were triggered by the NDFB cadres at the behest of Ranjan Daimary by keeping the local leadership out of the loop. Thereafter, a General Assembly meeting of the outfit was held and chaired by NDFB 'Speaker' B. Benga. The meeting was attended by top leaders, including the outfit's 'General Secretary' Govinda Basumatary. After revamping its office-bearers, the outfit's 'General Secretary' Govinda Basumatary stated on December 16, "Ranjan Daimary has not been removed. He is the 'Commander-In-Chief' of the NDFB, and we are ready to listen to his advice even today."[76]

However, on December 27, in an e-mail to the media, Daimary said that, "I am still the chairman of the NDFB, and I will continue my efforts for the self-determination of the Bodos. The NDFB-BLT clash is over, and as such I request the ex-BLT cadres not to target the NDFB cadres. I have also ordered the NDFB cadres not to target any ex-BLT members."[77] On December 28, 2009, a day after Daimary's statement, the outfit's Publicity and Information Secretary, S. Sanjarang, said in a press release that B. Sungthagra alias Dhiren Boro was its 'President', and confirmed the rift within the outfit.[78]

Meanwhile, as a final outcome of the rift within the outfit on January 1, 2009, the NDFB expelled its founder president, Ranjan Daimary *alias* D.R. Nabla, after replacing him with B. Sungthagra *alias* Dhiren Boro as its new chief. The new NDFB president, Sungthagra, criticising the alleged involvement of Daimary in the October 30 serial bomb blasts in Assam, said on January 1,2009, that the NDFB would have no truck with the former chief and his accomplices. "The NDFB, in a unanimous decision of the National Council, has expelled D.R. Nabla and his associates with immediate effect as a disciplinary action," he stated. "We are shocked and surprised that Mr. D.R. Nabla *alias* Ranjan Daimary, as per the statement of Ajay Basumatary, who has been recently arrested along with three others in Goalpara district, is proved to be directly involved in a series of bomb blasts in Assam on October 30 where many innocent civilians were brutally killed without any reason. The killing was inhuman and unfortunate which reveals nothing but his love for sadism. He not only committed crimes against humanity but also violated the ceasefire which he himself declared unilaterally on October 8, 2004. The act is undoubtedly an act of terrorism and can never be part of revolutionary struggle." The expulsion came a day after the cease-fire between the NDFB and the Centre expired.[79] This shows that the Pro-talk faction of the NDFB had taken such harsh decision on the apprehension that if it maintains any relationship with the Anti-talk faction, the ceasefire agreement might be withdrawn.

The split in the NDFB was confirmed when the anti-talk faction of the NDFB constituted its new 'Executive Committee' on November 18, 2009, with Ranjan Daimary as the 'President', Dinthi Gwra Narzary as 'General Secretary', 'Captain' Sangbijit as 'Commander-of-Staff' and Barbai Basumatary as 'Assistant Publicity Secretary'.[80] Meanwhile, the new Executive also finalised the nomenclature of the Anti-talk faction as the NDFB-R. The NDFB-R suffered a setback when the outfit's Chief, Ranjan Daimary, was arrested on April 17, 2010 in Jinaighati town in Sherpur district of Bangladesh and was handed over to the Border Security Force (BSF) at a border post in Dawki in Meghalaya.[81] Daimary was named as the prime accused by the Central Bureau of Investigation (CBI) in the serial blasts of October 30, 2008. The NDFB-R suffered another major blow on December 11, 2010 when security forces arrested its deputy commander-in-chief B Jwangkhang alias George Boro in Aizawl, Mizoram. He was one of the key accused of the October 30, 2008 serial bomb blasts in Assam.[82]

There occurred another split in the NDFB-R. The group led by the 'chief' of Bodoland Army (the armed wing of the faction), I.K. Songbijit, on November 20, 2012, announced the formation of a nine member "Interim National Council", with Songbijit as its self-proclaimed "Interim President". Other members of the "Interim Council" included 'Interim Vice-President' B. Naison; 'Interim General Secretary' B. Saoraigwra; 'Deputy Military Secretary' B. Jwngshar; 'Assistant Finance Secretary' B. Sansula; 'Assistant Forest Secretary' B. Sibigiri; 'Assistant Organising Secretary' H. Leba; 'Assistant Publicity Secretary' C. Rwikha; 'Member' B. Dwmwilu; and 'Captain' G. Bidai as the 'Deputy Chief of Bodoland Army'. This decision was taken at the general meeting of the NDFB held on November 13 and 14 at an undisclosed location.[83] Later, the NDFB-S also removed its 'President' Songbijit Ingti Kathar and elevated it's 'Interim General Secretary' B Saoraigwra to the top post. A Karbi by ethnicity, Songbijit is reportedly holed up in Myanmar. He was sidelined when the outfit took the decision to massacre the Adivasis. The heinous crime was executed under the direction of G Bidai, 'Deputy Chief' of the outfit's 'Armed Wing'. A group led by former 'General Secretary' B Saoraigra of NDFB-S has dissolved the

NDFB's 'Interim Council' formed in 2012, forming a new 'General Council' ousting IK Songbijit, as reported by *The Sentinel* on June 26, 2015. In an e-mailed statement to the media, B Saoraigra, the new 'President' of the 'General Council', said, "The 'General Assembly' (of the outfit), held on April 14 and 15, has vowed to revamp our national struggle and declare that the former Interim National Council of NDFB-S is dissolved.[84]

Thus, at present, the NDFB has three factions, viz., NDFB- Progressive (NDFB-P), also known as Pro-Talk Faction, led by Dhiren Boro, NDFB-R led by Ranjan Daimary, and NDFB-S led by B. Saoraigra.

It is important to note here that leadership of the NDFB has been frequently changing due to arrests, encounters, surrenders and splits in the outfit. Many of the founder leaders were arrested and found missing after Operation All Clear in Bhutan. Due to lack of safe hideouts, many front ranking leaders also surrendered. Some leaders were even dissatisfied with the progress of the ongoing talks and criticised the lavish lifestyle of the topmost leaders. This led political differences among the leaders and eventually resulted in splits and change of leadership.

Conclusion

Thus the demands raised by these organisations varied from autonomy in the form of Union Territory to a separate state for the Bodos to be carved out of Assam. However, none of these moderate demands articulated by such organisations could be fulfilled. This led to disillusionment among an articulated section of the Bodos and hardened their stance towards the Indian state. Eventually, this section formed an outfit called the Bodo Security Force (BdSF), which was later rechristened as the NDFB. Moreover, the ABSU, once an ardent follower of non-violence and moderate politics, was also dissatisfied with the inadequate responses to their demands from the Union and State Governments over the years, and formed the Bodo Volunteer Force which indulged in extremist activities.

The study showed that in terms of its organisational structure, the NDFB is hierarchical in nature. Its organisational activities are concentrated in the Central Headquarters and the 'Chairman' of the NDFB who is also the Chief of the Bodoland Army who enjoys supreme authority over the organisation. Below the Central Headquarters, there are territorial directorates, which are responsible for certain geographic zones and group leaders are organised according to military designations, e.g., Commandant, Captain, Commander, Area Commander, etc.

Ranjan Daimary was elected as the first President and Commander-in-Chief of the NDFB. On 15 December 2008, a meeting was held at Serfanguri designated camp in Kokrajhar district and a decision was taken to change the leadership of the NDFB. B. Sungthagra alias Dhiren Boro was elected as the new President and Govinda Basumatary as the General Secretary of the outfit. However, on 27 December 2008, Ranjan Daimary sent an e-mail to the media and claimed that he was the President of the outfit. Finally on 1 January 2009, the NDFB expelled its founder President, Ranjan Daimary after replacing him with B. Sungthagra *alias* Dhiren Boro as President. There was also a split in the Daimary faction of the NDFB, called the NDFB-R. The group led by the 'Chief' of Bodoland Army, I.K. Songbijit, on 20 November 2012, announced the formation of a nine member "Interim National Council", with Songbijit as its self-proclaimed "Interim President". It is observed that the main reasons for the split in the NDFB are political differences and struggle for supremacy among the leadership. The NDFB changed its leadership due to arrests, death of leaders in encounters and surrenders of the leaders.

It may be noted that although Ranjan Daimary was the founder President of the NDFB and spearheaded the organisation for more than twenty years from 1986 to 2008, his supremacy within the organisation was challenged due to his political differences with a section of the leadership. However, in spite of the setbacks faced by the Ranjan Daimary faction of the NDFB due to two splits, Daimary continues to be an important force to reckon with. As stated by the senior Union Home Ministry official and interlocutor P.C. Haldar, "the Centre felt that a final settlement could be worked out when the Ranjan Daimary faction of the NDFB is also on board."

As laid down in the Constitution of the NDFB, one of its major demands is to establish a "Sovereign Bodoland". After the 30th October, 2008 Assam serial blasts, the NDFB split into two factions; thereafter, the demand for Sovereign Bodoland was raised only by the anti-talk faction of the NDFB. Ranjan Daimary was anti-talk prior to his arrest. However, after his arrest Daimary was ready to hold talks with the Government and agreed to rethink on the core demand of 'Sovereignty'. Daimary had, however, said that the outfit's Constitution would have to be amended to remove the 'sovereignty' clause before going ahead with the talks. Later, the NDFB-R has not spelt out clearly whether the faction has dropped the demand for sovereignty or not. The NDFB-P dropped the demand for Sovereign Bodoland and advocated separate in tune with the sentiments of the Bodo people. However, the NDFB-S had committed to continue their struggle for 'Independent Bodoland'.

References

1 Sharma, C. K. (2000). The Bodo Movement: A Preliminary enquiry into the role of the middle class and the State. In Girin Phukan (ed.), *Political dynamics of North-East India.* (pp.128-42). New Delhi: South Asian Publishers.

2 Azam, K. J. (1981).*Political Aspects of National Integration,* Meerut: MeenakshiPrakashan. p.83.

3 Nadal, S.N. (1982).*Contemporary Capitalism and the Middle Classes,* Moscow: (n.d.).

4 Baruah, A. K. and Sengupta S. (eds)(2013).*Social Forces and Politics in North East India*, Guwahati: DVS Publishers.

5 Sudhir, J. G. (1994). 'The Bodo Movement in Assam: Unrest to Accord'. In *Asian Survey*, Vol.34, No.10,(pp. 878-92).California: University of California Press. Retrieved from http://www.jstor.org/stable/2644967

6 Brahma, S. (2004).'The Chatra Sanmilan as an Architect of the Boro Nationality'. In *Mugani Sakhi*, (n.d.): All BodoStudents 'Union.

7 Basumatary, B. (2005, February 3). 'Political Aspiration and Developments of Boros in the Post Independence Era'. *The Bodo*(pp.150-54). Mouthpiece, Bodo Sahitya Sabha, Bijni.

8 Basumatary, B. K. (1992).*Plains Tribal before the Simon Commission.*Harisinga: Becon Publishers.

9 Baglari, B. (2007).'A Brief Historical Account Leading to the Signing of Two Bodo Accords'.*Udangsri*(pp. 62-64).(n.d.): NDFB Information and Publicity Wing.

10 Sonowal,G. (2001, January 6-7).'The Rise of Tribals in Assam and the Role of SonowalKachari in the Rising of Tribals'. (An article in Assamese language "*AsomorJanjatiJagaranAruJanajatiJagaranatSonowalKacharir-Bhumika*) in the Souvenir of the fifth bi-anual Session of the Margherita District tribal Sangha held at No. 2 MahangDeuriGaon , Tinsukia.

11 Roy, A. (1995). *The Boro Imbroglio.* Guwahati: Spectrum Publishers.

12 Moshahary,R. N.(1993).'Boro Sahitya Sabha: A Brief Historical Survey'. Seminar paper of *North-East India History Association*, 14th Session, Jorhat.

13 Lahiri, M. (1991).*Boro Thunlaini Jarimin (*History of Bodo Literature*).*

Kokrajhar: Ansumui Publisher.

14 Bhattacharya,P.C. (1966). Introduction. In Bhaben Narzi, *Boro-KachariSamajaru Sanskriti* (Assamese). Guwahati

15 Moshahary,*op.cit.*

16 Roy, *op. cit.*, p.60.

17 *Ibid.* p.156.

18 The NDFB opposed the Decision of Bodo Sahitya Sabha.

19 Prakash, V. (2008).*Terrorism in India's North-East: A Gathering Storm* (Vol.I.).Delhi: Kalpaz Publications. p.266.

20 Sharma, *op.cit.,*p.134.

21 Prakash, *op.cit.*, p.266.

22 Sharma, *op.cit.,*p.134.

23 Chaudhury,Medini. The Nemesis of Insensitivity-The Bodoland movement (Unpublished Manuscript). p.42.

24 Roy, *op. cit.*, pp.60-61.

25 Sharma, *op.cit.,*p.135.

26 A Memorandum submitted by the UTNLF to the President of India, Gauhati, 29th May, 1984.

27 Dutta,P.S. (1993). *Autonomy Movement in Assam: Documents.* New Delhi: Omsons Publications.

28 Dutta, A. (1997). 'Politics of Identity and Nation Building in North East India'. InGirinPhukan&N.C. Dutta (eds.). *Political Dynamics of North-East India.* New Delhi: South Asian Publication. pp.180-181.

29 Dutta*, op.cit.*,pp.180-181.

30 Narzary,B. (2007).*UpendraNath Brahma: Life and Philosophy*, Chirang: Chirang Publication Board. p. 30.

31 Information collected from a former ABSU member.

32 Mandal (Basumata), S. N.(2011).*History and Culture of the Bodos.*Jalpaiguri:n.d. p.103.

33 Memorandum submitted to the Prime Minister Rajiv Gandhi by BPAC, New Delhi, January, 1989.

34 A memorandum submitted by ABSU to the President of India, the Prime Minister of India and the Home Minister of India, New Delhi, November 10, 1987.

35 Sharma, *op.cit.,*p.135.

36 Brahma, Y.Z. (2001). *Bodoland Movement: A Dream and Reality*. Kokrajhar: All BodoStudents' Union. p.46.

37 'Leaders wiser from mistakes'. (2003, February 11). *The Telegraph.*

38 BTC Memorandum of Settlement signed on 10th February, 2003.

39 Election Commission of India. List of Successful Candidates in Assam Assembly Election in 1951. Retrieved from http://www.elections.in on 21st December, 2014 at 11.40.

40 Election Commission of India. List of Successful Candidates in Assam Assembly Election in 1957. Retrieved fromhttp://www.elections.in on 22nd December, 2015 at 12:03.

41 Election Commission of India. List of Successful Candidates in Assam Assembly Election in 1962. Retrieved from http://www.elections.in on 22nd December, 2015 at 12:03.

42 Election Commission of India. List of Successful Candidates in Assam Assembly Election in 1967. Retrieved from http://www.elections.in on 22nd December, 2015 at 12:03.

43 Mukherjee,S.K. (1992). The Plains Tribal Council of Assam. In L.S. Gassah (ed.)*Regional Political Parties in North-East India,*Shillong,

44 Election Commission of India. List of Successful Candidates in Assam Assembly Election in 1972. Retrieved from http://www.elections.in on 22nd December, 2014 at 12:03.

45 Choube,S.K. (1985). *Electoral Politics in North East India*, Chennai (Madras): MadrasUniversities Press. p.61.

46 Election Commission of India. List of Successful Candidates in Assam Assembly Election in 1978. Retrieved from http://www.elections.inon 23rd August, 2013 at 22:48.

47 *Statistical Report on General Electionof the LAC of Assam*(1978). Election Commission of India. Delhi:Election Commission of India.

48 The Memorandum to the Prime Minister Indira Gandhi, submitted by the UTNLF, New Delhi, 10/07/1985.

49 *Statistical Report on General Election of the LAC of Assam*(1983). Chief Election Officer. Dispur, Assam:Election Commission of Assam.

50 The Three Member Expert Committee on Bodo Issues, submitted by ABSU and BPAC, Kokrajhar, 8th April, 1991; Why Separate State? (1987, November 10).Memorandum submitted to the President of India and

the Home Minister of India, by ABSU.

51 *Statistical Report on General Election of the LAC of Assam* (1985), Chief Election Officer, Dispur, Assam:Election Commission of Assam.

52 PTCA was formed on 27th February, 1967, and the UTNLF came into existence on 13th June, 1984, few months before the 1985 Assam Legislative Assembly election. For further details see Roy, *op.cit.*p.61.

53 Sharma, *op.cit.* p.139.

54 Sonowal, *op.cit.* p.56.

55 Boro, D. (2015).*The Lockup is My Home* (Rahul Dev Brahma, Trans.).Kokrajhar:Words n Words. p.91.

56 Lt. Col Chadha, V. (2005). *Low Intensity Conflicts in India.* United Service Institution of India.New Delhi: Sage Publications. p.267.

57 Prakash, *op.cit.*p.261.

58 NDFB (2002). *The Constitution of NDFB* (2nded.). (n.d.): National Democratic Front of Bodoland. p.2.

59 NDFB-P (2011, July). *Voice of Boroland.* (n.d.): NDFB-P Publicity Wing.

60 For details see B. Swmkhwr (2012, September 27). 'A Brief History of the National Democratic Front of Bodoland (NDFB)'. An unpublished article.

61 NDFB (2002), *op.cit.* p.3.

62 B. Swmkhwr, *op.cit.*, pp.2-4.

63 Chadha, *op.cit.* p.269.

64 NDFB(2002), *op.cit.* p.6.

65 Sonowal, *op. cit.,* p.57.

66 B. Swmkhwr, *op. cit.*, pp.2-4.

67 Sonowal, *op. cit.,* p.58.

68 NDFB (2002). *The Manifesto of the National Democratic Front of Bodoland* (2nded.). (n.d.): Publicity Wing. p.12.

69 NDFB(2002), *op.cit.* pp.5-8

70 Sonowal, *op. cit.*p.58.

71 'Rebel in police custody'. (2002, December 7). *The Telegraph.*

72 'NDFB expels Daimary'.(2009, January 2).*The Telegraph.*

73 'Bodo top gun held in Sikkim hideout swoop'. (2002, January 2). *The*

Telegraph.

74 'Bodo rebel leaders held in Calcutta hotel'. (2003, May 1). *The Telegraph.*

75 Bhaumik, S. (2009). *Troubled Periphery: Crisis of India's North-East.* Sage Studies on India's North-East. New Delhi: Sage Publication. p.127.

76 'NDFB appoints new chief'. (2008, December 16). *The Telegraph.*

77 'Daimary asserts authority'. (2008, December 28). *The Telegraph.*

78 'NDFB rift'. (2008, December 29). *The Telegraph.*

79 'NDFB expels Daimary'. (2009, January 2). *The Telegraph.*

80 *Centre for Development and Peace Studies.* Incidents 2009. Retrieved from http://cdpsindia.org/assam_incident1.asp on 13-08-2014 at 10:55.

81 'Top Assam police officials interrogate NDFB chief'. (2010, May 1). *The Assam Tribune.*

82 'NDFB leader held in Mizoram'.(2010, December 12). *The Telegraph.*

83 'NDFB-R stares at split'. (2012, November 21). *The Telegraph.*

84 'Songbijit 'ousted' from NDFB'. (2015, June 27). *The Sentinel* (Guwahati).

*****

3

Major Demands, Strategies and Role of NDFB

In previous chapter, an attempt has been made to trace the emergence of the NDFB, the organisational structure and the leadership patterns were also highlighted. For an understanding of the role of the NDFB, it is important to focus on its major demands and strategies to achieve the same. The NDFB has been demanding the fulfillment of the historical rights and aspirations of the Bodo community. It is seen that the NDFB has been switching their demands in the light of the situation or depending on their leadership. Since its formation, the NDFB has been demanding Bodoland and at present they are looking for possible options like, sovereignty, statehood, a union territory or even an honourable solution like rehabilitation of the NDFB cadres.[1]

The Constitution of the NDFB defines the aims and objectives of the organisation as:

(i) To Liberate Bodoland from the Indian Expansionism and Occupation;

(ii) To free the Bodo Nation from Exploitation, Oppression and Domination;

(iii) To establish a Democratic Socialist society, promote Liberty, Equality and Fraternity; and

(iv) To uphold the Integrity and Sovereignty of Bodoland."[2]

Apart from the above, the NDFB has also been demanding the introduction of Roman script for the Bodo language.[3] However, after the acceptance of the Devanagari script by the BSS, the NDFB also dropped its demand for adopting Roman script. The demand for Roman script was part of the 1st Edition of the Constitution of the NDFB. However; it was skipped in the 2nd Edition of its Constitution and it was mentioned that Bodo, as well as English, should be the official language of it, and preference will be given to the Roman or English script for the Bodo language.[4] However, the NDFB Vice-President, Dhiren Boro, in his autobiography "*The Lockup is My Home*" stated that 'the Roman script is not all an issue of the NDFB' and believe that it was an issue of the community as a whole

It is observed that the NDFB often stated that it would join talks if the Union Government would include 'historical rights' and the 'right to self-determination' of the Bodo people in Assam on the agenda.[5] When BLTF was in due process to sign BTC Accord, the NDFB criticized the new Accord on the ground that it will "never fulfill the hope and aspiration of the Bodo people" and the outfit vowed to continue "armed struggle" till the "goal" is achieved. Its Vice-President stated that:

> *"BTC is an agreement between the BLT and the Government; NDFB has nothing to do in it. While accepting the BTC they did not even feel the need to know our opinion. Therefore, the NDFB will not accept this accord but it has no intention of opposing it or of creating any hindrance against the creation of BTC. The organisation has not opposed even the BAC Accord."*[6]

Therefore, even after the BTC Accord was signed they stick to their basic demand. Further, on August 3, 2003, outfits arrested 'General Secretary' Govinda Basumatary reiterated the demand for a 'sovereign' Bodoland and talks in a foreign country as preconditions to come to the negotiating table. When the NDFB felt that the Government had slowed down the discussion process, it reacted and reiterated its demand for a 'Sovereign Bodo State' on June 27, 2005. The NDFB declared that the principle and ideology of NDFB "are the liberation of Bodoland, and thereby the talks with the Indian Government would be based on the solid rock of our principle and ideology."[7] The NDFB reiterated the demand just before the coming into the ceasefire agreement so that the government might take the Bodoland issue seriously. Though the NDFB was in the peace talks, yet on March 12, 2007, it refused to submit the charter of demands as a precondition for initiating peace talks with the Union Government. Thus, it sought to satisfy its constituency by persisting with the Bodoland demand.[8]

Meanwhile, on May 1, 2008, the NDFB submitted its charter of demands keeping liberation of Bodoland as a pre-condition to Prime Minister Manmohan Singh in New Delhi. However, on May 2, 2008, the Assam Government warned the Union Government that if it accepted the NDFB charter of demands, including 'liberation' of Bodoland, to start a dialogue with the outfit, it would strengthen ULFA's argument to sit for talk only if 'Sovereignty' was discussed.[9] However, gradually the rift widened among the leaders of the NDFB due to political differences. Hence, some leaders were in favour of negotiating with the government, and some were against it. On October 3, 2008, on the occasion of the NDFB's 22nd anniversary at a designated camp at Kumguri in Kokrajhar district, the NDFB President Ranjan Daimary said they were in favour of peace and a negotiated settlement of the conflict but the Indian authorities at the centre were not responding properly and therefore threatened to pick up the gun at the Centre, accusing it of dictating to the outfit.[10]

As discussed earlier, the nature of the NDFB's demand for Bodoland has taken different forms due to split in the outfit. The split has brought significant changes in the aims and objectives of the outfit that was primarily the creation of a sovereign Bodoland. However, at present the NDFB-P faction of the NDFB has dropped the demand for Sovereign Bodoland; the NDFB-R has not clearly spelt out its stand about the demand, and the NDFB-S faction is persistently demanding the same. It is important to note here that there are a few demands for which all factions of the NDFB have been raising voice for the common cause of the Bodos through different statements.

Demand of the NDFB-R

After the October 30, 2008 Assam serial blasts, the NDFB split into two factions. Thereafter, the demand for Sovereign Bodoland was raised only by the anti-talk faction of the NDFB.[11] The anti-talk faction of the NDFB is also known as NDFB-R. In the pre-arrest period, NDFB-R Chairman Ranjan Daimary was anti-talk and his stand against any negotiation with the government was one of the major factors for the split. However, as Daimary was arrested, the outfit became ready to hold talks with the Government and agreed to rethink on the core demand of 'Sovereignty'. However, Daimary stated that the outfit's Constitution would have to be amended to remove the 'sovereignty' clause before going ahead with the talks.[12] The outfit had even turned down the offer of peace talks with the Government as the right to self-determination, historical rights of Bodo people and the dreams of the martyrs were not included in the proposed agenda submitted by the leaders of the NDFB-P. The NDFB-R had partially dropped the demand for sovereign Bodoland. This became evident when it's 'Publicity Secretary' B. Naijab disclosed on June 25, 2012 by stating that there was no alternative but to form a separate Bodoland.[13] Also on July 3, 2012, the NDFB-R declared that it was ready to begin peace talks with the Union Government without any precondition to solving the Bodo imbroglio. However, the NDFB-R had stressed the necessity of releasing its 'Chairman' from jail to participate in the peace process.

Demand of the NDFB-P

The Pro-Talk faction of the NDFB was rechristened as National Democratic Front of Bodoland- Progressive (NDFB-P), which was declared formally on June 29, 2010. After the formation of NDFB-P, B. Sunthangra alias Dhiren Boro, President of the outfit, clarified that the demand for sovereignty was dropped after studying the mindset as well as the sentiments of the Bodo people. The NDFB-P had changed the strategy and adopted the ideology of creating a separate state of Bodoland under Article 2 and 3 of the Indian Constitution. Interacting with the media persons on the occasion, the General Secretary of the NDFB (P) also said that the organisation has already held several rounds of talks with the Union Government on the issue of the demand for a separate state and the outcome of these talks have been positive till date.

On June 29, 2010, the NDFB-P narrated the logic behind a separate homeland for the Bodos within the framework of the Constitution of India. It observed that the demand was not a fresh one, rather it was raised since 1967 by the then PTCA which was revived from time to time by the ABSU. It claimed that Bodoland is a historical and political right of the indigenous Bodos,and the Government of India must award it on due time.[14] Apparently, the NDFB understands the government's predicament with statehood demands coming in from various quarters, the major problem being in Telangana.

The NDFB-P is adamant and would not be ready to compromise on the issue of a separate Bodoland. The outfit appealed to the Bodo people to unite and fight for it.[15] Meanwhile, on June 20, 2011, it renewed its demand for creation of a separate Bodoland state by carving out the entire north bank of the Brahmaputra Valley comprising the whole area from the Sonkosh River in the west to Sadiya in the east. The NDFB submitted a map of the proposed separate Bodoland state to the government through interlocutor PC Haldar. The outfit denied to compromise on anything short of a separate Bodo state.[16]

On July 14, 2011, a four-member team belonging to NDFB-P, comprising its General Secretary B. Swmkhwr, Home Secretary M. Gerema, Finance Secretary B. Detsung and Organising Secretary B.K. Olongbar, met the Governor of Assam and urged him to take necessary steps to break the stalemate in the talks for an early solution.[17] The NDFB-P even appealed to tribal t (MPs) to support the issue and sought their intervention to help the NDFB-P by raising the demand for creating Bodoland state as per the provisions of Articles 2 and 3 of the Indian Constitution in the 2011 summer parliament session.[18]

On February 8, 2012, the NDFB-P demanded that the future Bodoland State (as projected by the outfit) should have a Legislative Assembly with as high as 90% of the total seats in the Legislative Assembly and 100% of parliamentary seats reserved only for tribal people.[19] Later on February 16, 2012, the outfit held a discussion with Union Home Minister P. Chidambaram over the solution of its vexed problems and submitted a memorandum demanding an early political settlement. It also demanded new interlocutor who are either politician or statesman by replacing interlocutor P.C. Halder.[20] The NDFB-P was not happy with the functioning of the interlocutor P.C. Halder on the ground that they had waited for more than two and a half years but there was not much progress in the peace talks. Hence, on February 17, 2012, the NDFB-P suggested the names of three politicians – former Lok Sabha Speaker and NCP leader P.A. Sangma, Congress MP from Arunachal Pradesh Sanjay Takam, and former Nagaland Chief Minister S C Jamir – and Meghalaya Governor R.S. Mooshahary as Haldar's replacement. It was reported that since Haldar was also appointed as the interlocutor for initiating talks with the other rival faction of NDFB-P led by Ranjan Daimary, the pro-talk faction was worried and hence they requested for his removal.[21] However, later the NDFB-P softened its stand on the issue of changing the interlocutor for the peace talks with the outfit.

On July 16, 2012,the Central Government refused to create a separate Bodoland and had appealed to the NDFB-P to lay down arms within three months to ensure further progress in the dialogue process. However, in reply to Union Government's refusal on July 17, 2012, the NDFB-P stated that the question of submission of arms does not arise until the Memorandum of Settlement was signed. The NDFB-P dismissed the news that the Union Government had asked the outfit to lay down arms within three months to ensure progress in the talks.[22]

According to the NDFB-P, the Bodo people have every right to a separate state and observed that despite fulfilling all the conditions of statehood, the Bodo people are allegedly facing discrimination and denied their constitutional right. The NDFB made an allegation to the government that the Bodo people have been discriminated against just because of their 'non-Indian' origin. Further to them the denial of statehood to the Bodo people on the part of the Government of India is not only a historical injustice but also a gross violation of the Indian Constitution. The NDFB-P, for and on behalf of the suppressed, oppressed and marginalized people, has appealed to the Government of India to discuss the issue of the separate state of Bodoland in an all-party meeting.[23]

Thus the above statements of the NDFB-P show that it had been continuously voicing the demand for a separate state of Bodoland. However, on August 10, 2013,its, General Secretary Govinda Basumatary stated that the NDFB-P was ready for a compromise if the status of Union Territory is granted instead of Bodoland State. As stated by the General Secretary, "Give us a Union Territory, we will be satisfied. Between Sixth Schedule (status) and statehood, there is no other path to give us political power. So, Union Territory status is acceptable to us if the Government of India cannot provide us with a state." But later, on August 18, 2013, he denied the misquoted news and criticized a section of the press for making a 'deliberate attempt to spread misgivings among the people about the outfit's stand by stating that he (Govinda Basumatary) had scaled down the demand for statehood to that for Union Territory.[24]

After several rounds of failed talks, the demand of the NDFB-P is yet to be fulfilled. It is observed that at present the NDFB-P is in the process of negotiation with the Union Government on subjects like inclusion of all the indigenous tribal groups in Assam under the Sixth Schedule of the Indian Constitution; re-enforcement of the Bengal Eastern Frontier Regulation Act,1873 in order to check the influx of illegal migrants and encroachment of tribal lands in Assam; lifting of ban imposed on NDFB to create a congenial atmosphere for political dialogues;[25] fixing of 1951 as the base year for detection, deletion and deportation of illegal migrants and updating of the National Register of Citizens (NRC);[26] establishment of institutions like central university, agricultural university, national law university, medical college, IIT and IIM in Bodoland; creation of an airport; and creation of Bodo Regiment in Indian Army.

Demand of the NDFB-S

Meanwhile after a split in the NDFB-R into two factions, one group remained as the NDFB-R and the other faction changed the nomenclature as the NDFB-S. The NDFB-S had committed to continue their struggle for 'Independent Bodoland' and they had no relation with those armed guerrilla organisations that did not have similarity with the principle and ideology of the NDFB. The NDFB-S laid the pre-condition that "until and unless the Government of India would grant 'Independent Bodoland' through internationally monitored referendum, then it would not be possible for them to join the peace talk."[27]

The NDFB was formed with the sole objective of forming a sovereign Bodoland outside the Indian Union. However, it failed to acquire mass support because there were many Bodo organisations which demanded Bodoland as a separate state within the Indian Union. However, after the formation of BTC, many cadres of the NDFB became disillusioned and surrendered and negotiation with the Government was the only way left for the NDFB. The Operation All Clear in Bhutan also compounded challenges to the survival of the outfit. After signing a ceasefire agreement with the government, the NDFB toned down the sovereignty demand and raised more voice about negotiation on the Bodoland demand.

Demand for Rescuing Missing Cadres and Leaders

It is observed that the NDFB has been concerned about the missing cadres and leaders who have been found missing since 2003 Bhutan Operation All Clear. Meanwhile, on February 7, 2006, the NDFB refused to begin peace talks unless the Union Government provides information about the whereabouts of seven senior members missing during Operation All Clear. It appealed to the Union Government to prove its sincerity by providing information on the seven leaders. The missing militants included the outfit's Publicity Secretary B. Erakdao, B. Habrang, B. Fwjoukhang, Jwkhrub, Derhasa, Onsula and Udla. Daimary claimed that the missing leaders were taken into custody by the Royal Bhutan Army just before the start of Operation All Clear. According to the NDFB, the missing leaders might be "in the hands (custody) of either India or Bhutan".[28] On July 16, 2013, the NDFB-S urged the Bhutan Government to disclose the whereabouts of its leaders who went missing during 2003 Operation All Clear.

Demand to Stop Fake Encounters of Bodo Youths

The NDFB has been demanding to stop fake encounters as well as the torture of Bodo youths. According to them, there are many such incidents where innocent and ignorant Bodo youths who had no relation with the outfit were accused, arrested and killed by the security forces. However, the security forces have cleared that all the deceased persons were the cadres of the NDFB and were involved in many illegal activities. However, the outfit protested against the sporadic killings of common people in the name of the NDFB. As part of such protest, the NDFB-P called for 12 hours' Assam shut down on July 19, 2009. Again on August 3, 2009, the NDFB-R called a 12-hour Assam *bandh* (general shutdown) from 5am (IST) to 5pm on August 5 to protest against what it alleged were systematic killings of the Bodo community by the security forces.[29] The NDFB-R warned that the outfit would not remain silent to the alleged excesses by the security forces. In a telephonic conversation, B. Barbai, who claimed himself to be the Sergeant Major of the NDFB's General Headquarters, said the Assam Police and the Army have been continuing their killing spree of common people in the name of operations against the NDFB. He said more than 75 percent reports of the encounters claimed by the security forces were false.

Meanwhile, on November 1, 2010, the NDFB threatened to kill 20 or more people for every NDFB cadre killed by the security forces. In a press release, the NDFB stated:

> *"The Government of India/Assam has been killing innocent Bodo people doing fake encounters in the name of NDFB. School students, cultivators and simple living innocent Bodo people are killed by Indian forces. And these fake encounters are continuing. So the Bodoland Army, NDFB strongly warns the Government of India/Assam to stop the killing of innocent Bodo people in the name of fake encounters. We (NDFB), the Bodo people and the Bodoland Army, NDFB, bear all these for long years. The Government*

> *of India/Assam has done much against the Bodo people. Patience also has limit and now our patience is over.'*[30]

On December 8, 2014, the security forces, in an encounter, killed a suspected militant belonging to NDFB-S, identified as Biswajit Basumatary (28), at Daisungjhora in Chirang District. However, the slain militant's family members said that he had gone to his crop field at dawn and claimed he was not a militant. Jayanta Basumatary, President of the Chirang unit of the ABSU, also backed the family's claim. NDFB-S has termed the encounter of Biswajit Basumatary as 'fake' by Assam Police and Indian Army.

Though, it is hard to prove whether those encounters are fake or real, yet some of the encounters seem to be fake. According to media sources, 52 cases of fake encounters were registered in Assam in the period 2009-2013.[31] The Asian Commission for Human Rights (ACHR) stated that many such fake encounter cases are not being reported by the family members of the victims due to several reasons. The NEDAN Foundation took the initiative to study the real story behind the iron curtain of the recent encounters. Total 10 cases were done in different places of Kokrajhar in BTC, Assam. The main motive of study was to measure the height of exploitation of rights in the name of encounter which is false and was decorated by the officials as encounter and the study revealed the fake encounters in the name of the NDFB cadres.[32]

Demand for Equal Treatment to Organisations like ULFA

The NDFB-P had demanded a clarification from Union Home Minister P. Chidambaram over why ULFA was treated with kid gloves despite being a banned outfit, while rules were different for other militant groups. The NDFB accused the incumbents in Dispur of being 'chauvinistic'. The ULFA came to the negotiating table in February, 2011, when their leaders, led by Aranbinda Rajkhowa, met the then Prime Minister Dr. Manmohan Singh and the Home Minister, P. Chidambaram. At that time, the ULFA had not signed suspension of operation agreement, prompting questions from the NDFB which felt that the Central and State governments were biased. In a four-page letter, the NDFB asked the Ministry of Home Affairs, "How could the Centre and its top-ranking ministers hobnob frequently with the leaders of the proscribed ULFA, who have not yet signed the suspension of operations agreement, whereas such a deal was neither heard nor seen in case of other organisations?'

The NDFB complained that the government seemed to be treating other militant organisations already in negotiations but termed banned- as "untouchables". The NDFB-P complained that the ULFA cadres moved about freely with arms without signing a peace agreement, but those who had signed a treaty were subjected to frequent frisking and "torture" by Assam police. It alleged that there was one set of rules for NDFB, another one for ULFA. In a letter to the Centre, the NDFB stated, "In Assam, an Assamese fellow is exempted even if he commits all kinds of nonsense, just because he is an *Axomiya.* The Assamese are treated as above the law by the Assam Government, manned by the chauvinistic Assamese." The NDFB-P alleged that such privilege was only because ULFA was an outfit of the "elite species of Assamese people" that it was dealt with extra care.[33]

Demand for Detection, Deletion and Deportation of Illegal Migrants and Updating of National Register of Citizens (NRC)

The NDFB has been raising voice against the illegal migrants' issue. It accused both Assam Government and Central Government of being soft on the illegal influx issue for the sake of votes. The NDFB even criticized the Assam Government for its failure to protect the indigenous people and warned that the NDFB will not allow any Muslim immigrants from Bangladesh to live in tribal belt and blocks.[34] The NDFB-P cautioned that the violence between the indigenous people and Muslim immigrants would be repeated if illegal immigrants were not pushed back after updating the NRC, taking 1951 as the base year. It also questioned as to why the Union and Assam Governments are concerned only when there is conflict with Muslims, but why they are not serious when the clashes take place between Bodos and Adivasis and Dimasa and Karbis. The NDFB-R also said that the Government should take a tough stand against illegal immigrants from Bangladesh, and mere sealing of border and rehabilitation will not bring a permanent solution.[35] At a time when anti-foreigner mood was growing stronger in the state, on September 15, 2012, the NDFB-P stated that the Assam Accord was not an appropriate instrument for detection and deportation of 'aliens', as it did not have any constitutional validity. In a press conference on September 16, 2012, it announced that the Asom Sanmilita Mahasangha (ASM), Indigenous Tribal People's Front and the NDFB-P had decided to move jointly the Supreme Court challenging the amendments made in the Citizenship Act. The organisations have alleged that the amendments made in the Citizenship Act in 1985, 1986 and 2003 were illegal and unconstitutional. The NDFB appealed the Government should first identify the foreigners on the basis of the 1951 NRC before updating the NRC.[36]

The NDFB-P was of the opinion that unless 100 Assembly constituencies out of 126 were not reserved for the indigenous tribes of Assam, the whole state would soon be dominated by the illegal Bangladeshi migrants. The outfit felt this was necessary for the existence of the indigenous tribes in their homeland that is already partially captured by the illegal migrants. Further, the NDFB-P reiterated its demand on updating NRC. In a statement on January 3, 2014, Govinda Basumatary, General Secretary of NDFB-P, which is holding negotiations with the government for many years now, said that this should be done keeping 1951 as the base year instead of 1971 fixed by the government.

Demand for the Proper Implementation of Assam Land Revenue Regulation Act, 1886

The NDFB has also been demanding the proper implementation of Assam Land Revenue Regulation Act, 1886. It is essential to note that the land rights of the tribals as guaranteed under Chapter X of the Assam Land Revenue Regulation Act, 1886, have been continuously violated. Some non-tribal villages have come up in notified tribal blocks in the BTAD as well as in other parts of Assam, which is a clear violation of the Act. The NDFB condemned that the Government of Assam has never taken any measure to prevent the encroachment of tribal lands. After the formation of BTC, certain sections of Bodo leaders hoped that BTC Accord would safeguard the land rights and stop the land acquisition and alienation by the encroachers. However, under the Bodo Accord of 2003, land rights were given to both tribal as well the non-tribal people. The provision of the Accord runs as:

> *4.3. Safeguards for the settlement rights, transfer and inheritance of property, etc. of non-tribals will be suitably incorporated in Para 3 of the Sixth Schedule. Any such law as may be made by the BTC in this regard will not, in particular:*
>
> *(a) Extinguish the rights and privileges enjoyed by any citizen of India in respect of their land at the commencement of BTC, and*
>
> *(b) Bar any citizen from acquiring land either*

by way of inheritance, allotment, settlement or by way of transfer if such citizens were eligible for such bonafide acquisition of land within the BTC area.[37]

This provision of the Accord is being criticized widely. Tribals, in general, and Bodos, in particular, felt that it would bring another wave of land alienation to the tribals, thereby causing a further threat to their existence. The base of the Bodo economy is land, while 90% of the Bodos and other tribals depend upon agriculture for their livelihood; almost 70% of them are landless today due to indebtedness, poverty, and above all the entry of outsiders into essentially tribal areas.[38] Bodo leaders claim that the state government appropriated 600,000 acres for government projects like industries, offices,etc.[39] A report of Asian Centre for Human Rights has mentioned that total 23 revenue villages within Bijni Tribal Block currently under Chirang district have been gradually encroached upon allegedly by the Muslims in violation of the Assam Land Revenue Regulation, 1886.[40] In order to protect tribal land and to preserve their distinct identity in Assam, Gopinath Bordoloi Ministry took a remarkable step. Under his leadership, legislation was availed in 1946, and Chapter X was inserted in Assam Land & Revenue Regulation Act of 1886. Subsequently, 33 tribal belts and blocks were created. The number of tribal belts and blocks was increased up to 45 by 1964 which cover 12546557 Bighas or 1672873 hectares of land area.[41]

Meanwhile, Govinda Basumatary, the leader of the NDFB-P, said that there are 47 tribal belts and blocks in Assam where non-tribals cannot buy land, but, 60%of these belts and blocks have been encroached. Therefore, the NDFB-P had appealed to the Home Minister that these need to be cleared by implementing the Assam Land and Revenue Regulation Act, 1886 (amended in 1947).[42] The NDFB leaders have been aware that BTC was not successful enough to stop the encroachment and safeguard the tribal belts and blocks. Therefore, they have been demanding the proper implementation of the Assam Land and Revenue Regulation Act, 1886.

Other Demands

Meanwhile from 20 July 2012, there was an outbreak of communal violence in Kokrajhar and Chirang districts between Bodos and Muslims. In order to seek a permanent solution to the Bodo problem and the communal clash in lower Assam, the NDFB-P submitted a memorandum to Ms. Sonia Gandhi, Chairperson, UPA Government and the Indian National Congress. The major demands they laid in the Memorandum were the protection of tribal belt and blocks; and illegal migrants.[43] The People's Joint Action Committee on behalf of the NDFB-P strongly urged Prime Minister of India to urgently intervene in order to:

1. Stop the burning situation of communal clashes immediately;
2. Arrest the culprits involved in fomenting the communal clashes;
3. Order a CBI inquiry to investigate the whole matter leading to communal violence;
4. Provide adequate security arrangement in sensitive areas and to provide immediate sufficient relief materials including food, drinking water, clothes and medicines in the relief camps belonging to both the communities;
5. Provide adequate compensation to the bereaved families and injured victims of communal clashes.

Further NDFB-P mentioned that the BTC being devoid of Home Power is not capable of protecting the lives and properties of the people living within its jurisdiction at the time of untoward incidences.[44] The NDFB-P criticized that the BTAD authority could do nothing to save and protect the lives and properties of the people and had to remain a silent spectator. According to it,the provisions and the power of the BTAD are not enough to save and protect the existence and identity of the sons of the soil. Moreover, the NDFB-P declared that as the sons of the soil are Indians from the depth of their heart, they want to live with dignity and honour; wish the implementation of constitutional provisions under the Indian Constitution, and want to live life in peace in their inherited land, enjoying equal opportunity with other bonafide Indian citizens. Besides these, it appealed to Ms. Sonia Gandhi to take prompt and sympathetic action and placed some demands, viz.

1. Grant Bodoland state to save and protect the identity of sons of the soil of Assam and also for permanent peace in the region;
2. Ensure the NRC on the basis of 1951 Census report before rehabilitating the evacuated illegal migrants;
3. Implementation of Clause 10 of Assam Accord 1985;[45]
4. Make an impartial and unbiased inquiry into the recent communal clash by the CBI and find out the actual culprits who are working behind the smoke screen.

Strategies

As far as the strategies of the NDFB are concerned, it appears that the NDFB does not attempt to challenge government forces directly but acts to change perceptions as to the effectiveness or legitimacy of the government itself. This is done by ensuring the widest possible knowledge of the acts of terrorist violence among the target audience. The NDFB rarely attempts to 'control' terrain as it ties them to justifiable locations and reduces their mobility and security. They, as a rule, avoid direct confrontations with government forces. The NDFB uses methods that neutralize the strengths of conventional forces. Bombings and mortar attacks on civilian targets where military or security personnel spend off-duty time, ambushes of undefended convoys, and assassinations of poorly protected individuals are common tactics.

The NDFB does not discriminate between combatants and non-combatants, or if they do, they broaden the category of "combatants" so much as to render it meaningless. It often targets the non-combatants by using various means of violence.[46] It led the Bodo people's war for independent Bodoland against the Government, but many times they did not discriminate and even attacked people from their own community and even was involved in many fratricidal clashes.[47]

The subversive activities of the NDFB include damage to rail tracks, causing accidents leading to loss of life and property; creating terror among the travellers; and throwing the entire system out of gear.[48] Similarly, vehicles on the State and National Highways are often attacked, passengers and transport workers are killed or wounded, and sometimes abducted for ransom, and goods are looted.[49]

The next important target of the NDFB is resource-based industries like petroleum and tea that form the core of the modern organized sector in the region. As the articulation of economic grievances hovers around the idea of so-called regional colonialism based on the alleged drain on rich resources of the region, any violent political movement makes petroleum and tea as its target. Oil pipelines are often blown up, tea gardens are targeted for extortion and, sometimes, tea garden executives are abducted. Tea gardens constitute the soft targets of the NDFB as these are in the vicinity of forests and away from the populous localities.[50] It is easy to understand that disrupting industrial activities centring on petroleum and tea are bound to block the wheels of progress in the region. The attack by the NDFB on tea and petroleum is bound to convey a negative signal to the prospective investors.

Cadre Strength of NDFB

As mentioned earlier, the NDFB (formerly known as BdSF) started its training with 77 cadres. The 1st Batch training of NDFB had started on October 26, 1989 and it was completed on 14 November 1989. Prior to the All Clear Operation in Bhutan, the group was estimated to have 3500 members, mainly based in Bangladesh, Myanmar and Bhutan.[51] Till December 15, 2003, the NDFB cadres were based in the 12 camps located in southern Bhutan. However, a large number of cadres either surrendered or were arrested during and after the operations. The strength of the outfit was then estimated at about 2000.[52] Prior to the declaration of a ceasefire with the security forces, most NDFB cadres were based in its camps in Myanmar and Bangladesh. Additionally, there were several temporary camps in different locations of Arunachal Pradesh and in the Garo hills of Meghalaya. Even as the NDFB-R was in the process of preparing the list of its cadres and arsenal, the names of some of its members were unlikely to figure in the list as they were believed to have gone underground again.

According to intelligence sources, although the NDFB-R faction had submitted a list of its cadres earlier, the government had asked the outfit to provide photographs and mobile numbers of the cadres also for the verification process. When the report came out, the Ranjan Daimary faction of the NDFB was said to have cadre strength of at least 500 militants, including about 70 female cadres, armed with sophisticated weapons. The designated camps for the NDFB-R were likely to be set up in Udalguri, Baksa and Chirang, and not more than 175 cadres would be kept in one camp. Video surveillance facilities would be installed in all the camps to monitor the activities of these people belonging to the Ranjan Daimary faction of the outfit. According to intelligence sources, all the cadres would be provided a stipend of Rs 3,000 each.[53]

On March, 29, 2010, the Assam Forest Minister Rockybul Hussain stated in the Legislative Assembly that among the active militant groups the NDFB-R had 225 cadres.[54] Four arrested cadres of the NDFB-R had revealed on July 23, 2011, in police interrogation, that NDFB-R had camps in the Hakha area of Chin province in western Myanmar since September 2009 and till date 93 militants were undergoing training at that camp. On October 1, 2011, Sergeant Major Biranjay Boro, belonging to the NDFB-R, who had surrendered on September 29, before the Border Security Force (BSF) in Shillong, had revealed that at least 70 NDFB-R militants were in Bangladesh till his surrender. The BSF sources said that the NDFB-R had winded up its Khagrachari camp in Bangladesh, and the cadres had moved to a remote area along the Bangladesh-Myanmar border.[55]

The State Forest Minister in a statement at the Assam Legislative Assembly, on 6th March 2012, pointed out that the NDFB–R had 320-350 cadres; the NDFB-P had a total of 936 cadres who have been residing in the designated camp after the ceasefire agreement. However, on June 1, 2012, the news report quoted a security source saying that the NDFB-S had about 100 cadres. Forest Minister Rockybul Hussain, on December 16, 2013, said that six militant outfits, including ULFA-I and NDFB-IKS, are active in Assam with cadre strength of 760. Hussain, answering on behalf of Chief Minister Tarun Gogoi, also in charge of Home, said the other outfits are KPLT, KLO, MULTA and HuM - Assam unit. The NDFB-IKS had the highest number of cadres at 300, followed by ULFA-I with 240 militants, KLO had 100, and MULTA and HUJI had 40 each.

It appears from the above that there is no consensus about the exact number of cadres and camps of the NDFB-R, the NDFB-P and the NDFB-S. The press statement from the Union and State Governments provided some ambiguous information regarding the cadre strength as well as the bases of the NDFB. The ambiguity increased more when we observe the number of cadres that the Government sources had published and the number of arrested cadres.

Sources of Arms and Ammunitions

Security sources informed *The Assam Tribune* that the NSCN provided weapons to the NDFB to start the training. They also managed to snatch away some weapons from the forest guards and police personnel to increase their strength. Ranjan Daimary met NSCN (I-M) Chairman Issac Swu for the first time in Kathmandu in 1993, and Issac Swu sent Daimary to Bangladesh to contact some persons for the procurement of sophisticated weapons. In 1996, the NDFB established contacts with a clandestine arms dealer of China and paid an amount of Rs. 2 crore in advance for procuring around 2,000 sophisticated weapons. However, the security forces of Bangladesh managed to intercept two fishing trawlers, and the NDFB received only around 400 weapons.[56] These weapons were brought to Assam from Bangladesh from different routes through Meghalaya, Tripura and Mizoram. Sources said that the NDFB had also procured weapons from the ULFA. Sources also revealed that Daimary had also stayed in the bases of the NSCN in Thailand for quite some time and established contacts with some agents of the ISI in 1993. The ISI provided the NDFB with some communications equipment, explosives and timer devices. Daimari even met some senior persons of the Pakistan High Commission in Dhaka in 2004, and he knew some officials of the General of Forces Intelligence (DGFI), the intelligence agency of Bangladesh. The Chin National Liberation Army (CNLA), a militant outfit of Myanmar, is also responsible for supplying arms and ammunition to the NDFB. Moreover,the NDFB also looted arms from security forces and different sources. In 1998, it looted 84 weapons, in 1999 they looted 16 weapons and in 2000 they looted 13 weapons.

It is to be noted that the NDFB has been using different strategies to pressurize and intimidate the authority or to gain the attention of the concerned authorities. By the use of their strength i.e. cadres, arms and ammunition, they tried to fulfill their aspirations. The following are some of the strategies that have been used by NDFB since its formation:

Bandh

Bandh is the most familiar device used by democratic protesters who are usually moderate groups. However, there are many extremist groups in Assam who often called *bandh*. So, the NDFB also adopted this technique at various points of their struggle. It called for *bandh* either to fulfill their demand or to react to the governments' decision. However, those *bandhs* were not peaceful, rather full of bloodshed. There were some incidents where the NDFB cadres were killed or wounded when the police retaliated against militants who were enforcing the closure of shops and business establishment during the *bandhs*.[57] There were few occasions when the NDFB called rail-cum-road *bandh* (general strike). During such *bandhs,* the NDFB militants damaged portions of railway tracks resulting in the derailment of wagons. The train services were hit due to such derailments.[58] During *bandh* hours the NDFB also set ablaze vehicles and harmed the owners of the vehicles. The *bandhs* affected the normal movement of the civilians. The government issued notices to Government services not to abstain their normal duties. In reply, the NDFB also issued warning that if the outfit takes any action that caused the loss of life and property, the outfit would not be responsible, and only the Government should be responsible.

It is observed that there were many incidents where the NDFB called for *bandhs* but withdrew it midway due to non-response of the authority. There are numerous occasions where general masses even boycotted such calls for *bandh*. It is important for an organisation to get maximum support for such *bandhs*. However, that also depends on the issue for which the *bandhs* have been called. When the NDFB failed to get maximum support, it changed its stance and called of the *bandh*. It is seen that the NDFB usually called *bandh* on issues like creation of Bodoland, fake encounters, police atrocities, illegal migrants, etc. Though, sometimes the NDFB could not get maximum response in the whole of Assam; in BTC area it got maximum response due to fear psychosis.

Rallies

In 2005, the NDFB held a series of public rallies to evolve a consensus on their demand for sovereignty before starting negotiations with Delhi. The last of such rallies took place at Kokrajhar on August 28, 2005. Before Kokrajhar, rallies were held at Udalguri, Sonitpur, Baska, Jeraiguri (under Gossaigaon subdivision), Serfanguri, Ramphalbhil, Chirang and Bijni. The top brass of the NDFB leadership was present in those rallies. General Secretary Govinda Basumatary alias B. Swmhhr, Speaker Sunil Basumatary alias B. Bengra, Bodoland Army Commander-in-Chief B. S. Sushrauga, Deputy Commander-in-Chief B. Olongbar, Cultural Secretary M. Gerema, Finance Secretary B. Detsung, Operation Commander B. Bikaraja were present, among others, in those rallies. However, the Chairman of the outfit Ranjan Daimary was missing in those rallies.

The rallies managed to attract a good crowd. All Bodo Students' Union (ABSU) and Bodo Sahitya Sabha sent their representatives in these rallies. Some prominent personalities of the Bodo society were also invited as guests. The NDFB made it clear that it would not climb down from its demand of a sovereign Bodo nation. The leadership termed the Bodo Territorial Council (BTC) as a compromise and observed that the BTC can never fulfill the aspirations of the Bodo people.

The main purpose of these rallies was to seek the confidence and support of the people. The outfit released its manifesto and booklets on its Constitution and history of the Bodo people. It also appealed to other Bodo groups and organisations for support by forgetting all past differences and bitterness.[59]

The outfit also held few rallies on the illegal migrants' issue. One such rally was held on October 10, 2012, in Kokrajhar district, in which the NDFB demanded implementation of the provision of Chapter X of Assam Land and Revenue Regulation Act, 1886 (amendment 1947), clearing up of 47 tribal belts and blocks from encroachment and justice to the tribal people of Assam and people of other notified weaker sections who have rights over the land within the tribal belt and blocks.[60]

Fig. 3.1 Year-wise distribution of Security Force Personnel killed by the NDFB (1992-2015)

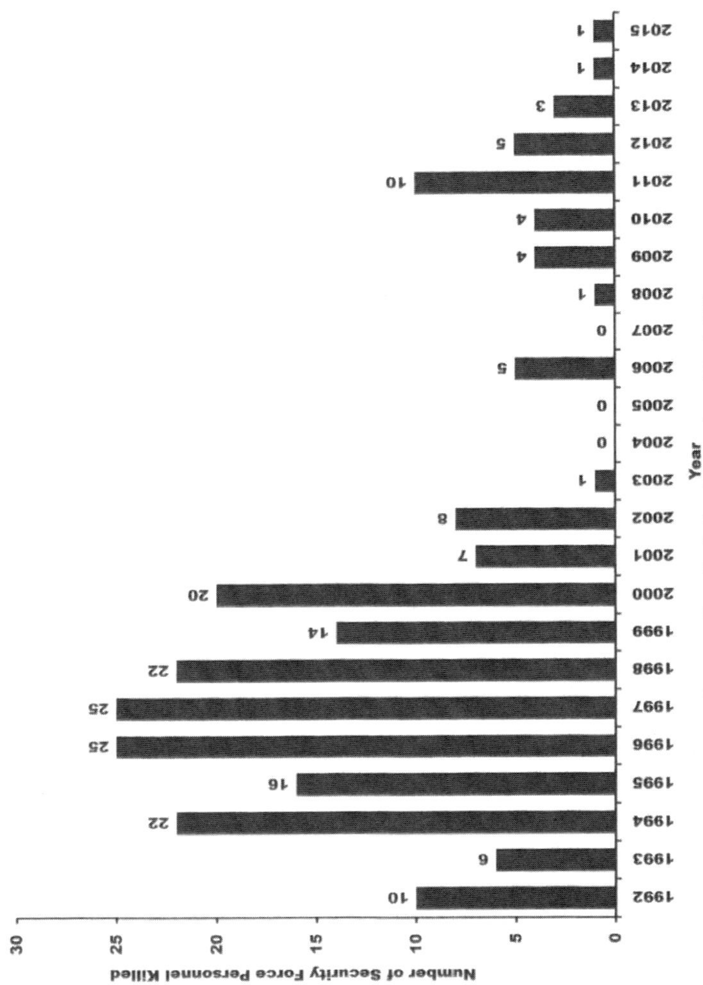

Source:South Asian Terrorism Portal [63]

Attacks on Security Personnel

As part of their strategy, the NDFB has been carrying out violence since its emergence and, as a result, many police personnel had lost their lives. There are incidents where the NDFB was in confrontation with the security force personnel and there was exchange of fire. The security forces vehicles are often targeted by the NDFB cadres using different sophisticated weapons, e.g., mortar, rocket launcher, etc. and even Improvised Explosive Device (IED).

The NDFB had sometimes claimed responsibility for such violence, and sometimes it denied. In 2000, the NDFB cadres were responsible for the deaths of twenty-nine security force personnel. It was responsible for maximum number of killings of security force personnel in the years 2002 and 2003, during which they killed 25 personnel in each year, and in 2004, 2005 and 2007 not a single security force personnel were killed (as shown in Figure 3.1).

In such violent attack on July 30, 2002, the NDFB laid an ambush near Durgapur village, Kokrajhar district, killing five security force personnel and two others. After two days, the NDFB Information and Publicity Secretary B. Erakdao claimed responsibility for the Kokrajhar massacre. Meanwhile, after two weeks on September 3, 2002, suspected NDFB terrorists set off an Improvised Explosive Device (IED) blast under a moving security force (SF)-patrol party-vehicle on the Kharigaon-Balazam river-bridge, Bishmuri police station limits, Kokrajhar district.

The NDFB had committed scores of incidents of violence like murders, bomb explosions, kidnapping for ransom, etc. which have had a serious bearing on the law and order situation of the state. According to the Union Home Ministry's 1996-97 report, a total of 201 persons were killed in Assam between April 1996 and March 1997, 174 which were attributed to the NDFB.

On July 26, 2010, the four Sashastra Seema Bal (SSB) personnel, including an assistant commander, were killed and three others injured in an ambush by the Ranjan Daimary faction of the NDFB at Amlaiguri under Panbari Police Station in Chirang District along the Bhutan border. A police spokesperson said militants of the NDFB attacked a vehicle of the SSB's 15th Battalion and decamped with two rifles and two pistols from the dead troopers. The SSB was deployed to guard the 605-kilometre-long India-Bhutan border in the Assam sector.[62]

Fig. 3.2 Year-wise distribution of Civilians killed by the NDFB (1992-2015)

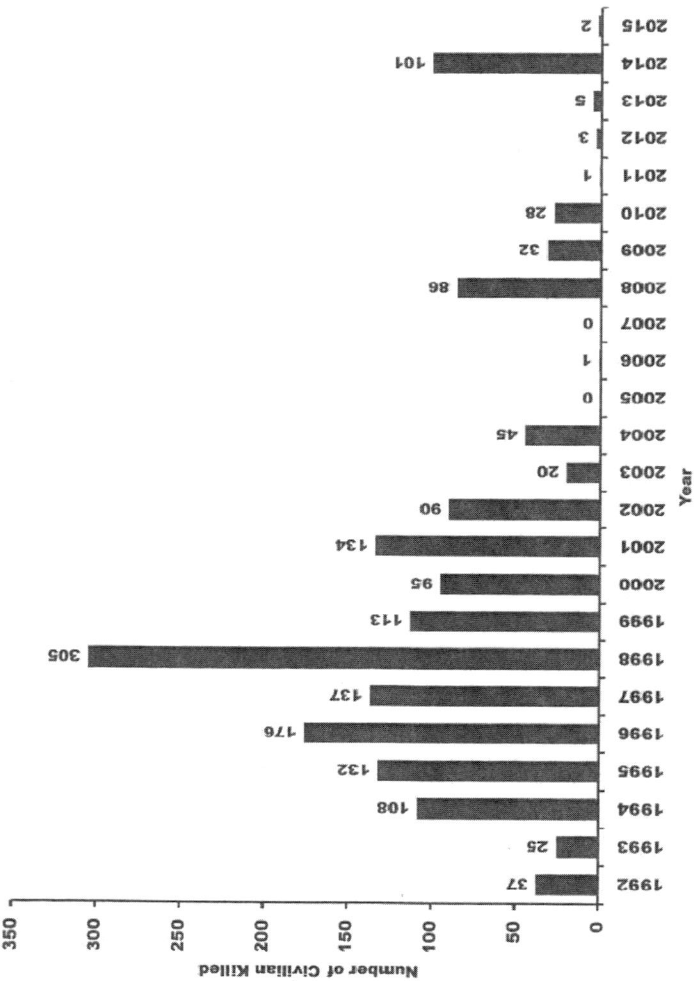

Source:South Asian Terrorism Portal (SATP)[63]

Attacks on Civilians

The NDFB was involved in numerous incidents of killing of civilians. In 1998, the NDFB killed maximum number of civilians and a total 305 civilians lost lives. On the other hand, in 2006, only one person was killed. It is to be noted that the ceasefire agreement between the NDFB and the Government was signed in 2005, as a result of which the NDFB had withdrawn all operations. However, it is observed that the NDFB carried out two types of attacks on the civilians viz., attacks on the civilians belonging to other communities, and attacks on civilians belonging to the Bodo community. It is important to note here that there are two forms of attack on the civilians from other communities, viz., attacks on the permanent inhabitants of Assam; and attacks on the temporary inhabitants of Assam.

There were many killing sprees where the NDFB was involved in killing civilians from other communities. It is observed that the NDFB often targeted the *Adivasis*. In 1998, the NDFB engaged in a killing spree in Kokrajhar district and killed 54 Santhal *Adivasis*. There was an ethnic clash between the Bodos and the Muslims in Udalguri in 2008 and 64 innocent people lost their lives. Though initially it was suspected that the NDFB had a hand in the clashes but, subsequently, they denied the allegation.[64]

Moreover, the NDFB often targeted inhabitants from other states, especially Hindi-speaking people from Bihar, Uttar Pradesh, Madhya Pradesh, etc. who are residing in the remotest places of Assam for business purpose. It is observed that incidents of killing of Hindi-speaking people often took place in response to perceived fake encounters. Meanwhile, on November 1, 2010, the NDFB threatened to kill 20 or more people for every NDFB cadre who was killed by security forces in the name of fake encounter.[65] Thus, the NDFB-R carried out a state-wide massacre on Hindi-speaking settlers in Assam in a revenge-killing spree after Mahesh Basumatary, who allegedly was a cadre of the NDFB-R, was killed by the Indian security forces in Sonitpur district of Assam. The massacres by NDFB militants took place in and around seven places of Assam. The NDFB-R claimed that Mahesh Basumatary was an innocent civilian and not linked to their organisation in any way, while the security forces claimed otherwise. A report aired in a local television news channel DY365 recorded the viewpoints of the victim's family and the village residents which matched the claims of the NDFB.[66]

In another revenge attack on 8 November 2010, at least 16 persons, including 13 Hindi-speaking people, were killed and several others injured when militants of the NDFB-R went on a killing spree at four places in

Northern Assam.[67] The massacre continued till next day and two Hindi-speaking persons of a minority community at Ultapani in Kokrajhar District on the Indo-Bhutan border were shot dead.[68] However, it may be noted that while most attacks on Hindi-speaking people were due to revenge, this particular killing was also due to an unwillingness to pay extortion money to the outfit. It is alleged that the Hindi-speaking community is usually targeted by militant groups, be it NDFB or ULFA, to draw Delhi's attention.[69]There were many such attacks on civilians from other states who have been residing for many years for business purpose or for other purposes but probably due to inaccessibility of such places such cases have failed to attract widespread publicity.

In 2014, on December 22, the NDFB-S warned security forces to stop attacks on its cadres. However, Assam Government officials as well as a few senior Ministers underestimate the strength of the outfit. The outfit accomplished the warning that was virtually ignored by the state authorities. Thus, on 23 December, militants belonging to NDFB-S killed 48 Adivasis at five different places in Sonitpur and Kokrajhar Districts. The December 23 attack by NDFB-S on remote *Adivasi* villages which resulted in 71 fatalities had also led to the displacement of more than 57,000 who were lodged in camps across Kokrajhar, Chirang and Sonitpur District. The IB Chief Syed Asif Ibrahim said on November 29, 2014, that in Assam, the militant outfit NDFB-S accounted for 85% of the civilian casualties in 2014.

The Assamese media brought allegations that such attacks on non-locals are a part of the strategy of the NDFB's ethnic cleansing operation. However, the term 'ethnic cleansing' refers to the forcible expulsion of an 'undesirable' population from a given territory, due to religious or ethnic discrimination, political, strategic or ideological considerations, or a combination of all these. Instead of using a negative term, which some political commentators consider a political euphemism, they prefer to apply a word with positive connotations (cleansing) to a morally objectionable act (forced population movement usually achieved through violence). At one end of the spectrum, ethnic cleansing is virtually indistinguishable from forced emigration and population transfer, while, at the other, it merges with deportation and genocide.

The objective of ethnic cleansing is to remove the conditions for the potential and actual opposition, whether political, terrorist, guerrilla or military, by physically removing any potentially or hostile ethnic communities. Although it has sometimes been motivated by the doctrine that claim an ethnic group to be literally 'unclean', more usually it has been a rational way of ensuring that total control can be asserted over an area. Ethnic cleansing is often also accompanied by efforts to eradicate all physical traces of the expelled ethnic group, such as by the destruction of cultural artefacts, religious sites and physical records.

From the above discussion, we can note some major characteristics of ethnic cleansing. They are as following:

1. Need larger population;
2. Forced emigration and population transfer;
3. A coherent way of ensuring that total control can be affirmed over an area; and
4. Efforts to exterminate all physical traces of the expelled ethnic group, such as by the destruction of cultural artefacts, religious sites and physical records.

However, if we go through the nature of Bodo politics, it is observed that Bodos have less population in comparison to other ethnic groups. Those ethnic groups claim themselves that such less populated (Bodo) ethnic group cannot have political autonomy like BTC. Repeated ethnic violence has affected more on the Bodo's demographic composition than other ethnic groups. So, it is observed that there is no forced emigration and population transfer. Moreover, Bodo nation is not looking for the total control, rather demanding political rights to safeguard and protect their own identity. It is important to note here that Bodos never tried to eradicate all physical traces of the expelled ethnic group by the destruction of cultural artefacts, religious sites and physical records. Further, there is a bias clause that media often used about the Bodos i.e. Bodo extremist. Anything that happened involving the NDFB, the media often described that as '*Bodo's involved in ethnic cleansing*' without taking the outfit's name.

Though theoretically, we cannot term those killings as ethnic cleansing but those killings were targeted civilians who belonged to other communities. Whatever terms the media and intellectuals used to describe those killings have little importance. However, it is true that those killings are part of the outfits' violent activities where civilians had suffered maximum casualties.

Fratricidal Killings

The NDFB was also involved in killing civilians from Bodo community that can be termed as fratricidal killings.[70] The formation of the BLTF with different political objectives was one of the major factors of these killings. In due process, in 1996, two rival groups, viz. the NDFB and the BLTF decided to annihilate each other. With this end in view, the NDFB launched operation *Doar* against their rival group, BLTF.[71] On the other hand, the BLTF launched operation *Srangsrang* against the NDFB.[72]The NDFB is at loggerheads with the other Bodo organisations like the All Bodo Students' Union (ABSU) and the Bodo Sahitya Sabha (BSS). In 1996, the BLTF killed a prominent woman activist claiming that her organisation was working as a front for the NDFB.[73] As the result of a decision taken on the January 10, 2001, in Bhutan, the NDFB decided to target members of the BLT, BSS, ABSU, Bodo People's Action Committee (BPAC), and the All Bodo Women's Welfare Federation (ABWWF), for selective killing.

It is observed that the NDFB was also involved in the killings of many of its former colleagues on the suspicion of spying or helping to Indian security forces. The formation of the BTC was another factor for the mutual distrust and rivalry. Those organisations, which were involved in the BTC Memorandum of Settlement (the NDFB perceived that the BTC could not fulfill the aspirations of the Bodos), became the victims of the NDFB. The split into three factions led to suspicions among the leaders of the NDFB, which often led to fratricidal killings or physical assault. A case was filed with National Human Rights Commission by the ABSU, and as per the complaint, there were 144 persons who were killed by a militant group backed by the ruling party who instructed the police not to investigate those cases. Later, the ABSU requested the intervention of the Commission on the matter.[75]

The Bodo National Convention (BNC) was formed in order to unite Bodos and to stop fratricidal killings. Though, it is observed that the number of fratricidal killings declined significantly. Besides the BNC, the Bodo Sahitya Sabha also tried to forge unity and to bring back mutual faith among the leaders of the various Bodo organisations. However, a class X student, Priya Basumatary, was killed on 20 August, 2014, by NDFB-S, suspecting her to be a police informer and alleged that she was in a relationship with a militant of NDFB-R. Meanwhile, on 22nd August, NDFB-S released the execution video of a girl whom they killed to avenge the killing of five of their cadres. As a reaction, BSS, Tribal Sangha and ABWWF staged a two-hour sit-in in front of DCs office on 29th August, protesting the killing of Priya Basumatary by NDFB-S and demanded an enquiry by the CBI. On 2nd September, NDFB-S General Secretary admitted that NDFB-S had killed Priya Basumatary for being an informer. Further, NDFB-S General Secretary stated that NDFB founder Ranjan Daimary was responsible for fratricidal killings and that he was also responsible for the killing of Priya Basumatary. In a statement, on September 14, 2014, the NDFB-S Chairman IK Songbijit stated that NDFB had split due to differences in idea and ideology among

Fig. 3.3 Year-wise distribution of the NDFB's Fratricidal Killings (2000-2015)

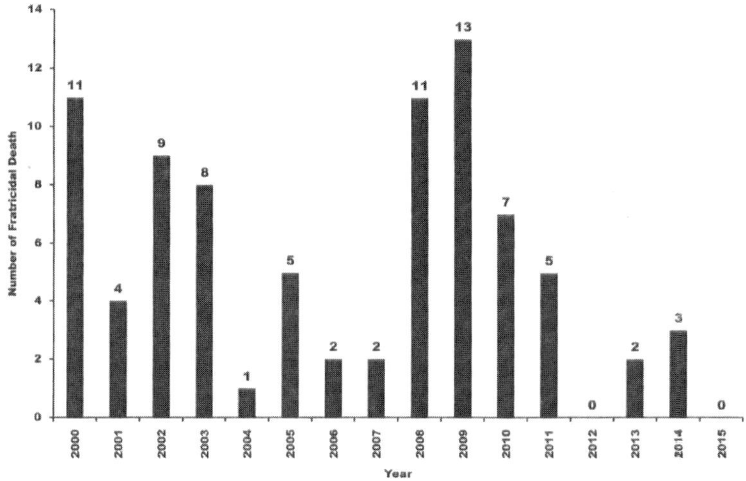

Source: South Asian Terrorism Portal (SATP)[74]

the leaders and added that due to this division, many innocent people lost their lives in the internecine fighting. The BTC Chief Hagrama Mahilary also once stated that NDFB had three factions and there were often fratricidal killings. That statement revealed the consistent infighting within the faction.

Bomb Blasts

The most dangerous and devastating strategy employed by the NDFB is bomb blast. They had exploded bombs on several occasions and killed many people to pressurize the Government as well as to terrorize the general masses. From 1999 to 2010, the NDFB was involved in 29 bomb blasts where more than 145 civilians lost their lives and 542 people were injured. In 2008, seven Bomb explosions took place in Assam where almost 88 people lost their lives and 300 hundred were seriously wounded. However, in the years 2003, 2006 and 2007, no such heinous incidents occurred (as shown in Figure 3.4).

Kidnapping

Kidnapping for ransom is a strategy that the NDFB has consistently been adopting since its formation. On March 17, 2003, the NDFB set March 20 as the deadline for the payment of ransom to release Custom Inspector and six coal exporters, abducted on February 28. Reports indicate that while a ransom of Rs. 3 million was demanded from the Customs department, and Rs. 50 million were demanded separately for the release of coal exporters.[77] On June 4, 2003, the NDFB terrorists abducted two Assistant Conservators of Forest from the Kuklung reserve forest area in Bijni subdivision of Kokrajhar district.[78]

On May 24, 2004, the NDFB terrorists abducted a contractor from Balisang area in Sonitpur district. On May 25, 2005, suspected NDFB and HNLC cadres abducted a trader from Moosyiem village in the Jaintia Hills district of Meghalaya. On December 22, 2006, a junior engineer of the Border Roads Organisation, M. Ganeshan, was abducted from Gitibari under Paneri police station in the Udalguri district. Involvement of the NDFB in the abduction is suspected.

In February, 2008, NDFB militants along with some other militants from Nagaland abducted two traders from the Panjan area under the Sarupathar police station in Golaghat district and took away INR 40,000 from them. On July 21, 2008, one trader, Pankaj Sarmah, while returning from Gogamukh to Dhemaji town, was abducted by suspected NDFB militants for ransom.

On March 3, 2009, two sons of the manager of Monmohinipur tea estate under Dhekiajuli Police Station in the Sonitpur District were abducted by suspected militants of the NDFB. Barun (9) and Karan (12), sons of garden manager Pamminder Sehra, were on their way to the Army School at Missamari, 10 kilometres from the tea estate, when the abductors waylaid their car at around 6.30 am (IST). The Dhekiajuli Police declined to comment on whether there was any demand for ransom from any militant outfit. However, sources in the tea industry said the NDFB had asked Monmohinipur tea estate authorities to pay a ransom of Rs. two million. On April 18, 2009, the NDFB militants abducted a businessman, identified as Mohammad Chabin Ansari, from Gormara village in the Dhekiajuli town of Sonitpur District. On May 9, Ratan Kumar Roy, a doctor who was kidnapped by suspected NDFB militants from his chamber on May 5, was released near Chapaguri in Chirang District. The Officer-in-Charge of Bijni Police Station, Pradeep Kumar Boro, said "Under mounting pressure from security forces, the militants found it difficult to keep him in captivity." However, Roy said a group of militants had taken him to attend to their ailing members and released him around 8pm (IST) at a village near Chapaguri. On June 11, businessman Lakshman Saha (45) who was abducted from his shop at Hatidhara Tiniali in the Dhubri District was reportedly released by the abductors after 25 days in captivity. Five unidentified youths reportedly came on two motorcycles at

Fig. 3.4 Bomb blasts, Persons Killed and Injuries caused by NDFB (1999-2010)

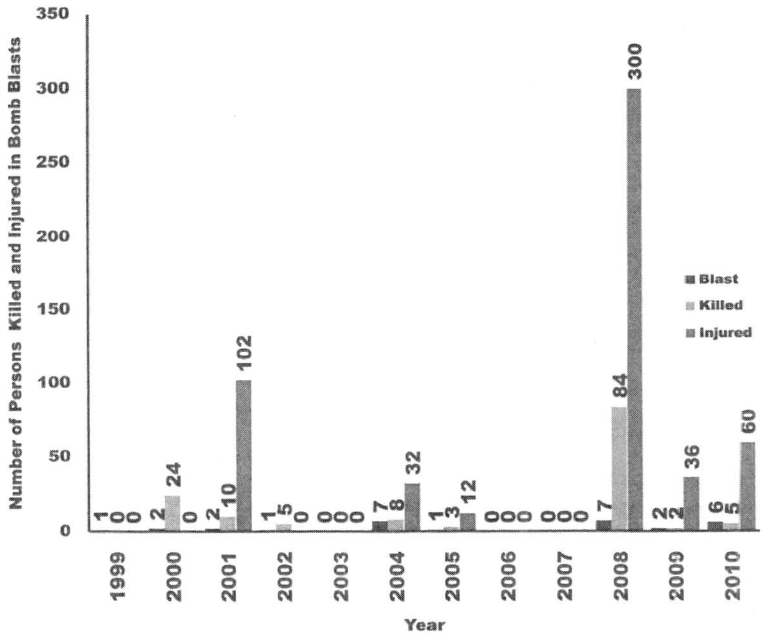

Source: South Asian Terrorism Portal(SATP)[76]

about 7.30 pm (IST) on May 14 and abducted Lakshman Saha at gunpoint from his shop at Hatidhara Tiniali and managed to escape to the Parbatjhora forest area under Kajigaon Police Station of Kokrajhar District in Bodoland Territorial Areas District (BTAD). According to sources, the abductors acted as hired men of the NDFB and handed Lakshman Saha to the NDFB. The same source claimed that Lakshman Saha was released after paying a ransom of INR 425000 though his family has denied the transaction. On November 17, P. Krishna Rao, project manager of the Gayatri-East Coast Insulation, who was abducted by suspected NDFB militants on October 16, 2009, was released near Karigaon in the Kokrajhar District. Rao, originally from the Krishna District of Andhra Pradesh, was supervising work on the East-West corridor project at Joypur near Karigaon when he was abducted by five motorcycle-borne militants. Sources said Rao walked from the spot he was released along the National Highway 31C to his company office at Kajalgaon after his release. He was subsequently driven to an undisclosed location by company officials with police security and was later said to have been taken to Guwahati. The abductors reportedly demanded INR 20 million in exchange of the abducted officer. It is not clear if ransom money was paid.

According to a police report, more than 30 people, including officials of the National Highway Authority of India, Railways, etc., were abducted by the NDFB in 2009, which affected implementation of the major projects. Sources said that all abduction cases were not being reported to police and only the abduction of high profile persons came to light through the media. Official sources said militants belonging to the anti-talks faction normally use the forest belt along the border with Bhutan and Arunachal Pradesh to keep the abducted persons by taking advantage of the fact that there is very little presence of security forces in that area and there have been instances when the kidnapped persons were shifted to Bhutan or Arunachal Pradesh whenever any major offensive is launched by the security forces.

The manager of Pabhoi Tea Estate at Biswanath Chariali in Sonitpur District, Bharat Singh Rathod, who was abducted from his bungalow in the garden on January 16, was released on January 21, 2014, by his captors at Namara near the Assam-Arunachal Pradesh border. NDFB-S is suspected to be behind the incident. Suspected militants belonging to NDFB-S abducted a businessman, Anup Das, on February 5, 2014, from Dukhungaon under the Runikhata Police Station in Chirang District. The NDFB-S militants abducted two volunteers on October 25, 2014, of Lutheran World Service India Trust from Patgaon Kausi Bazar in Kokrajhar.

On the basis of above mentioned incidents, we could reach the conclusion that the NDFB often target the rich persons who can afford ransom, persons who are not permanent domicile of Assam; and persons who are residing in inaccessible location from security forces. However, it is interesting to note that after release the kidnapped persons never confess about the ransom amount he/she or their family members had paid to the outfit and rather denied the fact.

Extortions

To generate funds, the NDFB relied on extortion bids, which they called either as donation or the "Bodoland Tax". The victims of the extortion were Government employees, businessmen, contractors, tea companies,etc. It is reported that in 1996, the NDFB collected over Rs. 20 crore from Barpeta, Bongaigaon and Kokrajhar and people had to pay in the range of

Fig. 3.5 Year-wise Distribution of Number of Persons Kidnapped (2003-2015)

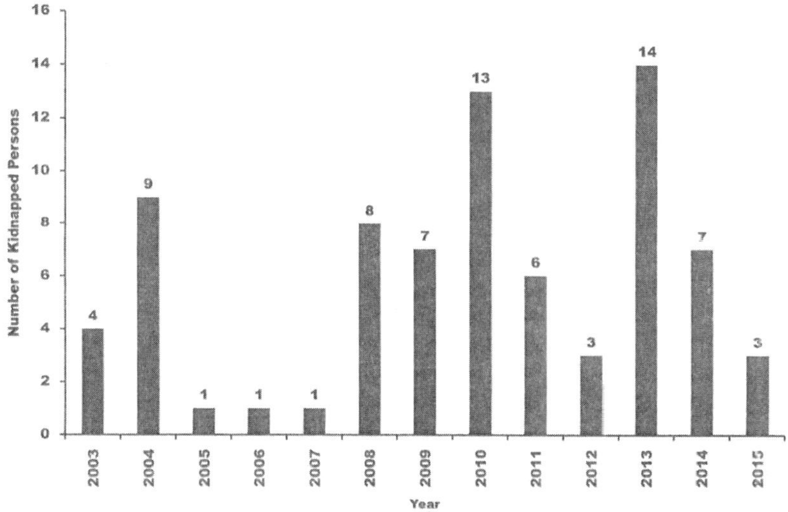

Source: South Asian Terrorism Portal (SATP)[79]

Rs. 2,000 to Rs. 5,000 in Bongaigaon district depending upon their financial position.[80] NDFB used to collect "tax" on a yearly basis. However, according to the NDFB, 'paying tax' for the 'cause' of Bodoland is a 'patriotic duty' for the people of Bodoland.

Meanwhile, on May 8, 2003, Williamson Magor & Co. Limited, a tea company based in Kolkata, West Bengal, was alleged to have paid a 'donation' of rupees one million to the NDFB, but the company denied that it had done so. On January 16, 2006, Hindi-speaking villagers living along the border of Assam's Nagaon and Karbi Anglong districts, under the banner of the Assam Bhojpuri Yuba Chhatra Parishad, sent intimation to the State Government seeking protection from the extortion drive by the NDFB in the area. Unidentified sources said that the NDFB's demand notes, ranging from Rupees 30,000 to Rupees 50,000, signed by a self-styled "collection-in-charge" Lt. D. Dethsrang have been distributed among villagers.

According to an NDTV report on December 12, 2007, the NDFB demands 6% from all projects, which falls under Bodoland territory. Every truck passing through the Bengal-Assam border at the Sri Rampur Gate has to pay up Rs.150. Each commercial taxi is charged Rs.150 per month. The NDFB takes a 2% cut from all salaried employees and charges Rs. 2-3 lakhs per annum from tea gardens. They have even charged 3% from the money meant for education projects like Sarva Shiksha Abhiyan (Education for All campaign).The NDFB claimed on July 6, 2009, that they had received rupees five million from the BTC chief Hagrama Mohilary ahead of the 2006 Legislative Assembly elections to help the BPF. The claim came within days of the opposition demand for Mohilary's arrest due to his admission earlier about having paid the NDFB. Mohilary, however, had immediately refuted the opposition's charge saying he had been misquoted. This is the first time that the NDFB has made any comment on the controversial episode, which was started by Mohilary himself soon after the 2009 parliamentary elections. In a press statement, issued by the outfit's Assistant Information and Publicity Secretary R. Daokha, the NDFB claimed receiving rupees five million in cash to work in favour of the BPF in the 2006 Assembly elections. The amount was received by M. Gerema, the Organising Secretary, and B. Bengga, the Speaker of the NDFB," the statement added.[81]

The Telegraph, quoting sources which interrogated Ranjan Daimary, reports that he used to receive nearly 0.6 to 0.7 million rupees every month from Assam, half of which was spent on running a camp at Khagracherri in Bangladesh and another in Myanmar. The rest he would use for his family's upkeep. However, the crackdown on timber smugglers in Assam's Sonitpur District has forced the NDFB to turn more and more to abductions to prevent its funds from running dry. Sonitpur District Police sources said the NDFB by a conservative estimate was collecting about 50,000 rupees everyday by way of "tax" from timber smugglers. On the question of massive extortions, kidnappings and killings by the NDFB-S in the BTC region, Songbijit claimed that not a single innocent person was killed by the NDFB cadres.[82]

However, sometimes the NDFB also denied the fact that the outfit was involved in extortion and appealed to the people of the region to be alert against fake organisations extorting money in the name of the NDFB and giving life threats. Such an incident happened on April 29, 2014, three young men identified as Mahatu, Manuj Giri and Kanu Gupta of Sirajuli were arrested for allegedly demanding money in the name of NDFB-S. In November 2014, at Amaniapara in Nalbari District, Buddha Basumatary had demanded INR 200000, in the name of NDFB-S, from a shopkeeper, identified as Dadhi Barman. He was nabbed and lynched by local people when he allegedly threatened Barman with a pistol. Meanwhile, following that incident, on May 29, NDFB-S warned that it would take stern action against those persons who were connected with the collection of 'tax' in their name. Though, on a few occasions the outfit denied the extortion bid yet it is true that they indulged in such activities to generate funds.

Strategic Alliances with Other Terrorist Groups

It has been alleged that the NDFB acts in collaboration with the ULFA. In this connection, the NDFB mentioned in a manifesto that "for effective fighting the NDFB is in favour of having alliance with other genuine struggling forces, having the same ideology and principle."[83] In 1999, the ULFA and NDFB formed a coordination committee for launching a united struggle. Also, the NDFB shares a close relationship with outfits like the Kamatapur Liberation Organisation (KLO), the Achik National Volunteers Council (ANVC) and the National Socialist Council of Nagaland-Khaplang (NSCN-K).[84] Prior to its dislodgment from Bhutan, the outfit was reported to have established working relationship with certain elements in Bhutan. Several Bhutanese officials were reported to have visited the training camps located inside Bhutan and have been alleged to openly aiding the NDFB cadres. The NDFB, along with the ULFA, on various occasions was found to be allegedly channelling its funds through the "Bhutanese diplomatic bag" to their leaders based in Southeast Asian capitals.[85]

Growing coordination between two militant groups based in neighbouring areas of West Bengal (North Bengal) and Western Assam's Bodoland Territorial Council (BTC) areas had prompted the Central Government to advise both the state governments of Assam and West Bengal to work out a joint strategy to deal with the groups effectively. A security source informed that the outlawed Kamatapur Liberation Organisation (which is active in few pockets in North Bengal) had struck coordination with the National Democratic Front of Bodoland (Sangbijit faction).

A media report on September, 2013 stated that the KLO had sent 30 of its cadres from Bongaigaon and Dhubri districts of western Assam to Myanmar for training with the help of NDFB (Sangbijit faction), raising concern among the security agencies. The KLO cadres have gone to Myanmar base of Nationalist Socialist Council of Nagalim (Khaplang) or NSCN-K to undergo training as the NDFB faction has provided all sorts of support for them.[86] The NDFB has also established a working arrangement with the National Socialist Council of Nagaland-Isak-Muivah (NSCN-IM), an insurgent outfit in neighbouring Nagaland.

In response to the support from the NDFB faction, the KLO helped the former in four incidents of abduction in BTC areas bordering West Bengal in the year 2013. The security agencies had information that the KLO was provided with explosives like TNT and improvised explosive devices (IEDs) by the NDFB faction at this crucial juncture when the area including parts of North Bengal and parts of Western Assam have become restive in view of agitation launched by several Koch-Rajbongshi organisations demanding a separate Kamatapur state. Security agencies feared that the KLO in coordination with NDFB (Sangbijit) may strike terror in Assam and parts of North Bengal taking advantage of the fluid situation.

On July 15, 2010, the CRPF claimed of having established a link between the NDFB and the Manipur-based People's Liberation Army (PLA) with the arrest of three PLA militants, including self-styled Captain R.K. Tumba alias Benjamin. A CRPF official involved in the operation said documents indicating links between the two outfits had been recovered from the arrested militants.[87] On March 14, 2014, on the occasion of its 'Army Day,' (March 16) ULFA-I 'Commander-in-Chief' Paresh Barua had expressed his gratitude to NSCN-K, CorCom of Manipur, KLO, NDFB and other "brotherly organisations" for their cooperation and help extended to the ULFA over the years. By extending support to the NDFB-S mass killing on December 23 and 24, on December 24, 2014, Paresh Baruah, the ULFA-I leader, also the mentor of NDFB-S leader I K Songbijit, in an interview on December 24, stated the massacre on December 23 as 'collateral damage'. He stated that "These killings of civilians are part of the strategy in any war." Thus, the NDFB has strategic alliances with other extremist groups of North-East region and followed the principle "Foe's foe is a friend of the NDFB and Foe's friend is a foe of the NDFB."

Role of the National Democratic Front of Bodoland

Regarding the role of the NDFB, it may be noted that although it has been demanding a 'Sovereign' Bodoland, there is no likelihood of fulfillment of this goal within the framework of the Indian Constitution. However, the NDFB has been using 'sovereignty' as a bargaining strategy to pressurize the government to take the Bodo question seriously. The extremist posture adopted by the NDFB forced the government to sign two autonomy accords within the span of a decade, even though earlier autonomy demands were completely ignored by the government.

However, the NDFB was opposed to the signing of both the accords and criticized organisations like the ABSU and the BLTF who supported the negotiations. In 1993, the Central Government invited the Bodo leaders who had sent friendly and frequent feelers for an honourable resolution of the conflict as well as the Government of Assam to sign on what came to be known as the "Bodo Accord", in Kokrajhar. The Accord created what it called the "Bodoland Autonomous Council", that was to comprise an area covering 2000 villages and 25 estates stretching from the Sankosh river to Mazbat Pasnoi on the north bank of the river Luit (Brahmaputra), via a Government of Assam notification (No. TAD/BAC/26/93/18).[88] There was also an internal split within the broad spectrum of political discourse in the Bodo community, with an armed section of the movement declaring the Accord to be "sell-out" of the original goal of an ethnic homeland for the Bodo community. The NDFB denounced the Accord and vowed to continue what it perceived as the resistance to colonialism.[89]

Meanwhile, on February 10, 2003, a new Accord was signed to create Bodoland Territorial Council. The NDFB neither welcomed nor rejected the Accord. But it termed it as an "insult to the Bodo nation" and "a faulty pact that had the backing of a 'handful of opportunists and Bodo people with leanings towards Delhi".[90] It criticised that the BTC has more provisions and guarantees for all-round security of the non-Bodos than the Bodo people themselves.[91] This is because the NDFB felt that the preservation of Bodo identity would not be possible without the achievement of a 'Sovereign Bodoland". This observation of the NDFB may have a big negative impact on the non-Bodos staying within the BTC area. The ABSU has been repeatedly requesting the NDFB to end the gun culture and to start a dialogue with the government. But the outfit's hawkish stand on the new Accord indicates that it has other ideas.[92]

It is observed that the NDFB as an underground extremist group never participated in electoral politics. However, some mainstream political parties like the Bodoland People's Front (BPF), the Bodo People's Progressive Front (BPPF), the United Progressive Democratic Front (UPDF), etc. brought alleged that the backed some candidates who could raise issues on behalf of the NDFB if elected to the State Assembly. On the whole, the NDFB kept the Bodoland issue alive and has been motivating some articulate sections of Bodos to fight for the cause of the Bodo nation. It appears that the NDFB has been playing the role of an opposition in Bodo politics by criticizing the functions of the BAC and later the BTC.

Conclusion

Though the NDFB lost its unified voice on the Sovereign Bodoland issue, all the factions of the outfit raised unified voice on some common issues like demand to rescue of missing cadres and leaders in Operation All Clear launched in Bhutan, demand to stop fake encounters on Bodo youths, demand for equal treatment with organisations like ULFA, demand for deletion and deportation of illegal migrants by updating the NRC, demand for proper implementation of the Assam Land Revenue Regulation Act, 1886, etc. In addition, the NDFB has also been demanding the introduction of Roman script for the Bodo language. However, after acceptance of the Devanagari script by the Bodo Sahitya Sabha and its endorsement by the Government of India in 2004, the NDFB removed this demand from the Constitution, but reiterated that Bodo as well as English will be the official languages of the NDFB and either English or Roman script will be its official script.

It is observed that over the years, the NDFB has been using different strategies to pressurize and intimidate the authority or to gain the attention of the concerned authority. By the use of its strength i.e. cadres, arms and ammunition it tried to mount pressure on the Government. The NDFB adopted strategies like bandhs, rallies, attacks on security personnel, attacks on civilians, fratricidal killings, kidnapping, extortions, attacks on non-locals and bomb blasts. In carrying out such activities, the NDFB has maintained strategic alliances with other extremist groups like ULFA, NSCN-K, NSCN-IM, PLA, KLO, etc.

Regarding the role of the NDFB, it may be noted that although it has been demanding a 'Sovereign' Bodoland, there is no likelihood of fulfillment of this goal within the framework of the Indian Constitution. Nevertheless, the NDFB has been using 'sovereignty' as a bargaining ploy to pressurize the government to take the Bodo question seriously. The extremist stance adopted by the NDFB forced the government to sign two autonomy accords within the span of a decade, even though earlier autonomy demands were completely ignored by the government. It is true that the NDFB was opposed to the signing of both the accords and criticized organisations like the ABSU and the BLTF who supported the negotiations. This is because the NDFB felt that the preservation of Bodo identity would not be possible without the achievement of a 'Sovereign Bodoland". Thus it seems that the NDFB kept the Bodoland issue alive and has been motivating some articulate sections of Bodos to fight for the cause of the Bodo nation. It appears, therefore, that the NDFB has been playing the role of an opposition in Bodo politics by criticising the functions of the BAC and later the BTC.

References

1 Langer, A. (2011, July 16).'A Bodo homeland within the Indian Constitution is a possibility'(An interview with Ranjan Daimary).*Tehelka*. Retrieved from http://www.tehelka.com on 21-09-2013 at 12:30.

2 NDFB (2002). *Constitution of the National Democratic Front of Bodoland* (2nd ed.). (n.d.): Publicity Wing.

3 NDFB (1998). *Constitution of the National Democratic Front of Bodoland*"(1st ed.).(n.d.): Publicity Wing,

4 NDFB (2002). *op.cit.* pp.4-8

5 South Asian Terrorism Portal (2002). Incident Involving National Democratic Front of Bodoland. Retrieved October 21, 2015, from http://www.satp.org.

6 Boro, D. (2015).*The Lockup is My Home* (Rahul Dev Brahma, Trans.).Kokrajhar: Words n Words. p.72.

7 'NDFB ups 'sovereign' ante - Outfit not to settle for separate state or Union Territory'. (2005, June 28). *The Telegraph.*

8 'NDFB Shuns charter Demand'. (2007, March 13). *The Telegraph.*

9 'Delhi warned on Bodo talks'. (2008, May 3). *The Telegraph.*

10 'NDFB reiterates 'war' option'. (2008, October 4). *The Telegraph.*

11 'NDFB tussle behind blast: Police'. (2008, December 31). *The Telegraph.*

12 'Daimary ready for talks-NDFB leader will rethink demand for sovereignty; panel pushes for unconditional dialogue'. (2010, May 5).*The Telegraph.*

13 'NDFB-R stresses statehood-Ranjan Faction says no alternative to Bodoland'. (2012, June 26).*The Telegraph.*

14 'Bodoland to ensure security for all: NDFB-P'. (2010, June 30). *The Assam Tribune.*

15 'NDFB-P pushes for statehood'. (2010, October 4).*The Telegraph.*

16 Kashyap,Samudra Gupta . (2011, Jun 21). 'NDFB pro-talk faction renews its demand for Bodoland state'. *Indian Express*. Retrieved from http://www.indianexpress.com/ on 16-09-13 at 19:49.

17 'NDFB-P meets governor - Team seeks Patnaik's help to expedite peace process'. (2011, July 15). *The Telegraph.*

18 Chatterjee, Shib Shankar.(2011, August 1). 'Indian Militant Group Appeals to Leaders of Indian Parliament for Separate State'. *News Blaze*. Retrieved from http://newsblaze.com on 28-06-2015 at 1:51.

19 'Roadmap to Boroland'. (2012,February 8). *Bodosa.*

20 'NDFB-P team to meet Chidambaram'. (2012, February 17). *The Telegraph.*

21 'NDFB-P demands removal of P C Haldar'. (2012, February 18). *Times of Assam*. Retrieved from https://www.timesofassam.com/on 22-02-2014 at 22:15.

22 'NDFB-P links arms surrender to pact'. (2012, July 18). *The Telegraph.*

23 'NDFB-P demands separate Bodoland'. (2012, December 8). *The Assam Tribune.*

24 'NDFB-P sticks to state demand Remark misread: Outfit chief'. (2013, August 19). *The Telegraph.*

25 A Charter of Demand of the NDFB-P submitted to Union Government India in 2012. NDFB-P. (2012, July). *Voice of Boroland; Let us die for Bodo Nation but Let not Boro Nation die for us!.* *VOL-II*, Issue-07.Dwimu:Information & Publicity Wing NDFB-P. p.5.

26 'Citizenship Act amendments to be challenged in SC'. (2012, September 17). *The Assam Tribune.*

27 An interview with NDFB-S Chairman I.K. Songbijit by Chief Editor of '*Times of Assam*' *Dhruba Jyoti Deka,* Published on: Saturday, August 10, 2013, 09:34AM IST Retrieved from https://www.timesofassam.com on 14-09-2014 at 10:10.

28 Brahma Choudhury, Pritam. (2006, February 8). 'NDFB adopts new talks line-Outfit seeks facts on missing leaders before dialogue'. *The Telegraph.*

29 'Bandh Call'. (2009, August 4). *The Telegraph.*

30 'NDFB faction dares forces'. (2010, November 2). *The Telegraph.*

31 Joshi,Sandeep. (2013, July 15).'555 fake encounter cases registered across India in last four years; Rise in disturbed areas like Naxal-affected States and the north east'. *The Hindu (*New Delhi).

32 NEDAN Foundation (2013), *Iron Curtained Encounters: Human Rights Violation*, Facts and Incidents bought out by Dwimalu Narzary and Namita Basumatary on behalf of NEDAN FOUNDATION, Kokrajhar. Retrieved August 18, 2015, from http://nedan.in

33 Dholabhai,Nishit. (2011, May 18). 'NDFB slams Govt 'softness for ULFA- Outfit questions preferential treatment, writes to Union Home ministry'. *The Telegraph.*

34 Brahma Choudhury, P. (2006, August 29). 'NDFB shoots with book-Outfit livid over continuous migration'. *The Telegraph.*

35 Guthal, R. (2012, July). Message. *Voice of Boroland: Let us die for Boro Nation but Let not Boro Nation die for us!.* Vol-II Issue:07. Dwimu: Information & Publicity Wing NDFB-P. p.1.

36 'Citizenship Act amendments to be challenged in SC'. (2012, September 17)).*The Assam Tribune.*

37 Memorandum of Settlement on Bodoland Territorial Council, 2003.

38 ABSU Memorandum Submitted to Honourable Prime Minister Rajiv Gandhi under the title "*Why Separate State of Bodoland*".

39 Das, J.N. (1989, July-September). 'Udayachal Movement in Assam'. *Indian Journal of Political Science*(pp.335-36),50:3. Madras.

40 Asian Centre for Human Rights (2012, September). *Assam Riots: Preventable but not Prevented.* Janakpuri, New Delhi: Asian Centre for Human Rights. p.21.

41 Bordoloi, B.N. (1986).*Alienation of Tribal Land Indebtedness.* Guwahati, Assam: Tribal Research Institute. p.15.

42 'NDFB-P renews demands'. (2012, July 17). *The Telegraph.*

43 According to the NDFB those aliens who encroached illegally after 1951 they are the illegal migrants.

44 *Voice of Boroland, op.cit.*

45 According to the Assam Accord signed by AASU, AAGSP and the Union Government in 1985, the 10th Clause will ensured "that relevant laws for prevention of encroachment of Government lands and lands in tribal belts blocks are strictly enforced and unauthorised encroachers evicted as laid down under such laws." Details are available in "Part II (A), "The Assam Gazette", June 23, 1999/313, p.1.Retrieved from http://aasc.nic.in/on 12-09-2013 at 20:02.

46 In **Figure 3.1**, **Figure 3.2** and **Figure 3.3**, the Killing of Security Force Personnel, Killing of Civilians, Fratricidal killings were shown year-wise, these are the evidence which proved that the NDFB engaged in violence with both combatants and non-combatants.

47 'Fears of Fratricide in Bodo Heartland'. (2007, April 4).*The Hindu;*Talukdar, Sushanta. (2009, November 19). 'Bodoland shuts down to protest fratricidal killings'. *The Hindu.*

48 Roy Burman, J.J. (2010). The Bodoland Ethnic Conflict. C.J. Sonowal (ed.) *Quest for Identity, autonomy and development: The Contemporary trends of ethnic and tribal assertion in Assam* (Vol.2). New Delhi: Akansha Publishing House. p.276

49 On 3rd May, 1998, 14 Adivasis including six women were killed and four others injured by a group of 15 NDFB terrorists, after dragging them out of a bus near Bishmuri point on National Highway –31 in Kokrajhar. South Asian Terrorism Portal (1998). Incidents Involving the NDFB. Retrieved September 17, 2014, from http://www.satp.org/.

50 'Old link in tea rebel payoff'. (2003, May 4). *The Telegraph;* 'Tea garden owner killed in Sootea'. (2012, November 14). *The Assam Tribune.*

51 Prakash, *op.cit.,*p.383.

52 *Ibid.,* p.384.

53 'Some NDFB-R rebels joined outfit's hard line faction'. (2013, September 17). *The Times of India.*

54 '7 militant groups active in State'. (2010, March 30). *The Assam Tribune.*

55 '70 NDFB cadres still in B'desh'.(2011, October 2).*The Assam Tribune.*

56 South Asian Terrorism Portal, *op.cit.*

57 'NDFB Screams truce 'murder'-Rebel dies in police firing during strike'. (2006, April 26). *The Telegraph.*

58 'Train services hit after derailments'. (2011, August 2). *The Assam Tribune.*

59 NDFB keen on sovereignty; National Democratic Front of Bodoland held a series of rallies to evolve a consensus on their demand for sovereignty. (2005, September 16-30). *North East News Agency,* Major Events Vol. 2 Issue No. 1. Retrieved 11 November, 2013, from http://www.nenanews.com/.

60 'Twin rallies decry illegal migration'. (2012, October 12). *The Telegraph.*

61 This Bar Diagram is drawn on the basis of the "Incident Involving the NDFB" (compiled from news report and are provisional) available in the *South Asian Terrorism Portal* by quantifying all those incidents where the NDFB was killed Security Force Personnel.

62 2 SSB officers, 2 jawans killed in NDFB ambush. (2010, July 27). *The Assam Tribune.*

63 This Bar Diagram is drawn on the basis of the "Incident Involving the NDFB" (compiled from news report and are provisional) available in the *South Asian Terrorism Portal* by quantifying those incidents in which the NDFB killed Civilians, retrieved 21 October, 2016, from http://www.satp.org.

64 'NDBF denies role in Bodoland clashes'. (2010, October 6). *The Telegraph.*

65 'NDFB faction dares forces'. (2010, November 2). *The Telegraph*

66 'Six more fall to NDFB vendetta- Outfit warns of killing spree'. (2010, November 10). *The Telegraph.*

67 '16 gunned down in Bodo outfit's eye-for-an-eye attacks'. (*2010, November 9). The Telegraph.*

68 'Six more fall to NDFB vendetta- Outfit warns of killing spree'. (2010, November 10). *The Telegraph.*

69 'NDFB targets migrants-Daimary faction guns down four of a family, Pro-talks group confident of ceasefire extension'. (2009, July 1). *The Telegraph.*

70 'Fears of Fratricide in Bodo Heartland'. (2007, April 4). *The Hindu.*

71 Chakladar, *op.cit.* p.63.

72 *Ibid.,* pp.280-285.

73 The activist, Ms. Golapi Basumatary was a well-known and respected activist who was the general secretary of the Bodo Women's Justice Forum and was a known figure not only in the Bodo areas but in other parts of Assam as well. The killing of human rights activists, trade union leaders and others who try to use the democratic spaces to articulate dissent, is a deliberate state policy in Assam, according to reports of voluntary human rights groups (MASS 1999).

74 This Bar Diagram is drawn on the basis of the "Incident Involving the NDFB" (compiled from news report and are provisional) available in the *South Asian Terrorism Portal* by quantifying those incidents in which the NDFB killed civilian from own community. , retrieved from, http://www.satp.org on 13/11/2014 at 18.53PM.

75 National Human Rights Commission (Law Division), Case No. 126/3/0/2010. (2010, December 27).

76 This Bar Diagram is drawn on the basis of the "Bomb Explosions in Assam" (compiled from news report and are provisional) available in the *South Asian Terrorism Portal* (SATP) by quantifying all those bomb blasts in which the NDFB was responsible, retrieved from http://www.satp.org on 21-10-2012 at 20:39.

77 'Abduction-hit customs staff suspend work'. (2003, March 18). *The Telegraph.*

78 'Two forest officials abducted'.(2003, June 4), *The Telegraph* .

79 This Bar Diagram is drawn on the basis of the "Incident Involving the NDFB" (compiled from news report and are provisional) available in the *South Asian Terrorism Portal* by quantifying those incidents in which the NDFB kidnapped, retrieved from http://www.satp.org on 13/11/2013 at 18.53PM.

80 'Extortion bid hit lower Assam'. (1996, December 4). *The Assam Tribune.*

81 'Mohilary paid us Rs 50 lakh: NDFB.' (2009, July 7). *The Telegraph.*

82 An interview with NDFB-S Chairman I.K. Songbijit by Chief Editor of '*Times of Assam*' *Dhruba Jyoti Deka,* Published on: Saturday, August 10, 2013, 09:34AM IST Retrieved from https://www.timesofassam.comon 14-09-2014 at 10:10.

83 *The Manifesto of the National Democratic Front of Bodoland*, *op.cit.*, p.17.

84 Burman.*op. cit.*, p.276.

85 Prakash. *op.cit.*p.384.

86 'KLO strikes coordination with NDFB faction'. (2013, September 7). *The Shillong Times.*

87 'High alert in Guwahati following bomb explosion'. (2010, July 16). *The Assam Tribune.*

88 The Bodoland Autonomous Council Act 1993, Institute for Conflict Management, South Asian Terrorism Portal (SATP) retrieved from http://www.neportal.org on 11/11/2002 at 11:22.

89 Roy, *op.cit.*, p.76.

90 Singh,M.A. (2004, February 21).'Challenges before Bodo Territorial Council'.*Economic and Political Weekly*. p.785.

91 'Leaders wiser from mistakes'. (2003, February 11). *The Telegraph.*

92 Talukdar, S. & Brahma Choudhury. P. (2003, February 17). 'ABSU woos last outfit standing'. *The Telegraph.*

*****

4

Support Base of NDFB and its Relationship with other Bodo Organisations

In the previous chapter, the major demands, strategies and the role of the NDFB were discussed. In this context, it is necessary to examine the nature and extent of support for the basic demands of the NDFB. For an understanding of the support base of the NDFB, a survey was conducted in Kokrajhar, Chirang, Baksa and Udalguri districts. A sample of 200 respondents—50 each from Kokrajhar, Chirang, Baksa and Udalguri districts were selected through systematic random sampling. The data obtained from the respondents with the help of structured questionnaire was quantified for statistical analysis.

Respondents' Perception towards the BTC

Before taking up an analysis of the support base of the NDFB, it is necessary to examine the respondents' perception about the role of the BTC which was formed as an alternative autonomy arrangement to accommodate the political aspirations of the Bodos. It is worth mentioning that performance of the BTC has a direct bearing on the persistence of the Bodoland demand.

The BTC was created to fulfill the economic, educational and linguistic aspirations of the Bodo community, preserve their land rights, promote their socio-cultural identity and speed up infrastructural development in the BTC region. As a mark of honour to the Bodo Accord 2003, ABSU withdrew its demand for a separate state of Bodoland. However, this Accord also failed to fulfill the aspirations of all sections of the Bodos. The NDFB opposed it and considered the formation of the Bodoland Territorial Council as an exercise in futility. The organisation carried out various violent and disruptive activities to register its dissatisfaction with the Accord. However, in 2005, a section of the NDFB declared a unilateral ceasefire and negotiations were started between the NDFB and the Government of India. The creation of BTC was challenged not only by some sections of the Bodos, but non-Bodos also vigorously opposed it. However, a major cause of concern for the BTC was to satisfy the people of Kokrajhar, Chirang, Baksa and Udalguri districts. It is important to mention that the demand for Bodoland was made for the entire north bank of the Brahmaputra River, but only four districts were included in the BTC. As a result, the Bodo population of the areas, which were ignored by the Government as well as by the Bodo leaders,was dissatisfied, particularly with the Bodo leaders who surrendered to the bargaining policies of the government.

Fig. 4.1 Respondents' Perception on BTC (in percentage)

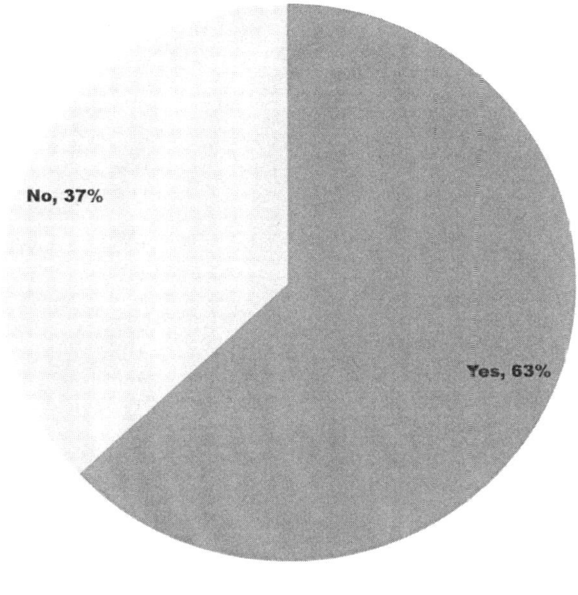

In reply to the question whether BTC has fulfilled the aspirations of the respondents (as shown in Figure. 4.1),63% respondents felt that BTC has somehow fulfilled their aspirations, but 37% felt that BTC has failed to fulfill the same.

Table 4.1 Educational qualification-wise perception on BTC for the aspiration fulfillment of Bodos

Perceptions	Total Respondents Perception	Educational Qualification of the respondents				Total
		Below Primary	Matriculate	Graduate	Post Graduate/ professional	
Yes	63%	19.0%	54.0%	27.0%	.0%	100.0%
No	37%	45.9%	35.1%	16.2%	2.7%	100.0%
Total	100%					

However, the feeling of satisfaction and dissatisfaction also varied in terms of the respondents' educational qualifications (as shown in Table 4.1). The respondents who felt that BTC had fulfilled the aspirations of the Bodos, included 54% Matriculate, 27% Graduate, and 19% educated up to Below Primary level. While, the respondents who believed that BTC could not fulfill the aspirations of the Bodo's, included 45.9% educated up to Below Primary, 35.1% Matriculate, 16.2% Graduate and 2.7% Post-Graduate. The study revealed that a majority of the less educated respondents percieved that BTC could not fulfill the aspirations of the Bodos. On the other hand, a majority of Matriculate and Graduates respondents percieved that BTC had fulfilled the aspirations of the Bodos. This implies that the BTC has never succeeded in promoting the interests of the least section of the Bodos.

Occupation is an important variable that influenced the opinions on the performance of the BTC. They hope that their political representatives would adopt major policies for development that could improve the whole economic scenario.

The perception of the respondent varied depending on their occupation and their present economic status (as shown in Table 4.2). Among the respondents who felt that BTC fulfilled the aspirations of the Bodos, 49.2%were Housewives, 28.6% were Self-employed, 9.5% were Govt. employees, 9.5% were cultivators and 3.2% were Student. On the other hand, among the respondents who opined that the BTC had failed to fulfill the aspirations of the Bodos, 51.4% Cultivators, 16.2% Housewives, 16.2% Students, 10.8% Self-employed, and 5.4% Govt. employee. The majority of Housewife respondents perceived that BTC had fulfilled the aspirations of the Bodos. However, the majority of cultivator respondents believed that BTC could not fulfill the aspirations of the Bodos. It is observed that a significant number of Self-employed respondents felt that the BTC had fulfilled the aspirations of the Bodos. This shows once again that the BTC could not provide concrete benefits to poorer section of the society like cultivators.

Table 4.2 Occupation-wise perception on BTC for the aspiration fulfillment of the Bodos

Perception	Perception of the Total Respondents	Occupation of the respondent					Total
		Cultivator	Govt. employee	Self-employed	Students	Housewife	
Yes	63%	9.5%	9.5%	28.6%	3.2%	49.2%	100%
No	37%	51.4%	5.4%	10.8%	16.2%	16.2%	100%
Total	100%						

The study revealed that the household annual income brought some variance in the respondents' perception on the fulfillment of aspirations by the BTC (as shown in Table 4.3). Out of the total respondents who perceived that the BTC fulfilled the aspirations of the Bodos, 52.4% have Rs.50001-100000, 19% have Rs.100001-300000, 17.5% have Rs. 20001-50000, and 11.1% have Rs.<20000 annual household income. Among the respondents who perceived that BTC did not fulfill the aspirations of the Bodos, 70.3% have Rs. 20001-50000, 18.9% have Rs. 50001-10000, 10.8% have Rs.100001-300000 annual household income. Those respondents, whose annual income is Rs. 20001-50000, had maximum dissatisfaction towards the BTC and felt that BTC did not fulfill the aspirations of the

Table 4.3 Household Annual income-wise perception on BTC for the aspiration fulfillment of the Bodos

Perception	Perception of the Total Respondents	Household Annual income of the respondents				Total
		<20000	20001-50000	50001-100000	100001-300000	
Yes	63%	**11.1%**	**17.5%**	**52.4%**	**19.0%**	100.0%
No	37%	.0%	70.3%	18.9%	10.8%	100.0%
Total	100%					

Bodos. On the other hand, respondents, whose annual household income is more than Rs. 50001, were satisfied with BTC and perceived that BTC fulfilled the aspirations of the Bodos. This clearly shows that the BTC has been more beneficial for the higher income groups rather than for those with lower household income.

However, out of the respondents who felt that the BTC had fulfilled their aspirations (as shown in Figure 4.2**)**, 57.14% thought that the BTC had created opportunities for development, and another 42.86% respondents felt that the BTC had preserved the self-identity of Bodo community. Meanwhile, those respondents who are not satisfied with the BTC and feel that the BTC could not fulfill the aspirations of the Bodos, did not comment on this issue and responded as "don't know."

Bodos have been facing problems in terms of education, employment, language, etc. since 1947. The literacy trends (as shown in Annexure III) of five major Bodo inhabited districts and the other districts of the state for the three successive census years of 1991, 2001 and 2011 varied significantly. In the state of Assam, 52.89% of the total population was literate, whereas 45.92% of the population was literate in the Bodo inhabited districts in 1991. However, the rate of literacy varied significantly across the districts in the state.

Lowest literacy rate of 40.47% has been observed in Kokrajhar district as against the highest literacy rate of 55.99% in Nalbari in Bodo inhabited districts that were the only districts having higher literacy rate than the state average. The male literacy rate was 39.79% in Kokrajhar, which was the lowest among the districts in Bodo inhabited districts (Kokrajhar,

Fig. 4.2 Respondents' perception on opportunities created by the BTC

Note: a= by giving the opportunity to develop,
b= to preserve the self-identity

Bongaigaon, Darrang, Barpeta, Nalbari) and male literacy was highest at 54.68% in Nalbari district. Female literacy in the Bodo inhabited districts was only 24.59% that was the lowest among the districts in Bodo inhabited districts and female literacy was highest at 35.83% in Nalbari. However, there was a literacy gap of 30.09% between males and females in Bodo inhabited districts. Nalbari district shows the literacy gap between male and female of 18.85%, followed by 16.15% in Bongaigaon, 15.20% in Kokrajhar, 15.19% in Barpeta, and 14.87% in Darrang.

In 2001, the state literacy rate further increased to 63.25% leaving the same behind for Bodo inhabited districts to 57.82%. This has shown that during the decade of the 1990s, the literacy rate in the state has increased by 10.36%, while literacy rate has increased by 11.90% in Bodo inhabited districts. The Census report shows that literacy rate has increased more in the Bodo inhabited districts than other districts in the state. Literacy rate in Bodo inhabited districts ranges from 40.47% to 55.99% in 1991. The above analysis gives us literacy rate in the state of Assam in respect of Bodo inhabited districts and its situation in terms of literacy performance of total, and Bodo inhabited districts population in the state. Total literacy rate in other districts was 54.99% in 1991,which increased to 64.88% in 2001. It is seen that more than 70% of the districts other than Bodo inhabited districts have performed well in terms of literacy and had higher literacy than the state average in 1991.

It may be noted that female literacy rate in the state was 34.28% in 1991, which increased to 54.61% in 2001. On the other hand, the female literacy rate in Bodo inhabited districts was 28.44% and 48.50%, respectively, during the same decades. It is therefore important to know whether after the formation of BTC there was any improvement in literacy rate of Bodo inhabited districts, particularly Kokrajhar, Chirang, Baksa and Udalguri districts. In 2003, Chirang, Baksa and Udalguri districts were created, so, a comparative study of literacy trends will not be possible. However, 63% respondents believe that BTC has been developing since its formation, but 37% negate such belief (as shown in Figure 4.3).

But literacy trends of Kokrajhar district (as shown in Annexure III) shows 40.47% literacy rate (Male=39.79% & Female=24.59%) in 1991, 51.63%

Fig. 4.3 Respondents' perception towards BTC development (in percentage)

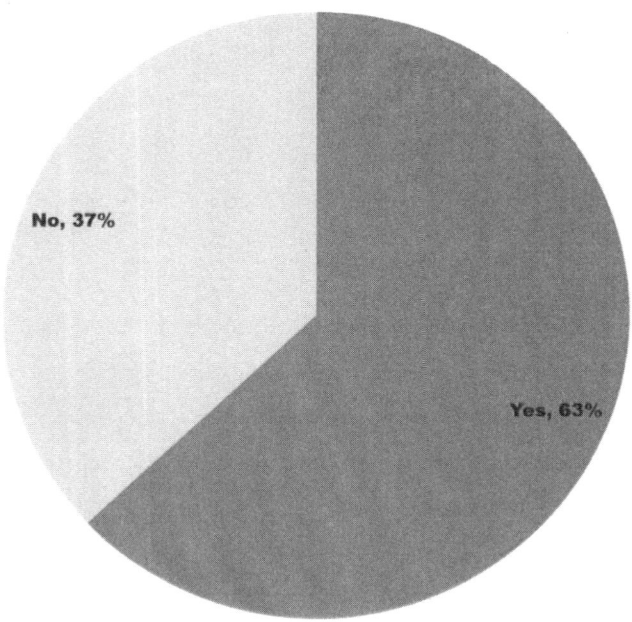

(Male=60.32% & Female=42.40%) in 2001 and 66.63% (Male=73.44% & Female=59.54) in 2011. It may be noted that there are marginal gaps between state literacy rate and that of the four districts of BTC. It is a matter of concern that every census shows that Kokrajhar district's literacy rate is lower than the state literacy of 52.89% in 1991, 63.25% in 2001 and 73.18% in 2011, respectively. Compared to it, the literacy rate in BTAD is 67.12%. Male literacy rate is 74.28%, and female literacy rate is 59.70%. Bodos, inspite of being the largest plains tribe in the state, are still lagging behind in terms of literacy rate (as shown in Annexure V). On the contrary, other tribes like Sonowal Kachari and Rabha are ahead of the Bodos in terms of literacy rate. Total tribal literacy rate that was 53.78% in 1991 in the state has increased to 62.52% in 2001.

The demand of Bodoland is a matter of depression towards the Government. The Bodo political representatives also failed to promote the issues. Over 90% of Bodo population depends on agriculture. Meanwhile, 79% respondents expected help (as shown in Figure 4.4) from the Bodo political representatives to receive government employment either for them or for their siblings, 15% respondents expected financial assistance to improve agriculture, and 6% respondents expected financial assistance to start business. This shows that maximum respondents were hopeful of receiving government employment with the help of their representatives.

Thus, respondents expected various opportunities i.e. employment, financial assistance to start a business and financial assistance to improve agriculture. BTC's policy deprives the general people in providing an opportunity to their relatives. In spite of such expectations, 91% respondents did not receive any opportunity, 4% received financial assistance to start business, 3% received financial support for agricultural development, and 2% were able to get government employment (as shown in Figure 4.5). This analysis shows that BTC failed to provide adequate opportunity for the people of the four districts under its jurisdiction.

It is also important to know the respondents' perception on the development brought about by BTC (as shown in Figure 4.6) in specific fields. On this issue, 37% respondents reacted that they do not know about whether BTC is developing or not, 22% respondents thought communication has been developing since the formation of BTC. Interestingly, 19% respondents thought that Bodos are developing educationally; 16% respondents thought Bodos are developing economically; 5% respondents thought that the literature of Bodos is developing; and the lowest i.e. only 1% respondents thought health and medical facilities have improved after

Fig. 4.4 Respondents' expectations from Bodo political leaders (in percentage)

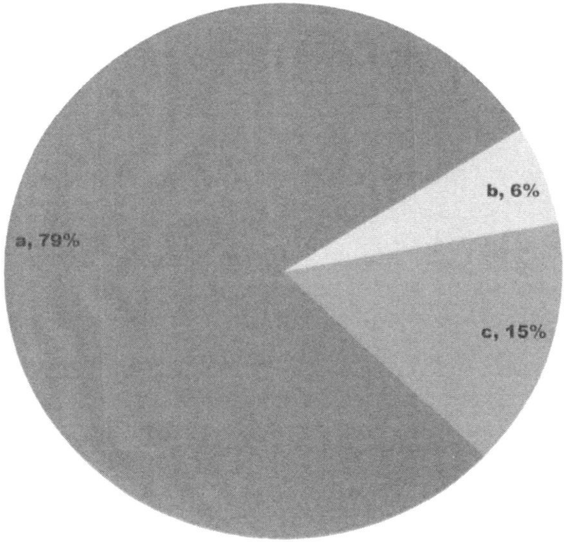

Note: a= Employment, b= Financial assistance to start a business, c= Financial assistance to improve agriculture.

the formation of BTC. Due to illiteracy, there are inadequate employment facilities in BTC region and this has led to economic underdevelopment. There is no large-scale industry in BTAD region except Bongaigaon Refinery and Petrochemical Ltd. The increasing rate of unemployment, coupled with growing trend of economic underdevelopment, has helped sustain extremism in the region.

There is no provision for direct appointment by BTC authorities and it has to wait for the State Government's approval to appoint even 4th Grade employees. Due to the absence of Home and Finance power, the BTC fails to function fully and fulfill the aspirations of the Bodos. The financial packages run the financial expenses of BTC that Union Government provides via the State Government. Due to lack of Home power, the BTC Government failed to stop some major ethnic violence that broke out in the region. The BTC cannot take immediate action and has to wait for the State/Union Government's approval to deploy armed forces during the conflicting situations.

Thus, the Bodo Accord 2003 could not resolve the core issues like illiteracy, underdevelopment, illegal migration and land alienation of the

Fig. 4.5 Distribution of respondents' receipt of facilities from BTC (in percentage)

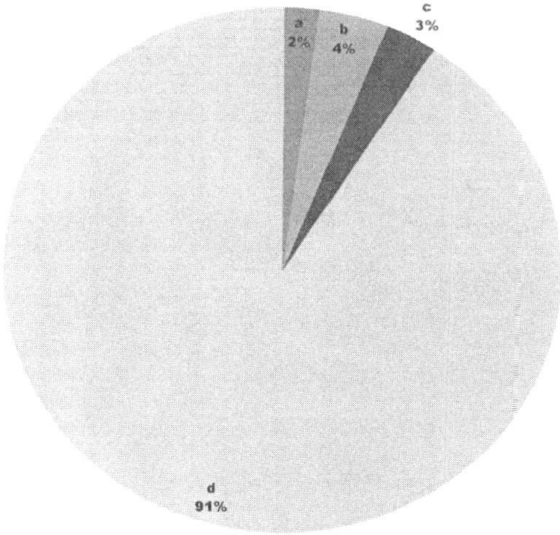

Note: a= Govt. Service, b= Financial assistance for business, c= Financial assistance to improve agriculture, d= Nothing

Fig. 4.6 Respondents' perception on development brought about by the BTC

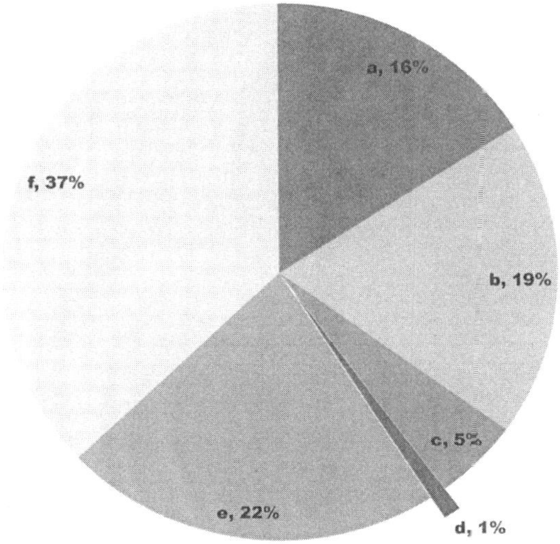

Note: a= Economically, b= Educationally, c= On Literature, d= Health & Medical Facilities, e= Communication, f= Don't Know

tribals in general. Meanwhile, 52% respondents (as shown in Figure 4.7) still feel that Bodos should continue Bodoland demand, while 48% respondents are not in favour of the continuation of the demand.

Fig. 4.7 Respondents' opinion on Continuation of Bodoland demand (in percentage)

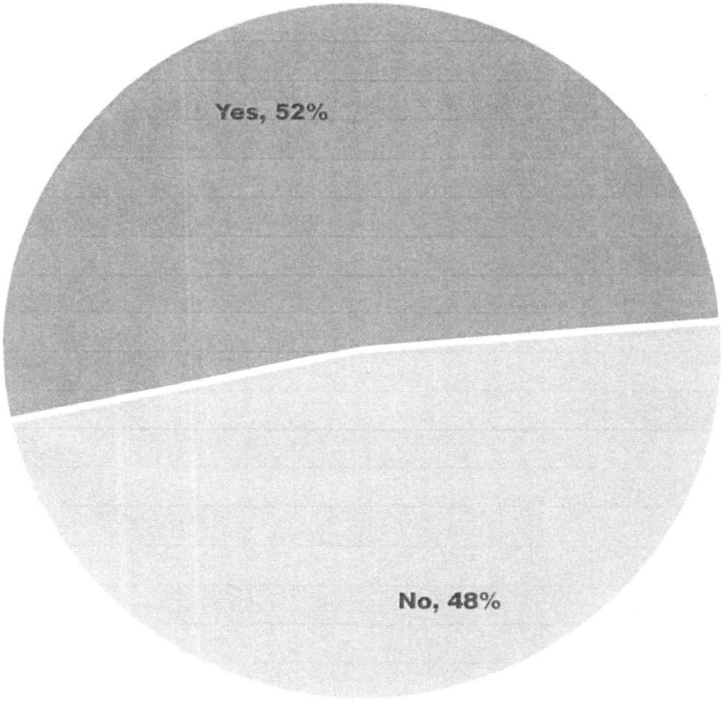

The respondents, who believe that BTC has already fulfilled the aspirations of the Bodos, are not in favour of the continuation of Bodoland demand (as shown in Table 4.4). Out of those respondents who feel that BTC has fulfilled the aspirations of the Bodos 76.19% are not in favour of continuation of Bodoland demand and only 23.81% respondents are in favour of continuation of this demand. All 100% respondents, who think that BTC had failed to fulfill the aspirations of the Bodos, are in favour of continuing the Bodoland demand.

Thus, from the above discussion, it can be concluded that one of the major factors responsible for the persistence of Bodoland demand is the BTC's failure to fulfill the aspirations of the Bodos.

Table 4.4 Respondents' fulfillment of aspiration on BTC and continuation of Bodoland demand (in percentage)

Opinion on Aspiration	Opinion of the Total Respondents	Opinion on demand Total		
		Yes	*No*	*Total*
Yes	*63%*	*23.81%*	*76.19%*	*100%*
No	*37%*	*100%*		*100%*
Grand Total	*100%*			

Support Base of the NDFB

Coming to the support base of the NDFB, it is interestingly to note that although different organisations are demanding Bodoland, yet the NDFB has been able to obtain more support than other Bodo organisations. However, out of the total respondents, 54% are in favour of peaceful movement, 35% in favour of violence, and 11% in favour of using both strategies for the achievement of Bodoland (as shown in Figure 4.8).

Fig. 4.8 Respondents' opinion on strategies to achieve Bodoland (in percentage)

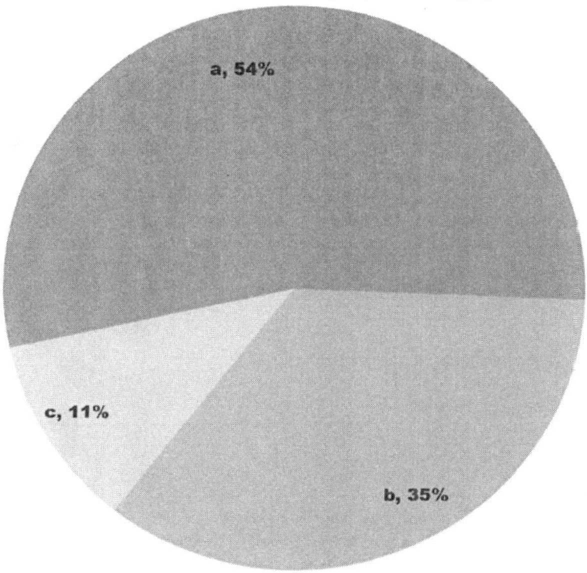

Note: a= by peaceful movement, b= by using violence, and c= both

However, age-wise respondents opined differently (as shown in Table 4.5) on the issue as to how Bodoland can be achieved. Out of the total respondent, 41% are in the age group of 41-60 years. Among them, 60.98% opined that Bodoland demand can be achieved only by peaceful movement, 26.83% opined that Bodoland can be achieved only by using violent methods, and another 12.20% opined that Bodoland can be achieved by using both peaceful and violent strategies. It is because people who are 41-60 years of age are more concerned about their families, and they want better result without taking the risk that could result in losing their near and dear one's life. Among the respondents who are in the age group of 26-40 years, 52.63% opined that Bodoland can be achieved only by using the strategy of violence, 31.58% opined that demand of Bodoland will be fulfilled only by using peaceful movement, and 15.79% opined that Bodoland can be achieved by using both violent and peaceful methods. Among the respondents who were of the age of 61^{+} years, 60.0% r opined that Bodoland can be achieved by peaceful movement and 40.0% opined using violence is the only means of achieving Bodoland. Among the respondents who are of 18-25 years, 83.33% felt that Bodoland can be achieved only by using violence and 16.67% opined that Bodoland can be achieved only by peaceful movement. This clearly shows that the respondents from higher age groups are in favour of peaceful methods while those belonging to lower age group support violent methods.

Table 4.5 Age-wise distribution of the respondents' opinion on strategies to achieve Bodoland (in percentage)

Age	Out of the Total Respondents	Strategies			Total
		By peaceful movement	By using violence	Both	
18-25 Years	6%	16.67%	83.33%	0	100%
26-40 Years	38%	31.58%	52.63%	15.79%	100%
41-60 Years	41%	60.98%	26.83%	12.20%	100%
61+ Years	15%	60.0%	40.0%	0	100%
Grand Total	100%				

However, depending on the respondents' educational qualifications, opinion also varied. Education is an important variable that changes the perspective of respondents' thinking. Thus, we can find varied responses depending on the educational qualification of the respondents (as shown in Table 4.6). Out of the total 47% Matriculate respondents, 51.06% supported peaceful movement, 38.30% supported violent strategies and 10.64% supported both violent and non-violent strategies to achieve Bodoland. Out of the 29% respondents who studied up to below primary, 72.41% supported non-violent, 20.69% supported violent and 6.90% supported both violent and non-violent strategies to achieve Bodoland. Out of the total 23% Graduate respondents, 43.48% supported violent, 39.13% supported non-violent and 17.39% supported both violent and non-violent means to achieve Bodoland. 100% Post-Graduate respondents felt that only violent strategy can be helpful to achieve Bodoland.

Table 4.6 Educational qualification-wise distribution of respondents' support for strategies (in percentage)

Level of Education	Out of the Total respondents	Strategies			Total
		By peaceful movement	By using violence	Both	
Below Primary	29%	72.41%	20.69%	6.90%	100%
Matriculate	47%	51.06%	38.30%	10.64%	100%
Graduate	23%	39.13%	43.48%	17.39%	100%
PG/ Professional	1%	.0%	100%	.0%	100%
Grand Total	100%				

Thus the study revealed that respondents, who are Graduate and are more intent to get Bodoland, support more violent strategies because they think only Bodoland can create opportunities to develop themselves.

As mentioned earlier that the NDFB had never been in any negotiation and signed any Memorandum of Settlement with the government. Though ABSU dropped the Bodoland demand in 2003 after BTC Accord, but ABSU denounced the BTC Accord and announced to launch a fresh Bodo movement from 2nd March 2010. ABSU held the several rounds of mass rally, demonstration and railway blockade. There are few leaders hankered after to consolidate their position and even start voicing for Bodoland.

Bodo National Convention (BNC) is an umbrella organisation consisting of 23 Bodo organisations initially established to bring peace in strife-torn Bodoland area. The BNC came into existence on 19 November 2010, with the objective to provide common platform for all Bodo organisations—civil, political and non-political organisations. Other objectives includes to fight for their common causes, including the demand for a separate state of Bodoland. An umbrella organisation, PJACBM, was formed on 31 March 2012, including the 52 tribal and non-tribal organisations, including those representing *Adivasis*, Gorkhas, and Bengali, Deuri, Mishing, Tiwa, Karbi, Rabha communities,to bring a long-term solution to Bodo conflict. The PJACBM, backed by the NDFB-P, for the first time, visualized that the proposed separate Bodoland state is not only for the Bodos but also for all non-Bodo communities living in the region.

Fig. 4.9 Distribution of respondents' support base for various organisations (in percentage)

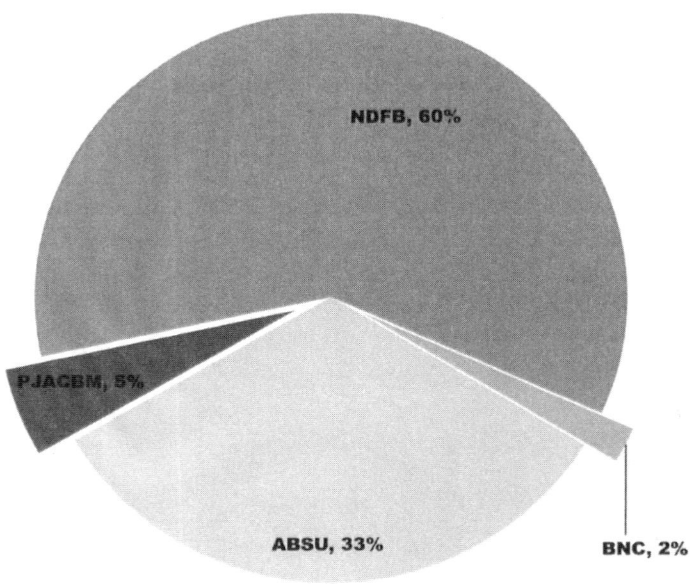

The survey revealed that 60% respondents supported the NDFB, 33% respondents supported the ABSU and 5% supported the People's Joint Action Committee of Bodoland Movement (PJACBM).Only 2% of the respondents support the Bodo National Convention (BNC), another umbrella organisation formed on 19 November, 2010 to bring peace in strife-torn Bodo areas (as shown in Figure 4.9).

However, respondents' support base varied depending on their age (as shown in Table 4.7). Among the respondents who are 18-25 years, 66.67% supported the NDFB, 16.67% supported ABSU and remaining 16.67% supported BNC. Among the respondents who are 26-40 years of age, 63.16% supported the NDFB, 31.58% supported the ABSU and 5.26% supported the PJACBM. Out of the respondents having 41-60 years of age, 48.78% supported the NDFB, 43.90% supported ABSU, 4.88% supported the PJACBM and remaining 2.44% supported BNC. Among the respondents who are 61^{+} years of age, 80% supported the NDFB, 13.33% supported the ABSU and 6.67% supported PJACBM. From the above analysis, it is proved that the NDFB is able to gain maximum support from every age group than any other Bodo organisation.

Table 4.7 Age-wise distribution of the respondents' support for various organisations for Bodoland demand (in percentage)

Age of the respondents	Out of the Total respondents	Organisations				Total
		ABSU	NDFB	BNC	PJACBM	
18-25 Years	6%	16.67%	66.67%	16.67%	.0%	100%
26-40 Years	38%	31.58%	63.16%	.0%	5.26%	100%
41-60 Years	41%	43.90%	48.78%	2.44%	4.88%	100%
61+ Years	15%	13.33%	80.0%	.0%	6.67%	100%
Grand Total	100%					

Education is also a variable that moulds the support base of various Bodo organisations. Depending on the level of education, respondents' opinion varied (as shown in Table 4.8). Out of the respondents whose level of education is below primary, 68.97% supported the NDFB, 27.59% supported the ABSU and 3.45% supported PJACBM. Out of the respondents who are educated up to matriculation, 57.45% supported the NDFB, 31.91% supported ABSU, 8.51% supported PJACBM and 2.13% supported BNC. Out ofthe graduate respondents, 52.17% supported the NDFB, 43.48% supported ABSU and remaining 4.35% supported BNC. One Post-graduate respondent (100%) supported the NDFB. So, from the above analysis, it can be concluded that while the level of education affected the support base of the NDFB. The NDFB was able to gain the consistent support from the majority of the respondents, irrespective of their educational qualifications.

Table 4.8 Educational qualification-wise distribution of the respondents' support for various organisations for Bodoland demand (in percentage)

Level of education	Out of the Total respondents	Organisations				Total
		ABSU	NDFB	BNC	PJACBM	
Below Primary	29%	27.59%	68.97%	.0%	3.45%	100%
Matriculate	47%	31.91%	57.45%	2.13%	8.51%	100%
Graduate	23%	43.48%	52.17%	4.35%	.0%	100%
PG/ Professional	1%	.0%	100%	.0%	.0%	100%
Grand Total	100%					

The support base of the Bodo groups who are demanding Bodoland depend on the ideology that the respective group had adopted. Among the respondents who supported the peaceful movement (as shown in Table 4.9), 44.44% supported ABSU, 42.6% supported the NDFB, 9.26% supported PJACBM and only 3.70% supported BNC. Among the respondents who felt that Bodoland can be achieved only through violence, 80% supported the NDFB and 20% supported ABSU. Though after BAC Accord, the ABSU fully dropped the extremist ideology yet few respondents support ABSU. Among the respondents who have felt that Bodoland can be achieved by using simultaneously violent and non-violent strategies, 81.82% supported the NDFB and 18.18% supported ABSU. From the above analysis, we can come to the conclusion that the respondents who supported the non-violent ideology, 44.44% supported the ABSU. Again out of the respondents who support violent ideology, 80% supported the NDFB. Among the respondents who had supported both violent and non-violent ideologies to achieve the Bodoland demand, 81.82% supported the NDFB.

Table 4.9 Distribution of respondents' opinion on strategy to achieve Bodoland and the organisation supported (in percentage)

Ideology	Out of the Total respondents	Organisations				Total
		ABSU	NDFB	BNC	PJACBM	
By peaceful movement	54%	44.44%	42.6%	3.70%	9.26%	100%
By using violence	35%	20%	80%	.0%	.0%	100%
Both	11%	18.18%	81.82%	.0%	.0%	100%
Grand Total	100%					

Therefore, one major doubt arises on the issue as to why 60% respondents (as shown in Figure 4.10) still support the NDFB, despite it being involved in numerous violent activities. However, 40% respondents are aware of the NDFB's activities, and they had not supported the NDFB. Among the respondents who supported the NDFB, 43.33% respondents supported it because there is no other option left to voice the demand for Bodoland, 30% respondents supported the NDFB because of its 'Die for Nation' attitude, and the remaining 26.67% respondents supported the NDFB because of its consistent demand for Bodoland.

It is important to note that splits in the NDFB also led to a division in the support base of the outfit (as shown in figure 4.11). While 51.67% respondents supported the NDFB-P, 48.33% supported the NDFB-R.

Respondents' support also varied in terms of the strategies to achieve Bodoland (as shown in Table 4.10). Among the respondents who had supported peaceful movement as a strategy to achieve Bodoland, 42.59% supported the NDFB-P,while 57.41% did not support any of these three factions. Respondents who had supported violence as a strategy to achieve Bodoland, 77.14% supported the NDFB-R and 2.86% supported the NDFB-P,while 20% respondents did not support any of the NDFB factions. Among the respondents who considered both violent and non-violent strategies as useful to achieve Bodoland, 63.64% supported the NDFB-P, 18.18% supported the NDFB-R and 18.18% did not support any faction.

Fig. 4.10 Respondents' reasons to support the NDFB (in percentage)

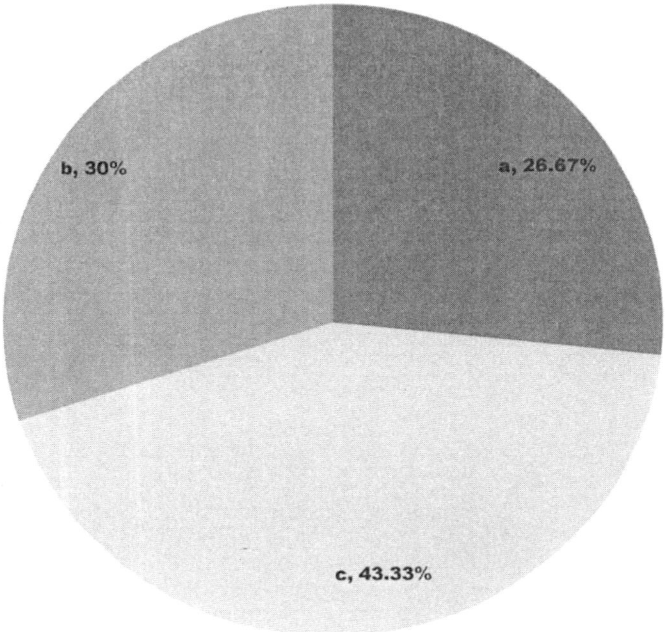

Note: a= because of consistency in demand, b= because of their 'die for Nation' attitude, c= because there is no any other option

An interesting fact which emerged from the study is that the NDFB-R is supported more by the respondents who are 18-25 and 26-40 years in age in comparison to those respondents who are 41-60 and 61^{+} years in age (as shown in Table 4.11). Out of the 40% respondents who are within the age group of 26-40 years, 62.5% support the NDFB-R and another 37.5% support the NDFB-P. Out of the 6.67% respondents who are in the age group of 18-25 years, 75.0% support the NDFB-R and only 25% support the NDFB-P. Out of the 33.33% respondents who are in the age group of 41-60 years, 60% support the NDFB-P and another 40% support the NDFB-R. Out of 20% respondents who are in the age group of 61^{+}, 75% support the NDFB-P and 25% support the NDFB-R. Thus, according to the survey, age is an important variable which has influenced the support base of the NDFB. The NDFB-R marginally lost support from the respondents who are 41 years or above in age. On the other hand, NDFB-P gained more support from the respondents who are 41 years or above in age.

Table 4.10 Distribution of respondent's opinion on NDFB Factions and the strategy (in percentage)

Strategies	Out of the Total respondents	Factions				
		NDFB-R	NDFB-P	NDFB-S	No support	Total
By peaceful movement	54%	.0%	42.59%	.0%	57.41%	100%
By using violence	35%	77.14%	2.86%	.0%	20.0%	100%
Both	11%	18.18%	63.64%	.0%	18.18%	100%
Grand Total	100%					

Fig. 4.11 Respondents' support to NDFB-R and NDFB-P (in percentage)

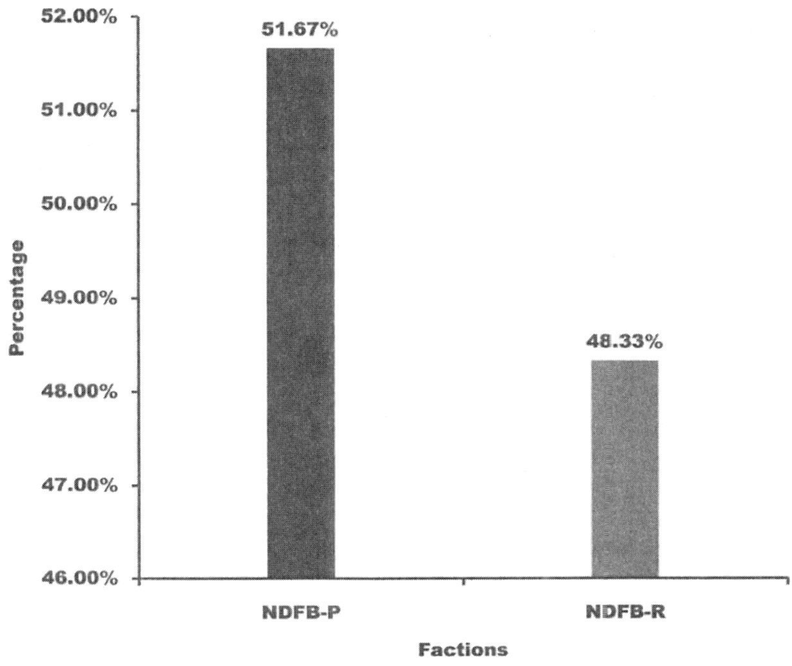

Table 4.11 Age-wise distribution of the NDFB's support base (in percentage)

Age	Out of total respondents who supported the NDFB	Factions of the NDFB			Total
		NDFB-R	NDFB-P	NDFB-S	
18-25 Years	6.67%	75.0%	25.0%	.0%	100%
26-40 Years	40.00%	62.5%	37.5%	.0%	100%
41-60 Years	33.33%	40.0%	60.0%	.0%	100%
61+ Years	20.00%	25.0%	75.0%	.0%	100%
Grand Total	100%				

It appears, therefore, that the level of education of the respondents shaped the support base of the NDFB (as shown in Table 4.12). Out of the respondents whose level of education is below primary, 65% supported the NDFB-P and 35% supported the NDFB-R. Among the matriculate respondents, 51.85% supported the NDFB-R and 48.15% supported the NDFB-P. Among the graduate respondents, 66.67% supported the NDFB-R and 33.33% supported the NDFB-P. Only one (100%) post-graduate respondent supported the NDFB-P. This may be interpreted to mean that the NDFB-R enjoys more support among respondents with higher level of education, i.e. upto graduation level. However, there is a deviation from this trend in the case of a 100% post-graduate respondent who supported the moderate faction of the NDFB.

Among the respondents who support the NDFB-R, 65.52% supported it due to the leadership of Ranjan Daimary, 27.59% supported it due to its steady demand; and 6.89% supported it due to its stable political ideology (as shown in Figure 4.12). Ranjan Daimary, the founder President of the NDFB, seems to have gained maximum popularity due to his prolonged struggle for Bodoland.

Among the respondents who support the NDFB-P, 87.5% support it due to its practical demand for a separate state of Bodoland, 6.25% support it due to the leadership of Govinda Basumatary, and another 6.25% support

Table 4.12 Educational qualification-wise NDFB's support base (in percentage)

Level of Education	Total numbers of the respondents who supported the NDFB	Factions			Total
		NDFB-R	NDFB-P	NDFB-S	
Below Primary	33.3%	35.0%	65.0%	.0%	100%
Matriculate	45.0%	51.9%	48.1%	.0%	100%
Graduate	20.0%	66.7%	33.3%	.0%	100%
Post-Graduate /Professional	1.7%	.0%	100%	.0%	100%
Grand Total	100%				

Fig. 4.12 Respondents' reasons to support the NDFB-R (in percentage)

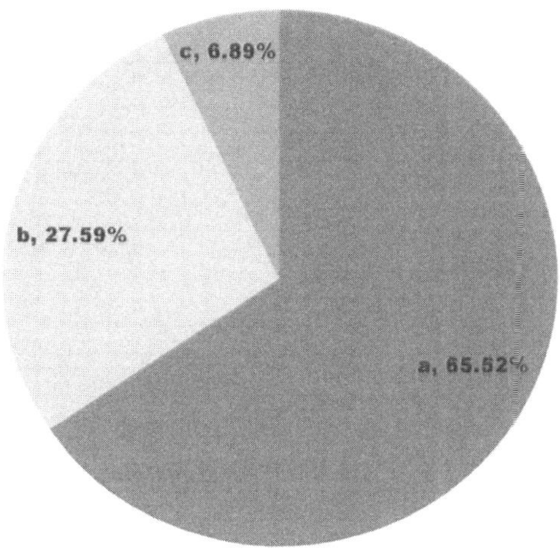

Note: a= Due to leadership of Ranjan Daimary, b= Due to steady demand, c= Due to stable political ideology

it due to its non-violent ideology (as shown in Figure 4.13). On the whole, those respondents who consider Sovereign Bodoland to be a non-pragmatic demand seem to support the NDFB-P.

Among the respondents who support the NDFB-R, 65.52% supported it due to the leadership of Ranjan Daimary, 27.59% supported it due to its steady demand; and 6.89% supported it due to its stable political ideology. Ranjan Daimary, the founder President of the NDFB, seems to have gained maximum popularity due to his prolonged struggle for Bodoland.

Fig. 4.13 Respondents' reasons to support the NDFB-P (in percentage)

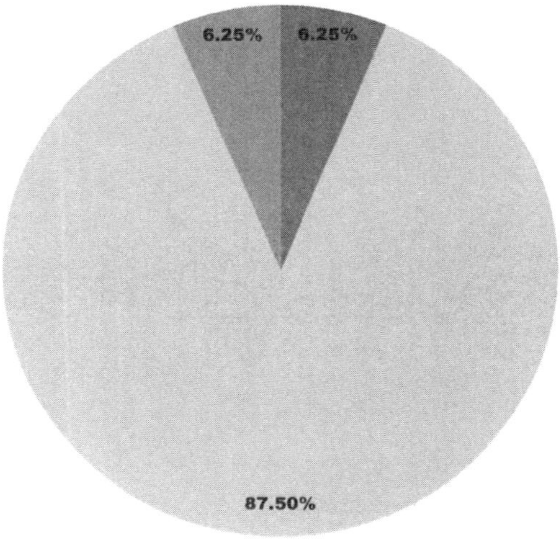

Note: a= Due to the leadership of Govinda Basumatary[1], b= Due to practical demand of Bodoland State, c=Due to newly adopted non-violence political ideology.

Thus, the persistence of the Bodoland demand is due to the failure of the BTC to fulfill the aspirations of the Bodos. Therefore, the majority of the Bodos are in favour of continuing the Bodoland demand. To continue the Bodoland demand, people are more concerned about the strategies that should be taken by the Bodo organisations. The NDFB has able to gain more support due to lack of other options to spearhead the Bodoland demand. After the split in the NDFB into two factions NDFB-R and NDFB-P, NDFB-P has gained more support because of its pragmatic demand of a Bodoland state within the Indian Union.

Role of the NDFB

The respondents' perceptions are varied about the role of the NDFB (as shown in Figure 4.14).While 43% respondents felt that NDFB played the role of motivating the Bodos to fight for Bodoland, 23% respondents believed that the NDFB played the role of social reformer, 5% thought that the NDFB brought the political awareness among the Bodos and 29% respondents had no idea about the role of the NDFB, so, they responded as "don't know".Therefore, it can be concluded that maximum number of respondents have the perception that the NDFB played an important role in motivating the Bodos to fight for Bodoland.

On the other hand, age-wise the respondents' perceptions were also varied (as shown in Table 4.13). Among the respondents who are 18-25 years of age, 50.0% felt that the NDFB is motivating the Bodos to fight for the Bodos, 33.33% thought that the NDFB has brought political awareness, and 16.67% responded as "don't know". Among the respondents who are 26-40 years of age, 42.11% responded as "don't know", 36.84% felt that the NDFB played the role of reforming Bodo society, and 21.05% think that the NDFB is motivating the Bodos to fight for Bodoland. Out of the respondents who are 41-60 years of age, 46.34% felt that the NDFB is motivating the Bodos to fight for Bodoland, 29.27% responded as "don't know",19.51%felt that the NDFB played the role of reforming Bodo society; and 4.88% felt that the NDFB has brought political awareness among the Bodos. Out of the respondents who are 61^{+} years of age, 86.67% felt that the NDFB is motivating the Bodos to fight for Bodoland, 6.67% felt that the NDFB played the role of reforming Bodo society; and 6.67% felt that the NDFB had brought political awareness among the Bodos. Thus, a majority of respondents of every age group acknowledged the role of the NDFB in motivating the Bodos to fight for Bodoland.

Perception of the respondents also varied in term of their educational qualification (as shown in Table 4.14). Out of the respondents who are educated below primary level, 48.28% perceived the role of the NDFB as motivating the Bodos to fight for Bodoland, 24.14% perceived the role of the NDFB as reforming Bodo society, 17.24% had responded as "don't know"; and 10.34% felt that the NDFB had brought political awareness.

Out of the matriculate respondents, 48.94% thought that the NDFB is motivating the Bodos to fight for Bodoland, 29.79% believed that NDFB is reforming Bodo society; and 21.28% had responded as "don't know" (as shown in Table 4.14).Out of the graduate respondents, 60.87% responded

Fig. 4.14 Respondents' perception on the role of the NDFB (in percentage)

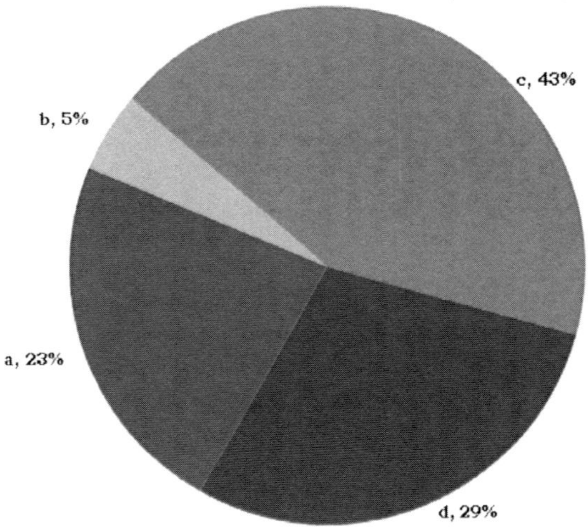

Note: a= Reforming Bodo society, b= Bringing political awareness, c= Motivating the Bodos to fight for Bodoland, d= Do not know

as "don't know", 21.74% responded as motivating the Bodos to fight for Bodoland, 8.7% responded as the NDFB is bringing political awareness; and another 8.7% responded as the NDFB is reforming Bodo Society. The only post-graduate respondent had perceived the role of the NDFB as they are motivating the Bodos to fight for Bodoland. From the above analysis, it is to be noted that irrespective of the respondents' educational qualification, maximum number of respondents perceived the role of the NDFB as motivating the Bodos to fight for Bodoland.

Opinion Regarding the Possible Delay and the Causes of Lack of Unity among the Bodos

Out of all the respondents, 31% felt that delay in solving the Bodoland demand is due to split in the NDFB, 26% believed that delay is due to lack of unity among Bodos, 24% thought that the delay is due to opposition of non-Bodos; and 19% observed that the delay is because of Government's unwillingness to solve the issue. Thus the lack of unity among the Bodos (as shown in Figure 4.15), split in the NDFB, the opposition of non-Bodos; and Government's unwillingness to solve the issue are considered to be the major causes of delay in solving the Bodoland issue.

Table 4.13 Age-wise distribution of the respondents' perception on the role of the NDFB (in percentage)

Age of the respondents	Perception of the total respondents	Role of the NDFB				Total
		Reforming Bodo Societies	Bring Political Awareness	Motivating the Bodos to fight for Bodoland	Don't know	
18-25Years	6%	.0%	33.33%	50%	16.67%	100%
26-40 Years	38%	36.84%	.0%	21.05%	42.11%	100%
41-60 Years	41%	19.51%	4.88%	46.34%	29.27%	100%
61+ Years	15%	6.67%	6.67%	86.67%	.0%	100%
Grand Total	100%					

Table 4.14 Educational qualification-wise distribution of the respondents' perception on the role of the NDFB (in percentage)

Level of education	Perception of the total respondents	Role of the NDFB				Total
		Reforming Bodo Society	Bring Political Awareness	Motivating the Bodos to fight for Bodoland	Don't know	
Below Primary	29%	24.14%	10.34%	48.28%	17.24%	100%
Matriculate	47%	29.79%	.0%	48.94%	21.28%	100%
Graduate	23%	8.7%	8.7%	21.74%	60.87%	100%
Post-Graduate/ professional	1%	.0%	.0%	100%	.0%	100%
Grand Total	100%					

Regarding the lack of unity among the Bodos, respondents' perceptions are varied. 52% thought "fight for leadership", 22% felt "being as a scattered community", 12% believed "elite competition", 9% thought "emerging the middle class" were the major causes of the lack of unity among the Bodos. However, remaining 5% respondents had no idea about the issue and responded as "don't know" (as shown in Figure 4.16). From the above analysis, it is to be noted that split and factionalism are the major characteristics of Bodo politics.

Total 22% respondents thought that Bodos have lack of unity because the whole community is scattered in different nook and corners of Assam (as shown in Figure 4.16). The Bodos have been demanding Bodoland comprising the whole north bank of the Brahmaputra River. However, if it is analysed minutely, it may be noted that the number of Bodos is less in the geographical area that the NDFB and other Bodo organisations are demanding as Bodoland. According to 2001 census, there is 8.89% Bodo population in the North-Bank of Brahmaputra River, and Bodo population covers 58.17% of the total tribal population of these districts.

Total tribal population in the state, according to the Census of India 2001, has been recorded as 33,08,570, accounting for 12.41% of state population (as shown in Annexure VI). The NDFB has been demanding Bodoland consisting the districts of Dhubri, Kokrajhar, Bongaigaon,

Fig. 4.15 Respondents' perception towards the causes of delay in executing the Bodoland demand (in percentage)

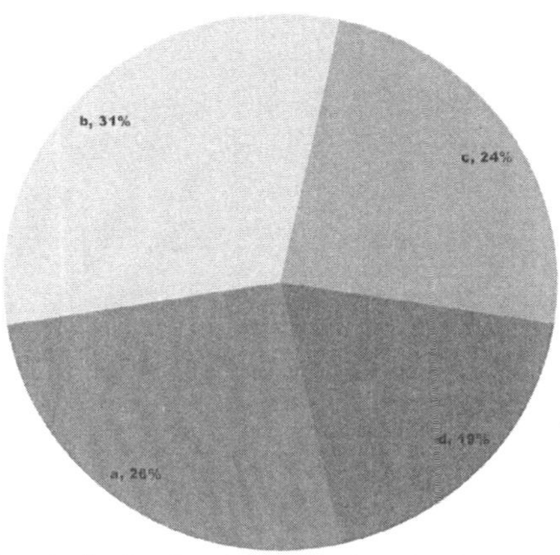

Note: a= Due to lack of unity in Bodos, b= Split in the NDFB, c= Due to opposition of non-Bodos, d= Governments' unwillingness to resolve the issue

Chirang, Barpeta, Baksa, Nalbari, Kamrup, Darrang, Udalguri, Sonitpur, Lakhimpur, Dhemaji. However, according to Census of India, 1991 and 2001, the Bodos are mainly concentrated in five districts of Assam, namely Barpeta Bongaigaon, Darrang, Kokrajhar and Nalbari. However, in other districts there is less number of Bodo population. According to 1991 census, these districts have population of 11296270, out of which tribal population is 1772619 and the number of Bodos is 1003385. Bodos cover 8.88% of the total population in these districts as against the state percentage of 5.05%.

In these districts, Bodos have the largest population among the STs,which cover 56.64% against the total tribal population of 41.12%. These 10 districts have a population of 13413079 (Census of India, 2001), out of which total tribal population is 2048744, and the total number of Bodos is 1191805.

Relationship with Other Bodo Organisations

Very often, Bodo political parties accused each other for having a relationship with the NDFB. It appears that the relations between NDFB and other Bodo organisations are sometimes close. Some of the opposition parties alleged that the National Democratic Front of Bodoland, as part of an understanding between the leaders of the NDFB and Hagrama Mohilary, the chief of BTC, had received incentive cash just before the election of 2006 and the amount was received by M. Gerema, the Organising Secretary, and B. Bengga, the Speaker of the NDFB. However, Hagrama Mohilary refuted the Opposition's charge saying he had been misquoted.[2] Bodoland People's Front (BPF) chief Hagrama Mahilary made a counter-allegation that the NDFB helped some Congress, BJP and AUDF candidates for the 2009 Lok Sabha election in lieu of money. Further Mohilary revealed that he had paid money to the NDFB in 2004 Lok Sabha polls.[3] The United Progressive Democratic Front (UPDF) also allegedly has relations with the NDFB. In the last BTC election, on 8th April 2010, Bodoland People's Front had alleged that the UPDF was contesting and campaigning in the elections with the help of the NDFB.[4] Thus, there are many allegations and counter-allegations on the relations of the NDFB with other organisations. For the present study, its relationship with BSS, ABSU and ABPF are discussed as follows.

Fig. 4.16 Respondents' perception on the lack of unity among Bodos (in percentage)

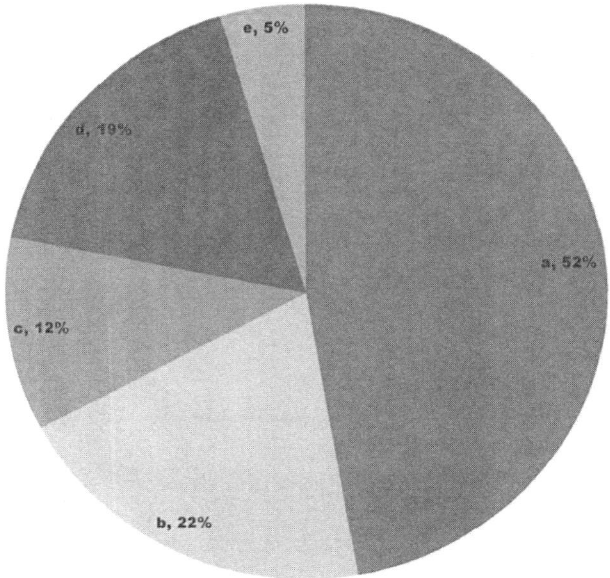

Note: a= Fight for leadership, b= Being as a scattered community, c= Elite competition, d= newly emerged middle class, e= Do not know

Relationship with the All Bodo Students' Union

From the day of its formation, there have been political differences that resulted in many fratricidal clashes between the NDFB and the ABSU. In fact, the formation of the NDFB was also against the decision of election of ABSU President. In February, 1986, at Bashbari (Kokrajhar) ABSU Conference, late Upendra Nath Brahma was elected as the President of the ABSU, but some dissidents of ABSU were against that decision, instead of that they were in favour of someone from the then Darrang district.[5] On the other hand, the ABSU does not support the demand of the NDFB on the ground that the Bodo people want only a separate state and that the demand for sovereignty has no popular support. The then ABSU President, U.G. Brahma, therefore, said that the NDFB should try to convince the people about the viability of their demand for sovereignty. An Anchalik ABSU President from Kokrajhar denied any relationship with the NDFB, but agreed that they had moral support for the NDFB on their demand of Bodoland state under the Indian Union. He further added that NDFB's demand for Sovereign Bodoland is a non-pragmatic demand. He even admitted that the NDFB had been indulging in many fratricidal killings. Regarding the role of the NDFB, he primarily mentioned about the social reformation policies that had been taken by the outfit.[6] A General Secretary of Anchalik ABSU also more or less agreed with the statement of their President.[7]

In protest against the NDFB's activities, sometimes different organisations held peace rallies. The All Bodo Peace Forum organised such a peace rally on June 17, 2005, at Udalguri, which was attended by thousands of Bodos in traditional attire who welcomed the cease-fire agreement that came into effect on June 1, 2005 for a period of one year and pledged the support of the masses for meaningful dialogue. The rally witnessing an unprecedented gathering of more than 40,000 people and was addressed by leaders of various North-East organisations including Harangse Sangtam, President Naga Hoho, Artrex Shimray, Chief Adviser, North-East Students' Organisation, Kanaksen Deka, President, Asom Sahitya Sabha and Urkhao Gwra Brahma, Rajya Sabha M.P.[8]

Bodo Sahitya Sabha

The Bodo Sahitya Sabha (BSS) President Brajendra Kumar Brahma said that the dialogue with the NDFB was imperative to find a permanent solution to the problems afflicting the state. He also said 'sovereignty' of Bodoland as raised by the Ranjan Daimary-led faction was not possible, and so the NDFB should think for a solution within the ambit of the Indian Constitution.[9]

The Bodo Sahitya Sabha organised a protest rally on 29 December, 2014, against killing innocents and urged the Centre to take strict action against the Songbijit faction of the National Democratic Front of Bodoland (NDFB-S) for its inhuman act. The protest was supported by Bodo organisations like the All Bodo Students' Union, All Bodo Women's Welfare Federation, All Assam Tribal Sangha, Tribal Youth League, All Bodo Employees Federation and the Dularai Bodo Harimu Afad.[10] The ABPF also organized a peace rally on 17 June, 2005, at Udalguri, to welcome the cease-fire agreement that came into effect on 1 June, 2005.

Thus, the support base of NDFB and its relationship with other Bodoorganisations had discussed in this chapter. It is seen that for the maximum number of the respondents perceived that Bodo aspirations were not fulfilled by the BTC and hence the Bodoland demand should continue. To raise the voice for Bodoland, maximum number of respondents supported the NDFB. Hence, in Chapter-V, an attempt is being made to analyse the responses of the BTC, the Union and State Governments to the demands made by the NDFB.

Conclusion

For an understanding of the support base of the NDFB, a survey was conducted in Udalguri district, which has been the main base of the NDFB. The survey showed that the formation of BTC could not fulfill the aspirations of all sections of the Bodos. However, according to 63% respodents, BTC fulfilled the aspirations of the Bodos. Out of the respondents, who perceived that Bodos should continue to demand for Bodoland, 54% are in favour of peaceful movement, 35% favoured violence, and 11% favoured both the strategies to achieve Bodoland.

The study revealed that in spite of the violent strategies adopted, 60% respondents supported the NDFB, 33% respondents supported the ABSU and 5% supported the People's Joint Action Committee of Bodoland Movement (PJACBM) and 2% respondents supported the Bodo National Convention (BNC). Moreover, 100% Post-Graduate, 68.97% educated below the primary level, 57.45% Matriculates, and 52.17% Graduate respondents supported the NDFB. It appears that the level of education of the respondents shaped the support base of the NDFB. The study revealed that the NDFB-R enjoys more support among respondents with higher level of education, i.e. upto graduation level. However, there is a deviation from this trend in the case of a single post-graduate respondent who supported the moderate faction i.e. the NDFB-P, which may be due to the respondents' realisation of the non-viability of the NDFB-R's demand for sovereignty.

It is interesting to note that a majority of the 60% respondents supported the NDFB out of which 43.33% respondents supported it because there is no other option left to voice the demand for Bodoland, 30% respondents supported the NDFB because of its 'Die for Nation' attitude, and the remaining 26.67% respondents supported the NDFB because of its consistent demand for Bodoland. However, 40% respondents did not support the NDFB. It is interesting to note that a majority of the respondents supported the NDFB on the ground that there is no other option. This implies that Bodos have become disillusioned and have lost faith in other organisations because of their failure to achieve Bodoland.

It is important to note that splits in the NDFB also led to a division in the support base of the outfit. Out of the respondents who supported the NDFB-P, 87.5% supported it due to its practical demand for Bodoland State. On the whole, those respondents who considered Sovereign Bodoland to be a non-pragmatic demand seem to support the NDFB-P. Among the respondents who supported the NDFB-R, 65.52% supported it due to the leadership of Ranjan Daimary. Ranjan Daimary, the founder President of the NDFB, seems to have gained maximum popularity due to his prolonged struggle for Bodoland.

Respondents' support also varied in terms of the strategies to achieve Bodoland. Among the 54% respondents who supported peaceful movement as a strategy to achieve Bodoland, 42.59% supported the NDFB-P and 57.41% did not support either of these factions. Among the 35% respondents who supported violence as a strategy to achieve Bodoland, 77.14% supported the NDFB-R and 2.86% supported the NDFB-P and another 20% respondents did not support any of the NDFB factions. Out of the 11% respondents who considered both violent and non-violent strategies as useful to achieve Bodoland, 63.64% supported the NDFB-P, 18.18% support the NDFB-R and another 18.18% did not support any faction. Thus the strategies that have been used by both the factions of the NDFB are important determinants of acquiring support from the respondents.

An interesting fact which emerged from the study is that the NDFB-R is supported more by the respondents who are 18-25 and 26-40 years in age in comparison to those respondents who are 41-60 and 61^{+} years in age. Thus, according to the survey, age is an important variable which has influenced the support base of the NDFB. The NDFB-R marginally lost support from the respondents who are above 41 years. On the other hand, the NDFB-P gained more support from the respondents who are above 41 years.

Regarding the role of the NDFB, the perception of the respondents varied in terms of age and education. However, according to the majority of the respondents, the NDFB is playing a major role in motivating the Bodos to fight for Bodoland. Respondents also acknowledged the NDFB's role in reforming the Bodo society and in arousing political awareness among the Bodos. It is felt by respondents that the amount of pressure exerted by the NDFB on behalf of the Bodo community resulted in the signing of two accords and that it is the NDFB's relentless struggle which has kept the Bodoland demand alive. Thus, it appears that the NDFB has major political differences with other Bodo organisations because of the fact that the latter do not consider the demand for sovereignty to be a viable one.

Regarding the relationship of the NDFB with other Bodo organisations, the study showed there are many allegations and counter-allegations on the relations of the NDFB with other Bodo organisations. However, study revealed that since the formation of the NDFB, there have been political differences which resulted in many fratricidal clashes between the NDFB and ABSU. ABSU does not support the demand of the NDFB on the ground that the Bodo people want only a separate state and that the demand for sovereignty has no popular support.

Former President of Bodo Sahitya Sabha (BSS), Brajendra Kumar Brahma, said that the dialogue with the NDFB was very important to find a permanent solution to the problems afflicting the state. He also said that 'sovereignty' of Bodoland as raised by the Ranjan Daimary-led faction was not possible, and so the NDFB should think for a solution within the ambit of the Indian Constitution. The Bodo Sahitya Sabha had stressed on holding of talks to carry forward the peace process. The ABPF also organized a peace rally on 17 June, 2005, at Udalguri, to welcome the cease-fire agreement that came into effect on 1 June, 2005. Thus, it appears that the NDFB has major political differences with other Bodo organisations because of the fact that the latter do not consider the demand for sovereignty to be a viable one.

References

1 Talukdar, S. (2010, November 20). New Body of Bodos to work for Statehood. *The Hindu*. Retrieved August 23, 2012, from http://ww.thehindu.com.t

2 Dhiren Boro is the President of the NDFB-P, however, it is observed that General Secretary of NDFB-P, Govinda Basumatary gained more popularity as the founder General Secretary of the NDFB.

3 'Mohilary paid us Rs 50 lakh: NDFB'. (2009, July 7). *The Telegraph*.

4 'NDFB helped Congress candidates: Mahilary'. (2009, April 27). *The Hindu*.

5 'UPDF Contesting in BTC Elections for NDFB'. (2010, April 5). *Bodosa*.

6 A personal interview with an ABSU delegate attended in the conference.

7 A personal interview with an ABSU Anchalik President.

8 A personal interview with an ABSU Anchalik General Secretary.

9 'Boycott cloud on Bodo Rally'.(2005, June 17). *The Telegraph.*

10 'Bodos want Daimary freed'.(2010, May 6). *The Telegraph.*

11 'Bodo groups warn NDFB-S against killings'. (2014, December 30). *The Telegraph.*

*****

5

BTC, Union and State Government's responses to demands raised by the NDFB

In the previous chapter, the support base of NDFB and its relationship with other Bodo organisations was discussed. The present chapter analyses the responses of the BTC, the Union and State governments to the demands made by the NDFB and it revealed that the Bodo aspirations were not fulfilled by the BTC and hence the Bodoland demand is persisting. In view of the NDFB's involvement in many bomb blasts, killing of civilians, kidnapping, extortion, killing of security forces, attack on railway tracks, etc., both the Union and State Governments have taken steps to neutralise the NDFB. However, the demand for Sovereign Bodoland was ruled out and the government refused to sit in the discussion table with such pre-conditions. The Union Government is in great dilemma to choose among the three factions of the NDFB, viz., NDFB-R, NDFB-P and NDFB-S, before signing the Memorandum of Settlement. This is because of the bitter experiences of the BAC Accord, 1993 and BTC Accord, 2003 when after signing a Memorandum of Settlement with one group another group came out with the demand for more concessions.

BTC Response to Bodoland Demand

It may be noted that the BTC has no power on Home and Finance subjects.[1] So, there is no direct response of the BTC to the NDFB's demands. However, on May 18, 2010, Hagrama Mohilary, the chief of Bodoland Territorial Council (BTC), welcomed the NDFB leader Ranjan Daimari's proposal for unconditional talks to resolve the issues between the Government and the NDFB leadership.[2]

It appears that the Bodoland Territorial Council (BTC) has been playing the role of a facilitator in the sense that the BTC authorities have taken some initiative to negotiate a settlement among the Union, State Government and the NDFB. The ruling political party of BTC, Bodoland People's Front (BPF) has also tried to unite the Bodos and formed the Bodo National Council (BNC) in response to the fratricidal killings that resulted from intra-group clashes.

Union Government's Responses

The Union Government and the State Government of Assam responded to the NDFB's demands in two different ways. On the one hand, the government tried to prevent violence by counter-terrorism operations and, on the other, it also invited the NDFB to join the peace process.

Ban on the NDFB

In response to the violent activities resorted to by the NDFB since its formation, the BTC, Union and State Governments had undertaken various measures to neutralise the violent situation. On November 23, 1992, for the first time, the Union Home Ministry imposed ban on the NDFB under provisions of the Unlawful Activities (Prevention) Act, 1967.[3]

According to Unlawful Activities (Prevention) Act, 1967, whoever does any act with intent to threaten or likely to threaten the unity, integrity, security or sovereignty of India or with intent to strike terror or likely to strike terror in the people or any section of the people in India or in any foreign country-[4]

a. By using bombs, dynamite or other explosive substances or inflammable substances or firearms or other lethal weapons or poisonous or noxious gases or other chemicals or by any other substances (whether biological radioactive, nuclear or otherwise) of a hazardous nature or by any other means of whatever nature to cause or likely to cause:

i. Death of, or injuries to, any person or persons; or

ii. Loss of, or damage to, or destruction of, property; or

iii. Disruption of any supplies or services essential to the life of the community in India or any foreign country; or

iv. Damage or destruction of any property in India or in foreign country used or intended to be used for the defence of India or in connection with any other purposes of the Government of India, any State Government or any of their agencies; or

b. Overawes by means of criminal force or the show of criminal force or attempts to do so or causes death of any public functionary or attempts to cause death of any public functionary; or

c. Detains, kidnaps or abducts any person and threatens to kill or injure such person or does any other act in order to compel the Government of India, any State Government or the Government of a foreign country or any other person to do or abstain from doing any act, commits a terrorist act.[5]

The NDFB involved in all prescribed form of violence that described in the "Unlawful Activities (Prevention) Act, 1967". As a result, it was necessary for government to impose ban on the NDFB due to the numerous incidents of killing civilians, security force personnel, and their alleged involvement in bomb explosions, fratricidal killings, kidnapping, extortion, etc.

The Interpol had also issued notices to NDFB leaders, i.e. in the year 1997, Interpol had issued notice against D.R. Nabla, alias Ranjan Daimary, the founder President of the NDFB.[6] Again on 1 January 2010, the Interpol issue a red corner notice against Chairman of NDFB-R, Ranjan Daimary, who is wanted as Daimary Ranjan alias Ronsaigra Nabla Doimari alias D.R. Nabla. Sources said that Daimary's name was put on the Interpol list after a talk between Centre's Interlocutor P.C. Haldar and the NDFB-P.[7] On 13 January, 2012, Interpol issued a Red Corner notice also to Rajen Goyari *alias* G Rifikhang, Vice-President of the NDFB-ATF for his alleged involvement in the use of weapons, explosives and acts of terrorism.[8]

In 2014, the Union Government extended the ban on all factions of the NDFB viz. NDFB-P, NDFB-R and NDFB-S for a maximum period of five years.

Counter-insurgency Operation against the NDFB

In 1994, for the first time to counter the violence mounted by the NDFB, army was deployed in the strife-torn areas of lower Assam. Operation Kranti was launched in Barpeta District to rid the 2,837 km^2 Manas Wild Life Sanctuary of the NDFB, who had held in those areas since 1986. Army operations were also conducted in Anand Bazar, Nagaon, Fatemabad, and Goardhana Mouza, as well as across the international boundary into Bhutan where Bodo factions reportedly took harbour.

Counter-insurgency Operations against the NDFB in Bhutan

Bhutan had committed itself to find a peaceful solution and pursued a series of dialogues with the separatist groups since 1998. Bhutan's official statement had called the entry of approximately 3,000 terrorists and setting up of their camps illegal. Every effort was made by the Royal Government to ensure their peaceful departure from the country. In this regard, the fraternal and good neighbourly relations between the Bhutanese people and the people of Assam have always been the primary concern and have, in fact, been a major factor in the Royal Government's decision to ensure that every effort is made to resolve the problem peacefully. It was with much regret and frustration that the Royal Government was unable to report any successful outcome of the talks to the National Assembly. Finally, during the 81st session of the Assembly, held from June, 28, to August 18, 2003, the Royal Government was mandated to make one last attempt at persuading the militants to leave the country. The resolution was clear in that, should the talks fail, then as a last resort, the Royal Bhutan Army would have to be given the responsibility of removing the militants from Bhutan.

Based on the above, the Home Minister, who was also the Prime Minister of Bhutan, invited the leaders of the three separatist groups to Thimphu for talks. Despite Bhutan's request that the top leadership should attend the talks, the two militant groups, namely the ULFA and the NDFB, sent mid-level representatives, while no response was received from the Kamtapur Liberation Organisation (KLO). Meanwhile, three rounds of talks were held with the NDFB, of which two rounds were held in October 2000 and May 2001, the latter being with the NDFB Chairman D.R. Nabla. On May

9, 2003, Chief of the Indian Army, General N C Vij, discussed activities of the ULFA, the NDFB and the KLO with Bhutanese authorities. On May 17, Bhutan King Jigme Singhye Wangchuk called upon the people to volunteer for the formation of a 'militia force' to counter Indian insurgent groups—ULFA, NDFB and the KLO—on its soil. NDFB had 12 camps scattered across the dense jungles of southern Bhutan, adjacent to Assam and West Bengal. While initiating the Operation All Clear (OAC), the Bhutan Government clearly pointed out that the action followed a protracted effort of persuading the terrorists to vacate the territory peacefully. The talks with the NDFB also did not yield any positive results. Subsequently, the fifth round of talks with the ULFA and the third round with the NDFB were held in October and November 2003. The NDFB categorically told the Bhutanese delegation that "they would have to come back" even if they left for the time being.[9]

Nevertheless, because of the sincere effort on the part of the Royal Government to find a peaceful solution, the Home Minister met separately with the ULFA in October 2003 and the NDFB in November 2003, and engaged in lengthy, substantive discussions. During the talks, the militants were told, with great restraint and patience, that the Royal Government cannot tolerate their presence any longer. They were reminded that their entry into Bhutan was no different from a foreign invading army, and their conduct showed no regard for Bhutanese laws. It was made very clear to them that they were not refugees seeking humanitarian protection, and that their refusal to leave would result in a senseless and fratricidal conflict. They were also told that the senselessness of a confrontation lay in the fact that Bhutan has nothing to do with their hopes and aspirations. Every life lost in the foreign soil of Bhutan for them would be a waste. They were advised to engage in serious reflection and consider the wisdom of continuing the armed struggle. They were also advised that the moment had arrived when they should try to find a solution within the constitutional framework of the Republic of India. Conducting a dialogue with the militants has never been easy, but Bhutan has been tolerant and patient in seeking a peaceful resolution of the problem. After six years of consistent and strenuous efforts to find a peaceful solution, the process of peaceful dialogue had been fully exhausted, and the Royal Government was left with no option but to give the Royal Bhutan Army the responsibility of removing the militants from Bhutan.

Earlier, the Bhutanese Government had given the terrorists a deadline (June 30, 2003) to abandon their camps. Likewise, before the OAC was launched, the government gave the terrorists a 48-hour notice "in the hope of avoiding bloodshed".[10] The unfavourable response of these groups to Bhutan's repeated offer of talks convinced the latter that the terrorists were acting as extra-sovereign entities on its territory. With no breakthrough, King Jigme Singye Wangchuk called upon his subjects to defend the country. The King also took unto himself the responsibility to safeguard the country's sovereignty from the Indian terrorist groups. Total disregard of the traditional authority was also mentioned in the official statement following the launch of the OAC. Meanwhile, OAC was launched and as a result in Tintala total 40 NDFB militants were gunned down in the December 16, 2003 Operation.[11] In this context, the Indian Chief of Army Staff, General N.C. Vij, was quoted as saying that 650 militants had been "neutralised"—either killed or captured—during the operation.[12] The NDFB Publicity Secretary B. Erakrdao was arrested during the operation. The other missing militants included B. Habrang, B. Fwjoukhang, Jwkhrub, Derhasa, Onsula and Udla. Ranjan Daimary claimed that the missing leaders were taken into custody by the Royal Bhutan Army just before the start of the Operation All Clear.[13] For the counter-insurgency operations, India sought help from Bhutan and warned them not to give shelter to any Indian terrorist group in their soil.

Counter-insurgency Operations against the NDFB in Bangladesh

Over the years, it appears that Bangladesh has become a safe haven for the Indian terrorist groups. Though Bangladesh denied the fact, but Indian Government pressurised them to act against the different outfits. The NDFB had been maintaining its bases in the Khagrachari area of Bangladesh. The outfit had some trained cadres as 26 batches of boys were trained in Bangladesh since 2004 and some trained militants seemed still at large, which was a major concern for the security forces. On 1 March 2007, Bangladesh Rifles (BDR) personnel arrested six NDFB militants along with a Bangladeshi national at Burunga of Nalitabari sub-district of Sherpur. The arrested cadres were identified as Mohishwar, Shombhu, Warao, Hor Kumar, Jiban Kumar, and Thandoi. They hailed from different districts of Assam. The Bangladeshi national was identified as Imrul Sangma. On 16 December 2008, Union Home Minister P. Chidambaram warned Bangladesh not to allow terrorist outfits from India to carry out anti-India operations from its territory. The Border Security Force (BSF), on March 11, 2010, said that Bangladesh had promised action against insurgents operating from its territory against India."We have handed over a list of insurgents likely to be in Bangladesh. I am confident of cooperation of the Bangladesh Rifles (BDR)," BSF Director General Raman Srivastava told reporters after the meeting held at New Delhi with BDR Chief Mainul Islam.[14]

On 30 September 2011, in a biannual conference of Border Security Force and Border Guards Bangladesh (BGB), held in Dhaka from September 25 to 30, the BSF handed over a fresh list of Indian terrorists hiding in Bangladesh to the BGB and demanded action against them even as the latter ruled out presence of rebels in Bangladesh. The BSF Director-General Raman Srivastava on September 30 said that BSF had furnished a fresh list of camps and hideouts of Indian terrorists hiding in Bangladesh soil like National Liberation Front of Tripura (NLFT), United Liberation Front of Assam (ULFA), All Tripura Tiger Force (ATTF), National Socialist Council of Nagaland-Isak-Muivah (NSCN-IM), National Democratic Front of Bodoland (NDFB), Hynniewtrep National Liberation Council (HNLC), People's Liberation Army (PLA), and United National Liberation Front (UNLF).On December 15, 2011, regarding the strategic alliance with Bangladesh for counter-insurgency, the BSF spokesman Ravi Gandhi had given them a list of Indian terrorists' camps, including the banned ULFA, NSCN-IM, NDFB, NLFT, HNLC, PLA and GNLA in Bangladesh with a hope to take action against the Indian terrorists.

After the arrest of NDFB Chief Ranjan Daimary, the Government of India provided information about the whereabouts of several other militant leaders in Bangladesh and was waiting for its response. Though the arrest of Ranjan Daimary was viewed as a major diplomatic victory for India, the Government kept mounting diplomatic pressure on Bangladesh to take action against the terrorists, particularly those belonging to the ULFA and the NDFB, who were still staying in Bangladesh.[15]

Counter-insurgency Operations against the NDFB in Myanmar

Myanmar has been the main base of the NDFB since its formation. On the basis of intelligence information, Indian Government pressurised Myanmar to operate against the NDFB as well as another terrorist group of North-East India. Cadres of the ULFA and NDFB are said to be hiding in the forest camps in Myanmar's Sagaing division where the NSCN-K has its headquarters. Source said Chidambaram would address a high-level security meeting with officials of the Army and other security agencies on April 3, 2010, after visiting Tirap and Changlang Districts, which border Myanmar, and have been affected by insurgency in an otherwise peaceful State. On November 9, 2013, Joint Secretary in the MHA, Shambhu Singh, said that Myanmar is not at all interested to take action against the northeastern militants based in that country.

Encounters in Assam

On December 29, 2009, *The Telegraph* reports that security forces launched a special operation in Assam's northern districts, particularly Udalguri and Sonitpur. The operation was targeted at the middle-ranking cadres of the NDFB-R who were involved on a recruitment drive from these two districts. The official said the outfit had started a recruitment drive recently to recover lost ground. There were many new unidentified NDFB cadres killed which indicated that they were new recruits. The success of their operations in the last few months against the NDFB was a big blow for the outfit. The NDFB had lost several armed wing cadres who were capable of carrying out major attacks. The NDFB had lost more than 40 cadres in encounters in the two Northern Districts and the Bodoland Territorial Area Districts (BTAD) since June 2009. At least 30 youths had joined the NDFB in November 2009. Those newly recruited cadres hankered after money that was promised by the outfit. Recruitment was done in a co-ordinated manner. A few cadres were entrusted with this responsibility and assigned areas where each would work.[16] Fresh recruitment of cadre by the NDFB was a setback to the insurgency operations launched by the Army.

In 2003, maximum 137 cadres were encountered by the security forces (including 40 cadres killed in Bhutan's Operation All Clear). In the years 1992, 2007 and 2008, minimum 1 (One) cadre in each year was killed by security forces. The reason behind the less number of encounters in 2007 and 2008 was the Suspension of Operation agreement that the NDFB had signed with the Government (as shown in Figure 5.1).

In 2009, more than 70 cadres were killed in encounters. Both the Government and the NDFB made allegations against each other on the violation of ceasefire ground rules. Though the NDFB is in ceasefire agreement with the Government since 2005, still security forces were involved in many counter-insurgency operations. Sources also revealed that 13 cadres of the anti-talk faction of the NDFB were killed in the counter-insurgency operations in January 2010, seven cadres were killed in February, five were killed in March and three were killed in April. It was also analyzed by the security forces that a few NDFB-P cadres were involved in unlawful activities despite their ceasefire agreement with the Government. [18]

Fig. 5.1 Year-wise Distribution of the NDFB Cadres Encountered (1992-2015)

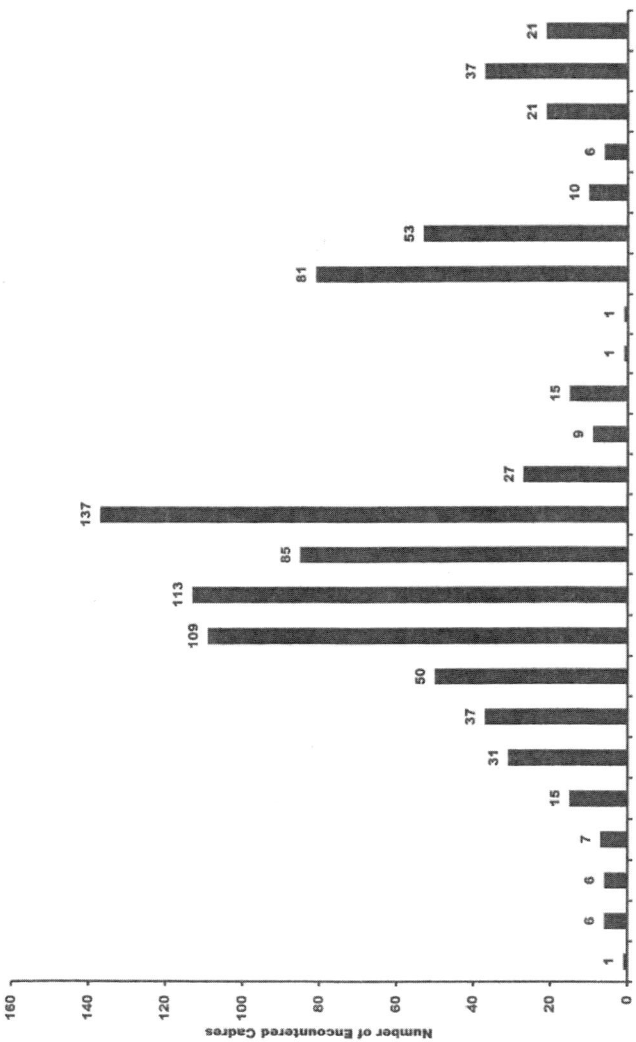

Source: South Asian Terrorism Portal[17]

Arrests of the NDFB Cadres

As a part of counter-insurgency operations, many NDFB leaders were arrested from different whereabouts. Following are some of the leaders who were taken into police custody and had taken action against them e.g. the NDFB 'General Secretary' B. Swmkhwr alias Govinda Basumatary was arrested in 2002. On January 1, 2003, the police arrested Dhiren Boro, 'Vice-President' of the NDFB from Tadung in Gangtok, Sikkim's capital, along with his wife, two children and two other NDFB cadres.[19] On January 2, 2003, NDFB 'Second Lieutenant' Sumit Basumatary was arrested from Samuktola Bazaar, near Siliguri in Jalpaiguri district of West Bengal.[20] On April 30, 2003, the Kolkata Police arrested the NDFB 'Speaker', Sunil Brahma alias B. Simong alias B. Benga and B. Buthang a'Captain' in the outfit's hierarchy was also arrested from a hotel in the Park Street, Kolkata and Rupees one million were recovered from their possession.[21] On May 15, 2003, the NDFB 'Deputy Commander-in-Chief' B. Olongbar alias Ajay Brahma was arrested from a local hospital in Guwahati while undergoing treatment under a false name.[22]

On November 19, 2008, the joint force of the CRPF and Army arrested Bipul Daimary, a 'Sergeant Major' of the NDFB, from Boglamari in the Baksa district.[23] On 26 May 2009, security forces arrested Indra Swargiyari, a 'Corporal' of the NDFB, from No. 3 Rayang Daruwa Basti near Jonai in Dhemaji District.[24]

Thus as a part of counter-insurgency policy, the security forces arrested many leaders and cadres of the NDFB. A maximum of 122 NDFB cadres were arrested in 1999 and in 2004; a minimum of 3 cadres were arrested. Samayee Narzarry, "Section Commandant" of the NDFB of Chirang district, and three others were arrested on September 14, 2009, in a joint operation by Chirang police and the army from Amteka in Chirang on Monday.[25] On November 8, 2009, the police arrested Mridul Goyari, an NDFB militant and accused in the October 30, 2008 twin blasts at Barpeta Road that claimed 21 lives, from Tezpur in Sonitpur District.[26]

On 1 May 2010, Bangladesh handed over Ranjan Daimary to India. Ranjan Daimary (50), wanted in numerous cases, was handed over at Dawki along the India-Bangladesh border in Meghalaya.[27] Following the arrest of the NDFB-R 'Chairman,' there were several setbacks as the outfits' many prominent leaders were arrested. On July 30, 2010, B. Barbai alias Bakul Brahma alias *B. Bihung*, an 'Assistant Publicity and Information Secretary', was arrested at Lankeswar under Jalukbari Police Station.[28]

Fig. 5.2 Year-wise Distribution of the NDFB Cadres Arrested (1998-2015)

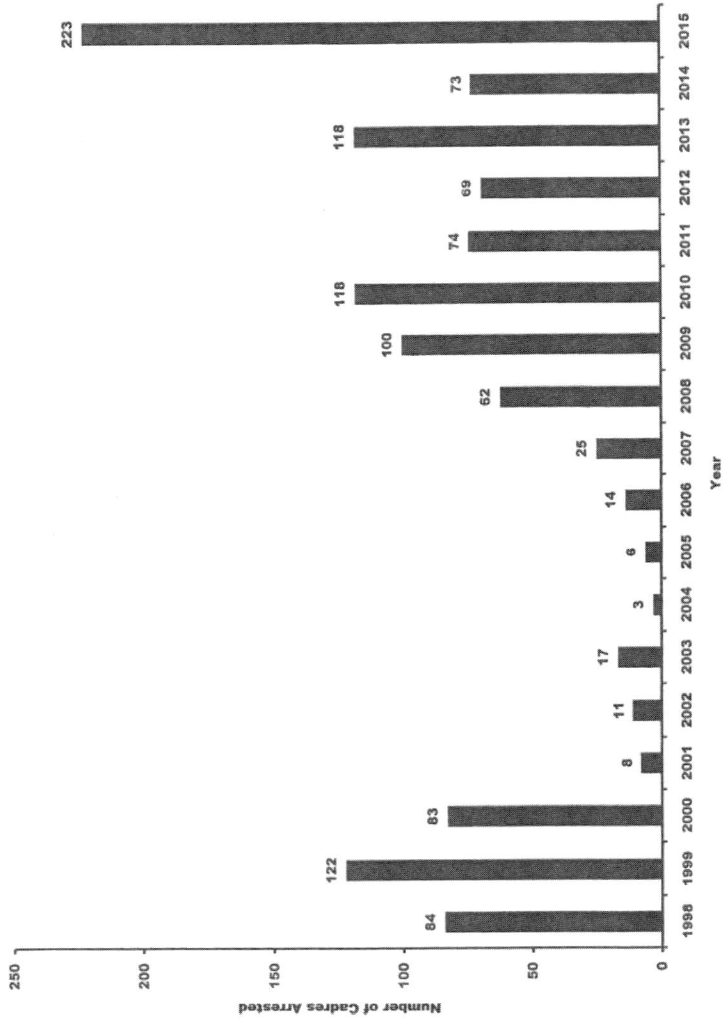

Source: South Asian Terrorism Portal[2]

On December 11, 2010, security forces arrested the self-styled deputy 'Commander-in-Chief' of the NDFB-ATF, George Boro, and a key accused in the October 30, 2008 serial blasts from Aizawl in Mizoram.[30]On February 10, 2011, Lachit Boro *alias* Haijang, a 'Commander', was arrested who had masterminded the serial killing of 20 people in Assam's Sonitpur District.[31] On March 12, 2012, SFs arrested Mihir Narzary *alias* Mwjib, 'Section Commander' of the NDFB-R (Sonitpur District), and Sunil Daimary from Karigaon in the same District.[32] Thus, the Government arrested NDFB leaders as well as cadres to intimidate the outfit, but the NDFB also tried to strengthen their power by recruiting the new and fresh cadres. Here it is important to mention that though the government from time to time declares the cadre strength of the NDFB, but there is a discrepancy between the total number of cadres and the number of arrested cadres.

During the period from 23rd December 2014 to 28th February 2015, total 214 numbers of cadres/linkmen of NDFB/S group were arrested and arms and ammunitions were recovered during the operations.[33]

Peace Talks

The government had undertaken many policies to tackle the violent situation in Assam. The peace process through negotiations started on January 1, 2001 when the NDFB and the ULFA were offered a 30-day safe passage by Assam Government.[34] However, the NDFB Chairman Ranjan Daimary remained opposed to any peace negotiations with the Government and rejected the amnesty offer of Assam Chief Minister Tarun Gogoi. The NDFB aslo rejected the general amnesty offer. On the other hand, realising the importance of peace, on February 25, 2004, Assam Government extended the period of 'general amnesty' to cadres of the NDFB to enable them to surrender.

On October 8, 2004, the Assam Government gave an offer for negotiations and in response, the NDFB announced a unilateral ceasefire on October 15 for six months.[35] On October 12, 2004, Assam Chief Minister Tarun Gogoi announced in Guwahati that NDFB had officially communicated its ceasefire offer to the government.[36] Both the State and the Union Governments were willing to begin the talks with the NDFB as early as possible. The government had tried to create a congenial atmosphere for discussion with the NDFB. Therefore, Assam Chief Minister Tarun Gogoi promised to offer safe passage to the representatives of the NDFB for talks with the government.[37] For that, the Assam Government even asked the NDFB to depute representatives to finalise the ground rules of the cease fire.[38]

As accused by the NDFB, security forces had encountered many NDFB cadres even in the unilateral ceasefire period. As a consequence, the outfit had threatened to pull out of the unilateral cease fire.[39] The Assam Government cleared that they would not declare a formal ceasefire with the NDFB unless the ground rules for the truce were formulated through discussions with representatives of the outfit.[40] The NDFB said that the outfit was not interested in holding talks with the Assam Government and that it would like to enter into direct negotiations with the Government of India.[41] Gradually, Ranjan Daimary also expressed his keenness for a peaceful solution to the conflict.[42] He sent an e-mail message to the local media in Guwahati and set a deadline of April 15, 2005 for the Union Government to respond to the outfit's unilateral cease fire.[43] However, due to the continuous opposition of the NDFB to the Union Government's decision to involve the Assam Government in the peace talks, there was a delay in the negotiations.[44]

In the hope for better results, the NDFB had extended the unilateral ceasefire declared by the militant outfit with the Centre for six months on April 16, 2005.[45] At the outset, the organisation set forth a condition that it would like the Union Government to appoint a 'special envoy' familiar with the history of the Bodo people for the peace talks. Finally, on May 25, 2005, the NDFB signed a tripartite agreement in New Delhi with the Government of India and the Assam Government.[46] The Suspension of Operation against the NDFB was valid up to May 31, 2007.[47] The NDFB representatives and senior Government officials met in Guwahati on June 17, 2005, to work out the modalities of the proposed peace talks.[48]

The Government of India, Government of Assam and the National Democratic Front of Bodoland had agreed to declare Suspension of Operations for one year with effect from 1 June 2005. The agreement was likely to be extended depending on the understanding between the Government and the NDFB. According to the terms of understanding, the NDFB should maintain peace and would not involve in any hostile or violent activity against the security forces or the civilians. The security forces would, in turn, not carry out any operations against the NDFB. The NDFB cadres would not carry arms or move in uniforms and would not give assistance to any other extremist groups.

A Joint Monitoring Group (JMG), comprising equal representatives from the Government of India, the Government of Assam and the NDFB would be setup to oversee the implementation of the agreement. Joint Secretary (NE) of the Ministry of Home Affairs would be the Chairman of the JMG. As per ceasefire norms, the NDFB would stay in designated camps, and the list of cadres and weapons in designated camps would be in the hands of the Assam police. There were many rounds of talks between the NDFB, State and Union Governments since they sat for the ceasefire agreement.[49]

The NDFB up to May 13, 2008, and after split, the NDFB-P faction sat in tripartite talks with the State and Union Governments. However, the outcome of those talks was only the extension of "Suspension of Operation" against the NDFB-P (as shown in Annexure II). The discussion and decision towards their demand are still pending. Both the NDFB and the Government accused each other of violating the ceasefire truce. On August 2, 2006, the NDFB threatened to pull out of the cease-fire with the Union Government, accusing the security forces of targeting its cadres without any provocation.[50] In reply, on August 10, 2006, the Union Government accused the NDFB of delaying the peace talks.

The NDFB, with whom the Government had a Suspension of Operation (SoO) agreement from July 1, 2005, witnessed a split in 2009. The NDFB 'Chief' Ranjan Daimary was expelled by the NDFB in January 2009 for his alleged involvement in the October 2008 serial blasts in Assam. On January 6, 2009, SoO was extended with more stringent conditions, and sustained operations were being carried out against the NDFB-R.[51] P.C. Haldar was appointed as Government of India representative for peace talks with the NDFB-P faction. On December 30, 2010, a faction of the NDFB, led by Ranjan Daimary, announced the unilateral cessation of hostilities to create a congenial atmosphere for peace talks with the Government.[52] On June 25, 2011, the NDFB-R threatened to pull out of the unilateral suspension of operations if its cadres were further targeted by the security forces.

On June 30, 2011, the NDFB-R terminated the unilateral cease-fire and Ranjan Daimary said, "The government did not give any importance to our NDFB's six-month unilateral ceasefire. Several NDFB members were killed during the ceasefire period. We'll not extend our six-month ceasefire period."However, only after one month of the withdrawal of unilateral ceasefire call, on July 26, 2011, the NDFB-R declared unilateral indefinite ceasefire. The ceasefire agreement came into effect from August 1, 2011, to find a durable and sustainable political solution through political dialogue and discussion.[53] But beginning of formal talks with the NDFB-R depended on the release of the Chairman of the outfit, Ranjan Daimary, who alone was in a position to win over most of the rebels of the outfit and to persuade them to join the peace process. The Central Government's interlocutor PC Haldar had conducted several rounds of informal talk with Ranjan Daimary in jail to find way for formal talk with the outfit. It was unspecified as to when the talk would start. The Central Government had ruled out a general amnesty for the members of NDFB-R, who were charged with involvement in violence, including the serial blasts in the state on October 30, 2008. On June 25, 2013, the Central Government was all set to launch peace talks with Ranjan Daimary, and released him from jail on June 23, 2013,after a six-month interim bail was granted to facilitate his participation in the peace process.

On July 18, 2013, the Central Government interlocutor P.C. Haldar began formal talks with the NDFB-R in Guwahati, but he warned that the dialogue could not be an excuse to carry on unlawful activities like extortion. Tripartite meetings were held with the representatives of the NDFB-P on 12.09.2013 and 20.02.2014 to discuss on its demand. The meetings also reviewed the functioning of Suspension of Operation arrangement and observance of Agreed Ground Rules. SoO agreement with the NDFB-P was extended up to 30.09.14. After the meeting, both sides claimed that the talks had kicked off on " positive note", but Daimary said that political issues did not come up and discussions were limited steps to carry the dialogue forward.

On October 8, 2013, the NDFB-R submitted the list of its cadres to the Government to sign the formal cease-fire agreement. However, the security forces were not ready to accept the list of weapons submitted by the outfit. The NDFB-R had submitted a list of 410 cadres with their addresses and the process of verification of it continued. On 10.09.2013 and 23.10.2013, meetings of Joint Working Group with NDFB-R were held at Guwahati for finalisation of Agreed Ground Rules of SoO Agreement with NDFB-R.[54] On October 21, 2013, the Union Government had decided to set a condition for surrender of complete firearms for signing SoO agreements with the outfit. The first outfit that could be affected by the new condition would be the NDFB-R, which was expected to sign a tripartite agreement with the Centre and the State Government on October 23.

Finally on 29 November 2013, the Centre and the Assam Governments signed an agreement for Suspension of Operation with the NDFB-R at the headquarters of the Special Branch of State Police at Kahilipara, Guwahati, in the presence of Sambhu Singh, the Joint Secretary (Northeast) in the MHA. Assam Home Secretary G.D. Tripathi, Additional Director-General of Police (special branch) Pallab Bhattacharyya, ADGP-law and order, A.P. Raut and a six-member delegation of NDFB-R leaders, led by Daimary, were also present. As per SoO Agreement, the outfit would deposit all arms held by them with the Government.[55] The Centre on 22 December 2014 extended the Suspension of Operation agreement with NDFB-P for six months till 30 June,2015. This followed tripartite talks with the representatives of the NDFB-P held on 22 December, 2014.[56]

Surrenders of the NDFB Cadres

Responding to the Central Government's peace process, a number of NDFB cadres surrendered to the authorities. The NDFB had shown a willingness to give up violence and seek solutions to their problems peacefully within the framework of the Constitution.

In 2004, a maximum of 190 cadres surrendered. However in 2006 and 2007, no cadres surrendered (as shown in Figure 5.4). On January 31, 2004, 91 cadres of the NDFB surrendered at Tamulpur in the Nalbari district. On May 10, 2004, 10 NDFB cadres led by 'Company Commander' of the outfit's 'Eastern Command', Gabba Basumatary, surrendered before the Army's 77 Mountain Brigade at Charduar in Sonitpur district along with a large number of arms and ammunition. In 2004, there was a wave of mass surrender in the NDFB.

The reasons for the maximum surrender in 2004 were because of "Operation All Clear" launched by Bhutan at the end of 2003 and also due to the all out counter-insurgency operation against the outfit. Another reason for the surrender was that due to lack of safe hideout places, many cadres preferred to lay down their arms.

Union Government Responses on Bodoland Demand

On July 28, 2009, *The Assam Tribune,* quoting the Union Government sources, reported that there had been no immediate plan to start a political dialogue with the NDFB, as its rival faction was on the run. Union Home Secretary, G. K. Pillai, during a workshop on 'Governance and Security: India's North-east and Bangladesh' at Jamia Milia Islamia in New Delhi said that the Union Government was keeping a close watch on the situation in the state. On July 30, 2009, the Union Government ruled out any possibility of separate

Fig. 5.3 Year-wise distribution of the NDFB's Cadres Surrendered (1998-2015)

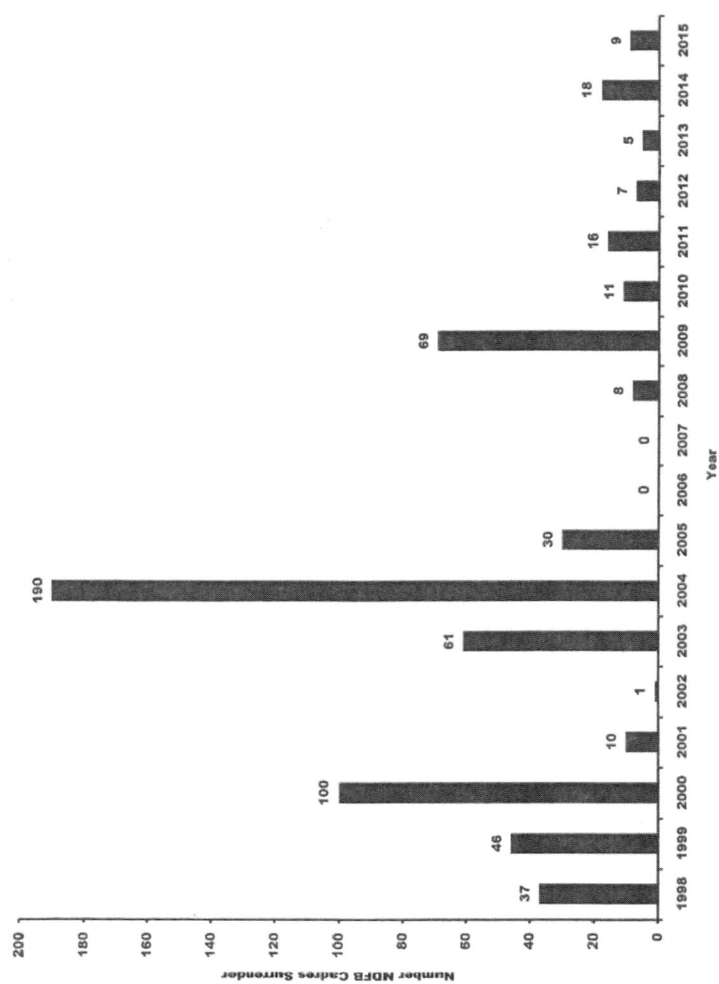

Source: South Asian Terrorism Portal (SATP)[57]

Bodo State. The Union Government made its stand clear that it hardly had anything more to concede after granting the status of the Autonomous Council under the Sixth Schedule of the Constitution to the Bodos. G K. Pillai also said that there was no question of carving out another state from Assam. "Statehood is ruled out," he said. Pillai said barring some financial powers to the council "here and there", there was not much left to concede. He added that the NDFB did not oblige when it was asked to join the negotiation while the Government was in talks with the BLT. "The request was conveyed to Ranjan Daimary. We had told them they would lose an opportunity if they did not join in, but they did not listen," he said, further adding if the NDFB thought it would get something more it was wrong.

On September 23, 2009, a tripartite peace talk among the Union and Assam Governments and NDFB was held in New Delhi.[58] Meanwhile, on November 4, 2009, Government had appointed Shri P.C. Haldar as Representative to negotiate with the NDFB. On December 1, 2009, peace talks with militant groups like Black Widow (BW), United People's Democratic Solidarity (UPDS) and the pro-talk faction of the NDFB were likely to be expedited as the Union Government's interlocutor for the peace talks, P.C.Haldar, had started the process and the Union Government was also reportedly keen on the early solution of the problems.[59] On December 16, 2009, P.C. Haldar held a meeting with the pro-talks faction of the NDFB in New Delhi. The Joint Secretary (Northeast) of the Union Ministry of Home Affairs (MHA), Naveen Verma, and other senior officials attended the meeting. The six-member NDFB delegation, led by its General Secretary, Govinda Basumatary, demanded a separate state. The deadlock in negotiations between the National Democratic Front of Bodoland-Progressive and the Centre continued with Delhi insisting on a resolution by the Assam Assembly for creating "Bodoland". There is also uncertainty over the ten other demands the NDFB-P had submitted to the Centre. . The Centre wrote to NDFB leaders, inviting them to the capital for "finalisation of the memorandum of settlement" which raised hopes of a breakthrough.

However, a three-hour marathon meeting between an eight-member delegation of the outfit and senior officials of the home ministry failed to finalise things on December 15, 2009. A few leaders of the outfit held another round of consultations at the ministry of home affairs on December 16, 2009. Talking to media person, an NDFB leader said, "Nothing has been achieved. The home ministry told us that Assam has stated that no resolution has been adopted by the state Assembly to create a separate state. The Centre says unless a resolution is passed by the Assembly, 'we cannot help'."

It may be noted that P.C. Haldar, attended the meeting which showed that the NDFB-P had dropped their insistent refusal to talk to him.[60] Sources in the home ministry said the premises of many of the demands were tenuous. The Centre is, however, examining the demand involving Chapter 10 of the Assam Land Revenue Regulation of 1886 in which 48 tribal belts and blocks were enlisted. The NDFB wants the implementation of the regulation so that alleged illegal migrants occupying tribal land can be evicted. The NDFB demand that four parliamentary constituencies – Guwahati, Lakhimpur, Tezpur and Udalguri – be declared reserved for Scheduled Tribes may also not cut ice with the government. The home ministry's stand is that it has no role in this, as the Election Commission will examine the issue.

On February 1, 2010, the Union Home Minister P. Chidambaram said that the Centre would like to talk to the NDFB without its Chairman Ranjan Daimary.[61] Accordingly, tripartite talk held on December 4, 2011, among the Central Government, the State Government and NDFB-P remained inconclusive over the demand for the separate state of Bodoland.[62]

An Expert Committee has been set up vide Ministry of Home Affairs Order dated February 26, 2014, under the chairmanship of Shri G.K. Pillai, former Union Home Secretary, to study/examine the demand of Bodoland State. The Committee consulted all sections of the society on the viability of the creation of a separate State of Bodoland.[63] The NDFB-P and the Centre held another round of talks on December 22, 2014, to thrash out a settlement on their demands and decided to "meet more often" to chalk out a roadmap to a possible solution. The broad contours of a settlement were apparently being worked out and several issues regarding autonomy, economic package and political rights of the ethnic population were discussed at the parleys. A meeting was held among NDFB-P Chief Govinda Basumatary, senior Union Home Ministry officials and interlocutor P.C. Haldar. The Centre felt a final settlement could be worked out when the Ranjan Daimary faction of the NDFB is also on the board. At the meeting, the possibility of increasing the number of seats in the Bodoland Territorial Council, which governs the Bodoland Territorial Areas District (BTAD), was also discussed. Officials were tight-lipped on the issue of a separate "Bodoland", which is the principal demand of all Bodo underground outfits and social organisations. An economic package is also being worked out for the BTAD.[64]

Government Response on Roman Script

According to the Constitution of the NDFB, a major demand of the organisation is adoption of Roman script for Bode language. However, Roman script was not originally the demand of the NDFB; it subsequently supported the demand of the Bode Sahitya Sabha and other allied organisations. The Chairman of the NDFB had threatened to kill Bineswar Brahma, President of BSS, if he failed to accept Roman script for the Bodo language, in a meeting held in Shillong on May 30, 1999.[65] The BSS accepted Devanagari script in the Simbargaon (in Kokrajhar district) Bodo Sahitya Sabha conference held from February 25 to 28, 2000.[66] The NDFB opposed the move and shot dead Bineswar Brahma on August 19, 2000, and he was killed by the outfit on the suspicion that he had advocated the use of Devanagari script for the Bodo language. In 2004, the Bodo language received recognition under the provisions of the 8th Schedule to the Constitution India. The decision of the BSS was taken on the Roman script issue finalised by the Government of India. Thus, the demand of the NDFB on this issue remained unfulfilled.

State Government Responses on the NDFB

The state government had responded to the demands of the NDFB many times. The state government had repeatedly rejected the demand of sovereignty and was not ready to hold talks with the pre-condition laid down by the NDFB. The Assam Government stated many times that they were ready to talk with the NDFB only if the outfit dropped the demand for sovereignty. However, when the NDFB-P dropped their demand of sovereignty and started the statehood demand, the State Government rejected the offer and declared that there will be no further division of Assam.

On March 5, 2007, Assam Forest Minister Rockybul Hussain stated in the State Legislative Assembly that the formal talks with the NDFB had not started because of the failure of the outfit to submit its charter of demands. After long confabulation among the leaders of the NDFB in April 2008, the outfit submitted the charter of demands. However, on May 2, 2008, the Assam Government warned the Centre that if it accepted the NDFB charter of demands, including 'liberation' of Bodoland to start a dialogue with the outfit, it would strengthen ULFA's argument to sit for talks only if 'sovereignty' was discussed.[67] On March 28, 2010, the Assam Government stated that they would have to take the lead role in the early completion of talks with militant groups of the state. Sources said that the Union Government had a very limited role in the process of talks with the militant groups like pro-talk faction of the National Democratic Front of Bodoland-Progressive, United People's Democratic Solidarity (UPDS), Karbi Longri North Cachar Hills Liberation Front (KLNLF), Dima Halim Daogah (DHD) and Black Widow (BW). Sources added that in case of the militant groups of Assam, the Union Government had already ruled out the possibility of division of Assam and asked the militant groups to seek solution of the problems within the geographical boundaries of the state.[68]

There were contradiction in the stand taken by the Assam Government towards the NDFB and its demands. For example, on May 2, 2010, Assam Chief Minister said that the Government was ready for discussion with the NDFB minus the demand for sovereignty if the outfit wanted. Followed by the involvement in unlawful activities, on November 13, 2012, Chief Minister Tarun Gogoi said operations against the NDFB-R would be intensified.[69]

In the context of the above discussion, it is observed that on the one hand, the government tried to prevent violence by counter-insurgency operations and, on the other, it also invited the NDFB to join the peace process. The Union and State Governments intensified counter-insurgency operations against the NDFB to reduce the strength of the outfit. The NDFB, the Union and the State Governments sat periodically for the permanent solution of the Bodoland issue, but the outcome was not more than an extension of 'Suspension of Operation'. In this regard, Ranjan Daimary's statement on September 14, 2008, assumes significnace, "India does not want to talk and resolve the Indo-Bodo problem peacefully and democratically. India just wants to prolong the ceasefire and wants NDFB to die a natural death."[70]

Conclusion

Both the Union and the State Governments responded to the NDFB's demands in two different ways in the sense that the governments tried to prevent violence by counter-insurgency operations, on the one hand, and they also invited the NDFB to join the peace process, on the other. In response to the violent activities of the NDFB, on 23 November 23, 1992, the Union Home Ministry imposed ban on the NDFB under the provisions of the Unlawful Activities (Prevention) Act, 1967. The NDFB still figures in the list of the banned organisations. Interpol also issued notices on Daimary twice in 1997 and in 2010.

In 1994, Operation Kranti was launched in Barpeta district against the NDFB. Apart from operations in Assam, the Union Government also sought cooperation from neighbouring countries like Bhutan, Bangladesh and Myanmar. The Royal Bhutan Government agreed and launched the Operation All Clear, gunned down 40 NDFB cadres including few top leaders of the outfit, and destroyed 12 camps of the NDFB. Though Bangladesh initially denied the existence of Indian extremists in their soil, later they agreed to cooperate with the Government of India and the arrest of NDFB President Daimary from Bangladesh and his handover to the BSF in India in India was considered to be a major diplomatic victory for the Indian Government. However, Myanmar Government refused to take action against Indian extremists and even denied the existence of any such outfits in their soil.

Moreover, there were a large number of encounters between the NDFB and the security forces since 1992 with a maximum of 137 encounters in 2003. However, the number of encounters was less in 2007 and 2008 because of the Suspension of Operation agreement that the NDFB signed with Government. As part of counter-insurgency operations, many NDFB leaders were arrested from different whereabouts.

It is evident that the core demand of the NDFB is not negotiable within the framework of the Constitution of India. In view of this, not much progress was achieved as far as the negotiations between the NDFB-R and the Union and State Governments are concerned. However, "Suspension of Operation" agreements were signed and renewed repeatedly from 25th May 2005 onwards. Although the pro-talk faction of the NDFB has dropped the demands for Sovereign Bodoland and has joined the peace process, the Government of India seems to acknowledge the fact that no lasting solution to the Bodo problem is possible without the involvement of Ranjan Daimary and his faction of the NDFB in the process.

Responding to Union Government's peace process, a large number of the NDFB cadres also surrendered before the authorities. In 2004, a maximum of 190 cadres surrendered. The reasons behind the maximum surrenders in 2004 was "Operation all Clear" launched against the outfit. It is apparent that due to lack of safe hideouts during the time of counter-insurgency operation, many cadres preferred to lay down arms.

An Expert Committee has been set up vide Ministry of Home Affairs order dated February 26, 2013 under the Chairmanship of Shri G.K. Pillai, former Union Home Secretary to study/examine the demand of Bodoland State. But, there are no tangible solutions even after many rounds of talks between the NDFB and the Government. Besides, the demand for Roman Script also remained unfulfilled because the decision of the BSS in favour of Devanagari script was finalised by Government of India. In 2004 Bodo language received recognition under the provisions of 8th Schedule in the Constitution of India with Devanagari script.

The Government of Assam had repeatedly rejected the demand for sovereignty and was not ready to hold talks with the pre-condition laid by the NDFB. The Assam Government was ready to talk with the NDFB only if the outfit dropped the demand for sovereignty. However, when the NDFB-P dropped its demand for sovereignty and raised the statehood demand, the State Government rejected the offer and declared that there will be no further division of Assam.

It may be noted that the BTC has no power on Home and Finance subjects. So, there is no direct response of the BTC to the NDFB's demands. It appears that the Bodoland Territorial Council (BTC) has been playing the role of a facilitator in the sense that the BTC authorities have taken some initiative to negotiate a settlement among the Union, State Governments and the NDFB. The ruling political party of BTC, Bodoland People's Front (BPF) has also tried to unite the Bodos and formed the Bodo National Council (BNC) in response to the fratricidal killings that resulted from intra-group clashes.

In the context of the above discussion, the role of the Indian State assumes a lot of significance. It has been observed that the mainstream ruling elite has taken an intolerant stance towards the legitimate aspirations for autonomy voiced by smaller nationalities like the Bodos.[71] Refusal to recognize small communities as nationalities has bred discontent among these communities inciting some aggressive sections to propagate anti-Indian ideas. Recent trends in northeast India show that extremist factions of aggrieved communities like Bodos have become thoroughly disenchanted with the existing arrangements and are seeking to explore new political frontiers beyond India.[72]

The dynamics of Bodo identity assertion reveal that the Bodo leadership was initially clamouring for territorial autonomy in the form of a union territory for all plains tribes of Assam. This was followed by the demand for a separate state of Bodoland. But both the demands met with a negative response from the Indian State. The autonomy accords which were signed in 1993 and 2003 were desperate attempts at conflict management. By then, a section of the Bodo youths had already embarked on a trajectory of extremist politics since prospects of democratic and constitutional options seemed bleak as far as fulfillment of their goals for self-determination was concerned. It is observed that unless this trend is reversed, there may be an acute crisis in the Indian political community. It may, therefore, be argued that in order to dilute the appeal of extremist politics resorted to by organisations like the NDFB, the Indian State needs to appreciate nationality aspirations within a framework of mutual understanding and trust and respect for the rights and interests of other groups inhabiting the "perceived" homeland of these nationalities.

References

1 Memorandum of Settlement, "Bodoland Territorial Council", 10th February, 2003.

2 'Hagrama offer to mediate'. (2010, May 19). *The Telegraph.*

3 Sudhir. op.cit.

4 The Unlawful Activities (Prevention) Act, 1967. Ministry of Home Affairs, Government of India. p.12. Retrieved November 9, 2015, from www.mha.in.

5 Ministry of Home Affairs, Government of India, *op. cit.*

6 South Asian Terrorism Portal, *op.cit.*

7 'Interpol issues Daimary alert- Red corner notice fallout of Haldar-NDFB talks - Fratricidal clashes feared'. (2010, January 3). *The Telegraph.*

8 'Interpol notice against NDFB leader'. (2011, January 14).*The Assam Tribune.*

9 Bhutan's Foreign Ministry in its statement on December 15, 2003 mentioned the 81st National Assembly resolution in this regard. The Militant Problem. (December 15, 2003). *The Kuensel.* Retrieved November 28, 2009, from http://www.kuenselonline.com/article.php?sid=3552.

10 'Security Troops Continue Operations to Flush Indian Militants Out of Bhutan'. (2003, December 20).*The Kuensel.* Retrieved November 28, 2009, from http://kuenselonline.com.

11 '124 killed in Bhutan operation'. *The Tribune.* Retrieve September 21, 2010, from http://www.tribuneindia.com.

12 'Myanmar Operation in sight'.(2004, January 3).*The Telegraph.*

13 Brahma Choudhury, P. (2006, February 8). 'NDFB adopts new talks line-Outfit seeks facts on missing leaders before dialogue'. *The Telegraph.*

14 'BDR assured action against NE insurgents: BSF'. (2010, March 12).*The Assam Tribune.*

15 Terrorism Update. *South Asian Terrorism Portal.* Retrieved July 21, 2014, from http://www.satp.org

16 'Cops target NDFB headhunters'. (2009, December 26) *The Telegraph.*

17 This Bar Diagram is drawn on the basis of the "Incident Involving the NDFB" (compiled from news report and are provisional) available in the *South Asian Terrorism Portal* by quantifying those incidents in which the NDFB were cadres killed in encounters, retrieved from http://www.satp.org on 13/11/2013 at 18.53PM.

18 'Pro-Talks rebel held'. (2009,May 27). *The Telegraph.*

19 'Top Boro leader held'.(2003, January 2). *The Hindu.*

20 'Assam moves court for Boro custody'. (2003, January 3). *The Telegraph.*

21 'Bodo rebel leaders held in Calcutta hotel'. (2003, May 1). *The Telegraph.*

22 Dialogue link in NDFB extortion'.(2003, May 16). *The Telegraph.*

23 'Arrested.' (2008, November 20). *The Telegraph.*

24 'Pro-talks rebel held'.(2009, May 27). *The Telegraph.*

25 'Rebels held'. (2009, September 15). *The Telegraph.*

26 'Remanded'.(2009, November 10). *The Telegraph.*

27 'Daimary arrest triggers hope of parleys'. (2010, May 3). *The Telegraph.*

28 'NDFB hires tech-savvy youths - Outfit's publicity cell busted in Guwahati, three Bodo rebels held in Baksa'. (2010, July 31). *The Telegraph.*

29 This Bar Diagram is drawn on the basis of the "Incident Involving the NDFB" (compiled from news report and are provisional) available in the *South Asian Terrorism Portal* by quantifying those incidents in which the NDFB were arrested. Retrieve January 12, 2016, from http://www.satp.org

30 'Serial blasts key accused arrested'.(2010, December 12). *The Assam Tribune.*

31 'Rebel reveals bomb plan - NDFB training Meghalaya militants on explosives'.(2011, February 16). *The Telegraph.*

32 'Rebels arrested'.(2012, March 13). *The Telegraph.*

33 This was stated by the Minister of State for Home Affairs, Shri Kiren Rijiju in a written reply to Shri Santiuse Kujur in the Rajya Sabha on 4th March, 2015. Retrieved March 3, 2015, from http://pib.nic.in

34 A Statement of Government of Assam on 7th November, 2004, detailed available in *South Asian Terrorism Portal*, "Incident Involving National Democratic Front of Bodoland". Retrieved January 14, 2016, from, http://www.satp.org

35 'NDFB formally appeals for ceasefire'.(2004, October 15). *The Assam Tribune.*

36 'No decision yet on NDFB truce offer: Gogoi'. (2004, October 13). *The Assam Tribune.*

37 'Truce thrust to early talks - Gogoi to bring NDFB to table soon'.(2004, October 20). *The Telegraph.*

38 'Dispur sets pace for Bodo peace parleys'. (2004, October 26). *The Telegraph.*

39 'Rebel death triggers NDFB ire'.(2004, November 7). *The Telegraph.*

40 A Statement of Government of Assam on 7th November, 2004, detailed available in *South Asian Terrorism Portal*, "Incident Involving National Democratic". Retrieved January 21, 2012, from http://www.satp.org .

41 A press statement signed by its spokesman S. Sanjarang,On 13th November, 2004, detailed available *South Asian Terrorism Portal.* Retrieved January 21, 2012, from http://www.satp.org .

42 The NDFB "President" Ranjan Daimary, in an interview with the Press Trust of India On 26th November, 2004. Retrieved January 21, 2012, from http://www.satp.org .

43 A email sent by the NDFB 'President' to media on 27th February, 2005, detailed available in *South Asian Terrorism Portal.* Retrieved January 21, 2012, from http://www.satp.org .

44 Press statements of the NDFB's spokesman S. Sanjarang,On 13th November, 2004 and again on 23rd May, 2005, detailed available in *South Asian Terrorism Portal.* Retrieved January 21, 2012, from http://www.satp.org .

45 'NDFB extends ceasefire'.(2005, April 17). *The Hindu.*

46 'Dispur rules out talks rush'.(2005, May 27). *The Telegraph.*

47 *Annual Report*, (2006-07). Ministry of Home Affairs, Departments of Internal Security, States, Home, Jammu & Kashmir Affairs and Border Management. p.17.

48 'NDFB peace process gains momentum'. (2005, June 20). *The Assam Tribune.*

49 *Public Information Bureau*(2005,May 25). Ministry of Home Affairs, Government of India. Retrieved February 26, 2015, from http://pib.nic.in/newsite/erelease.aspx?relid=9475

50 'Pull-out threat after killings-NDFB alleges violation of truce rules'. (2006, August 3). *The Telegraph.*

51 *Annual Report (2008-09*). Ministry of Home Affairs, Government of India. p.11.

52 *Annual Report (2010-11*). Ministry of Home Affairs, Government of India. pp.11-12.

53 'NDFB calls ceasefire'. (2011, July 27). *The Telegraph.*

54 *Annual Report*(2013-14). Ministry of Home Affairs, Government of India. pp.16-17.

55 'Daimary signs truce with Delhi, Dispur'. (2013, November 30). *The Telegraph.*

56 Press Information Bureau (2014, December 26).Centre Extends SoO Pact with NDFB-P for Further Six Months. Ministry Of Home Affairs, Government of India. Retrieved March 9, 2015, from http://pib.nic.in

57 This Bar Diagram is drawn on the basis of the "Incident Involving the NDFB" (compiled from news report and are provisional) available in the *South Asian Terrorism Portal* by quantifying those incidents in which the NDFB were surrendered , retrieved March 26, 2016, from http://www.satp.org

58 'Truce call-off hint on NDFB agenda'.(2009, September 23). *The Telegraph.*

59 'Delhi wants Nunisa to whittle demands'.(2009, December 2). *The Telegraph.*

60 'NDFB wants a Bodo state'.(2009, December 17). *The Telegraph.*

61 'Talks nod for Ulfa, NDFB'.(2010, February 2). *The Telegraph.*

62 'Govt begins talks with NDFB-P, DHD-N'.(2011, December 5). *The Assam Tribune.*

63 Shri Kiren Rijiju MoS (Home) gave this information in Rajya Sabha on July 23, 2014 in a written reply to a question by Shri Biswajit Daimary. Retrieved from http://pib.nic.in/ on 09/03/2015 at 12:30.

64 Dholabhai,N. (2014, December 23). 'NDFB accord on the horizon- Daimary group, Centre hold talks, to meet more often'. *The Telegraph.*

65 Narzary, R. (2013, December). Why 'Script' Movement of the Bodos: Revisiting Debates in Political Sociology. *Journal of Tribal Intellectual Collective India (*pp. 66-77)Daltri Journals, ISSN 2321 5437, Vol.1 Issue 2 No.5, p.74. Retrieved October 23, 2016, from http://www.ticijournals.org/JTICI/I2A5.php.

66 Record at a glance of the Previous Sessions, Bodo Sahitya Sabha. *The Bodos (pp.498-499)*39th Issue, 2014.The Mouthpiece,Bodo Sahitya Sabha.

67 'Delhi warned on Bodo Talks'. (2008, May 3).*The Telegraph.*

68 Choudhury,R. D. (2010, March 29). 'Peace talks moving at slow pace'.*The Assam Tribune.*

69 'Tea garden owner killed in Sootea'. (2012, November 14). *The Assam Tribune.*

70 'NDFB iterates 'war' option'.(2008, October 4). *The Telegraph.*

71 Baruah,A. K. (1991). *Social Tension in Assam: Middle Class Politics*, Guwahati: Purbanchal Prakash. pp.2-8.

72 Sengupta, S. (2014, August). Extremist Politics as an Instrument of Ethnic Assertions among the Bodos of Northeast India. *Journalism and Mass Communication.* (pp.527-534). Vol.4, No.8.

*****

Annexure-I

Memorandum of Settlement on Bodoland Territorial Council (BTC)

New Delhi, 10 February 2003

1. The Government of India and the Government of Assam have been making concerted efforts to fulfill the aspirations of the Bodo people relating to their cultural identity, language, education and economic development. Towards this end, a series of talks were held between Government of India, Government of Assam and Bodo Liberation Tigers (BLT) since March, 2000. As a result, it is agreed to create a self-governing body for the Bodo Areas in the State of Assam as follows:

2. Objectives

The objectives of the agreement are: to create an Autonomous self governing body to be known as Bodoland Territorial Council (BTC) within the State of Assam and to provide constitutional protection under Sixth Schedule to the said Autonomous Body; to fulfill economic, educational and linguistic aspirations and the preservation of land-rights, socio-cultural and ethnic identity of the Bodos; and speed up the infrastructure development in BTC area.

3. Area

3.1 The area of proposed BTC shall comprise all the 3082 villages and areas to be so notified by the State Government. The above mentioned villages and areas shall be divided into 4 contiguous districts after reorganisation of the existing districts of Assam within a period of 6 months of the signing of the agreement on the lines of the proposal given by BLT subject to clearance of the Delimitation Commission.

3.2 A committee comprising one representative each from Governments of India & Assam and BLT will decide by consensus on the inclusion of additional villages and areas in the BTC from out of 95 villages and areas on the basis of the criteria of tribal population being not less than 50%, contiguity or any other agreed relevant criteria within a period of three months of signing of this MoS.

4. Status of Bodoland Territorial Council

The provision of the Sixth schedule and other relevant Articles of the Constitution of India will apply to BTC, mutatis mutandis in terms of this agreement. The safeguards/modifications for the non-tribals in BTC area, inter-alia, will include the following:

4.1. Provision of para 1(2) of Sixth Schedule regarding Autonomous Regions will not be applicable to BTC.

4.2. A provision will be made in para 2(1) of the Sixth Schedule for increasing the number of members for BTC up to 46 out of which 30 will be reserved for Scheduled Tribes, 5 for non-tribal communities, 5 open for all communities and 6 to be nominated by Governor of Assam from the unrepresented communities for BTC area of which atleast two should be women. Nominated members will have the same rights and privileges as other members, including voting rights. Election from the 40 constituencies of BTC shall be on the basis of adult franchise. The term of the elected members of BTC shall be for 5 years.

4.3. Safeguards for the settlement rights, transfer and inheritance of property etc. of non-tribals will be suitably incorporated in para 3 of the Sixth Schedule. Any such law as may be made by the BTC in this regard will not, in particular:

a) Extinguish the rights and privileges enjoyed by an citizen of India in respect of their land at the commencement of BTC, and

b) Bar any citizen from acquiring land either by way of inheritance, allotment, settlement or by way of transfer if such citizens were eligible for such bonafide acquisition of land within the BTC area.

4.4. Provision will be added in para 6 of Sixth Schedule that in BTC area, language and medium of instruction in educational institutions will not be changed without approval of the State Government.

4.5. Provision of para 8 of Sixth Schedule regarding power to assess and collect land revenue and impose taxes shall be applicable to BTC.

4.6. Para 10 of the Sixth Schedule will not be applicable to BTC area.

4.7. Provision of Article 332(6) of the Constitution will be so modified that the existing status of representation of BTC area in the State Assembly is kept intact. After the creation of BTC, the Parliamentary & Assembly Constituencies shall be delimited by the Delimitation Commission in accordance with the provisions of the Constitution.

4.8. In the event, **Panchayati Raj** system ceases to be in force in the council area, the powers of the Panchayati Raj Institutions in such matters shall be vested with the Council.

The Amendments to the Sixth Schedule shall include provisions in such a manner that non-tribals are not disadvantaged in relation to the rights enjoyed by them at the commencement of BTC and their rights and privileges including land rights are fully protected.

5. Power and Functions

5.1. The Council shall have legislative powers in respect to subjects transferred to it as enumerated below. All laws made under this paragraph shall be submitted forthwith to the Governor and until assented to by him, shall have no effect. The BTC shall have executive, administrative and financial powers in respect of subjects transferred to it.

Subjects to be entrusted to BTC by Assam Government

1. Small, Cottage and Rural Industry; 2. Animal Husbandry & Veterinary; 3. Forest; 4. Agriculture; 5. PWD; 6. Sericulture; 7. Education (Primary Education, Higher Secondary Including vocational training, Adult

Education, College Education (General); 8. Cultural Affairs; 9. Soil Conservation; 10. Co-operation; 11. Fisheries; 12. Panchayat and Rural Development; 13. Handloom and Textile; 14. Health & Family Welfare; 15. Public Health Engineering; 16. Irrigation; 17. Social Welfare; 18. Flood Control; 19. Sports & Youth Welfare; 20. Weights and Measures; 21. Library Services; 22. Museum & Archaeology; 23. Urban Development – Town and Country Planning; 24. Tribal Research Institute; 25. Land & Revenue; 26. Publicity/Public Relations; 27. Printing & Stationery; 28. Tourism; 29. Transport; 30. Planning and Development; 31. Municipal Corporation, Improvement Trust, District Boards and other local authorities; 32. Welfare of Plan Tribes and Backward Classes; 33. Markets and fairs; 34. Lotteries, Theatres, Dramatic performance and cinema; 35. Statistics; 36. Food and Civil supply; 37. Intoxicating liquors, opium and derivatives etc.; 38. Labour and employment; 39. Relief and Rehabilitation; 40. Registration of Births and Deaths.

5.2. There shall be an Executive Council comprising of not more than 12 Executive Members, one of whom shall be the Chief and another one the Deputy Chief of the said Executive Council. There shall be adequate representation for the non-tribal members in the Executive Council. The Chief and the Deputy Chief of the Council shall have the status equivalent to the Cabinet Minister and the other Executive Members equivalent to the Minister of the State of Assam for protocol purposes in BTC area.

5.3. The BTC shall have the full control over the officers and staff connected with the delegated subjects working in the BTC area and shall be competent to transfer officers and staff within the BTC area. ACRs of these officers shall also be written by the appropriated BTC authority.

5.4. BTC shall also be competent to make appointments for all posts under its control in accordance with the rules of appointment followed by the Government of Assam. However, the posts, where recruitment is made on the recommendation of APSC, shall not be covered under this provision. The Council may constitute a Selection Board for appointments to be made by it and may also make rules, with the approval of the Governor of Assam to regulate appointments and to ensure adequate representation for all communities living in the Council area.

5.5. No posts shall be created by BTC without concurrence of the Government of Assam and it shall also abide by the decision of the Government of Assam in respect of abolition of/temporarily keeping vacant any post.

5.6. Development functions and bodies within the competence of BTC shall be transferred to BTC. In respect of DRDA, concurrence of Government of India will be obtained.

5.7. The offices of the Dy. Commissioner and Superintendent of Police will be outside the superintendence and control of BTC.

5.8. The State Government would provide an amount, to be decided every year on population ratio basis, as grants-in-aid in two equal instalments to the BTC for executing development works. The proportionate share for the BTC shall be calculated on the basis of the plan funds available after setting aside the funds required for earmarked sectors and the salary. This amount may be reduced proportionately if the state plan allocation is reduced or there is plan cut due to resource problem. In addition, the Council will be paid a suitable amount of plan funds and non-plan funds to cover the office expenses and the salaries of the staff working under their control. The BTC shall disburse the salaries of the staff under their control and would ensure strict economy in the matter.

5.9. BTC authority shall prepare a plan with the amounts likely to be available for development works, both under State share and Central share, covering any or all the activities of the departments under their control. The Council shall have full discretion in selecting the activities and choosing the amount for the investment under the same in any year covering all groups of people in a fair and equitable manner. This plan will be a sub set of the State plan and would be treated as its integral part. Once the plan of the State, including BTC plan, gets the approval of the Planning Commission the BTC authority will start execution of their plan in the BTC area. Modifications, if any, made by the Planning Commission in the BTC proposal, shall be binding on the BTC authority. The State Government shall not divert the funds allocated to the BTC to other heads and also ensure its timely release. BTC may have Planning Department to prepare the plans for BTC area to be submitted to Planning Commission through the Government of Assam.

5.10. The executive functions of the BTC shall be exercised through its Principal Secretary who shall be an officer of the rank not below of Commissioner/Secretary to Government of Assam. The sanctioning powers of the Government of Assam shall be vested with the Principal Secretary of BTC and sanctioning powers of head(s) of the Department(s) including for technical sanction shall be conferred on the senor most officer of that Department preferably not below the rank of Additional Director, who may be designated as Director of BTC for that department. The Principal Secretary and other officers shall exercise their powers under the overall guidance and supervision of BTC.

6. Law and Order

To strengthen the Police Administration, Government of Assam shall appoint an IGP for 4 districts of BTC and the jurisdiction of the DIG Kokrajhar shall also be modified to cover these 4 districts.

7. Revision of list of ST

Consequent to the inclusion of BTC area into the Sixth Schedule, the list of ST for the State of Assam shall be so modified so as to ensure that the tribal status of Bodos and other tribals living outside the BTC are does not get affected adversely.

8. Grant of ST status of Bodo Kacharis of Karbi Anglong and NC Hills districts

The Government of India agrees to consider sympathetically the inclusion of the Bodo Kacharis living in Karbi Anglong and NC Hills Autonomous Council area in the ST (Hill) List of State of Assam.

9. Development of Bodo Language

9.1. The Government of India agrees to consider favourably the inclusion of Bodo Language in Devanagri Script in the Eighth Schedule of the Constitution.

9.2. Bodo language shall be the official language of BTC subject to the condition that Assamese and English shall also continue to be used for official purpose.

10. Additional Development Package for BTC

10.1. The State Government, within the limitation of financial and other constraints, may offer or allow the Council to offer, possible and sustainable additional incentives for attracting private investment in the Council area and would also support projects for external funding.

10.2. In order to accelerate the development of the region and to meet the aspirations of the people, the Government of India will provide financial assistance of Rs 100 crores per annum for 5 years for projects to develop the socio-economic infrastructure in BTC areas over and above the normal plan assistance to the State of Assam. The size of the Corpus will be reviewed after a period of 5 years. Suitable mechanism will be built in the system to ensure that the funds are transferred to BTC in time and at regular intervals. An illustrative list of projects which may be considered to be taken up in BTC given below:

List of projects:

1. To establish a centre for development and research of Bodo language; 2. Upgradation of existing educational infrastructure by way of renovation/addition of buildings, providing modern facilities for teaching such as computers, science laboratories etc. from primary level to college level in BTC area; 3. A cultural complex to be established at Kokrajhar to promote and develop Bodo tradition and cultural heritage; 4. To establish a super-speciality hospital with all modern facilities at Kokrajhar Government Hospitals shall be established in all district, sub-divisional and block headquarter; 5. To establish sports complexes in all the district headquarters; 6. Food processing plants and clod storage facilities at Kokrajhar, Kajolgaon, Udalguri and Tamulpur; 7. Construction of a bridge over river Aai to connect Koilamoila, Amguri etc. with the rest of the district; 8. To build a Bodoland Bhawan in Delhi; 9. To set up integrated agro-processing park and textile-cum-apparel park; 10. Revitalisation of Kokilabari Agricultural Farm; 11. To develop adequate infrastructure to promote Manas sanctuary as an international

tourist spot; 12. To complete Champa, Suklai and Dhansiri irrigation projects; 13. To construct a highway on the Indo-Bhutan border from Jamduar to Bhairabkunda to connect remote places located adjacent to the border; 14. To set up model dairy, fishery, horticulture and poultry farms/training centres at different places in all the 4 districts to encourage youth for self-employment; 15. To enhance the existing facilities in veterinary hospitals in BTC area.

10.3. Government of India will provide necessary one time financial assistance required for development of administrative infrastructure in the newly created district headquarters, sub-divisional headquarters and book headquarters, besides the BTC Secretariat Complex at Kokrajhar

11. Centrally funded University

11.1. A centrally funded Central Institute of Technology (CIT) will be set up to impact education in various technological/vocational disciplines such as Information Technology, Bio-Technology, Food Processing, Rural Industries, Business Management, etc.

11.2. The CIT will be subsequently upgraded to a Centrally funded State University with technical and non-technical disciplines to be run by the BTC.

12. Relief & Rehabilitation

12.1. The BLT would join the national mainstream and shun the path of violence in the interest of peace and development. After the formation of the interim council of BTC, BLT will dissolve itself as an organisation and surrender with arms within a week of swearing-in of the interim council. The State Government would provide full support to relief and rehabilitation of the members of BLT who would surrender with arms in this process in accordance with the existing policy of the State. Financial support in such cases, however shall be limited to be provisions of the scheme prepared and funded by the Government of India. Withdrawal of cases against such persons and those related to overground Bodo movement since 1987 shall be considered according to the existing policy of the State of Assam.

12.2. The Government of India will initiate steps for review of action against the Bodo employees of Government of India and subordinate officers as well as in respect of Central Government Undertakings. Similar action would be taken by the Government of Assam.

12.3. Bodo youth will be considered for recruitment in Police, Army and Paramilitary forces to increase their representation in these forces.

13. Special Rehabilitation Programme for the people affected by ethnic disturbances

The Special Rehabilitation Programme (SRP) for the people affected by ethnic disturbances in Assam, who are at present living at relief camps in Kokrajhar, Bongaigaon etc. shall be completed by the Government of Assam with active support of BTC. Necessary funds for their rehabilitation shall be provided by the Government of India and lands which are free from all encumbrances required for such rehabilitation shall be made available by the BTC.

14. Interim Council

Immediately after signing of the agreement, Interim Executive Council for BTC shall be formed by Governor of Assam from amongst the leaders of the present Bodo movement, including the signatories to this settlement, and shall include adequate representation to the non-tribal communities in BTC area. The Interim Council shall not continue for a period beyond 6 months during which period election to the Council shall be held. Government of Assam shall dissolve the Bodoland Autonomous Council (BAC) and repeal the BAC Act.

15. Government of Assam will consider inclusion of all tribals including Bodos in RHAC/MAC/LAC in consultation with leaders of these Councils.

16. The Implementation of the provision of the Memorandum of Settlement shall be periodically reviewed by a Committee comprising representatives of Government of India, Government of Assam and BTC.

Signed on 10th February, 2003 at New Delhi in the presence of Shri L.K. Advani, Hon'ble Deputy Prime Minister of India and Shri Tarum Gogoi, Chief Minister of Assam.

(Hagrama Basumatary)	(P K Dutta)	(R C A Jain)
Chairman	Chief Secretary	Secretary (BM)
Bodo Liberation Tigers	Govt. of Assam	Ministry of Home Affairs
		Government of India

Annexure Page

1. Memorandum of Settlement - 1 – 9
2. List of Villages I 10 – 51
3. List of Additional villages II 52 - 55 demanded by the BLT.
4. List of Subjects to be entrusted III 56 – 57
5. Illustrative list of Projects IV

Source: The South Asia Terrorism Portal (Website)

Annexure- II

Chronological development of Peace Talks with the NDFB

Sl. No	Date/ Month/Year of Signature	Outcome	Period	With effect from	Valid Up to
1	25/05/2005	Suspension of operations	1 Year	01.05.2005	31.05.2006
2	27/05/2006	Suspension of operations	6 Months	31.05.2006	31.11.2006
3	01/12/2006	Suspension of operations	6 Months	01.1 006	31.05.2007
4	25/05/2007	Suspension of operations	6 Months	01.06.2007	30.11.2007
5	30/11/2007	Suspension of operations	6 Months	01.12.2007	31.05.2008
6	31/05/2008	Suspension of operations	3 months	01.06.2008	31.08.2008
7	30/09/2008	Suspension of operations	3 months	30.09.2008	31.12.2008
8	06/01/2009	Suspension of operations	6 months	01.01.2009	30.06.2009
9	31/12/2009	SoO with the NDFB-P	6 months	01.01.2010	30.06.2010
10	01/07/2010	SoO with the NDFB-P	6 months	01.07.2010	31.12.2010

11	31/12/2010	SoO with the NDFB-P	6 months	01.01.2011	30.06.2011
12	29/06/2011	SoO with the NDFB-P	6 months	01.07.2011	31.12.2011
13	18/01/2012	SoO with the NDFB-P	6 months	01.01.2012	30.06.2012
14	20/07/2012	SoO with the NDFB-P	3 Months	01.07.2012	30.09.2012
15	10/10/2012	SoO with the NDFB-P	3 months	01.10.2012	31.12.2012
16	15/01/2013	SoO with the NDFB-P	6 Months	01.01.2013	30.06.2013
17	12/09/2013	SoO with the NDFB-P	3 months	01.09.2013	31.12.2013
18	19/11/2013	SoO with the NDFB-R	6 months	01.12.2013	31.05.2014
19	31/12/2013	SoO with the NDFB-P	3 months	01.01.2014	31.03.2014
20	26/12/2014	SoO with the NDFB-P	6 months	01.01.2015	30.06.2015

Annexure-III

Comparison of Literacy Trends: Bodo Inhabited and Other Districts of Assam

(in percentage)

District	1991			2001			2011		
	Male	Female	Total	Male	Female	Total	Male	Female	Total
*Baksa							78.55	62.23	70.53
*Barpeta	41.55	26.36	43.24	64.83	47.07	56.24	70.72	59.04	65.03
*Bongaigaon	46.43	30.28	49.06	67.67	50.44	59.33	75.48	65.18	70.44
*Chirang							71.35	57.87	64.71
*Darrang	40.71	25.84	42.00	63.91	46.40	55.44	68.36	60.40	64.55
*Kokrajhar	39.79	24.59	40.47	60.32	42.40	51.63	73.44	59.54	66.63
*Nalbari	54.68	35.83	55.99	76.56	57.26	67.23	85.58	73.85	79.89
Cachar	56.44	39.55	59.16	75.73	59.41	67.82	85.85	74.62	80.36
Dhemaji	51.08	31.55	53.84	74.41	53.51	64.48	75.66	62.13	69.07
*Dhubri	36.45	21.95	38.36	55.91	40.04	48.21	64.20	54.26	59.36
Dibrugarh	55.31	39.92	58.32	77.30	59.95	68.96	82.59	69.52	76.22

Goalpara	40.09	28.93	46.81	64.86	50.85	58.03	72.67	64.53	68.67
Golaghat	54.33	40.00	58.54	77.14	60.99	69.38	84.20	72.18	78.31
Hailakandi	51.78	32.47	53.07	68.24	50.46	59.64	81.61	68.54	75.26
Jorhat	61.66	47.25	65.51	83.62	68.49	76.33	88.38	78.22	83.42
*Kamrup	61.47	44.95	65.04	81.16	66.31	74.16	77.64	67.69	72.81
*Kamrup (M)							91.26	85.82	88.66
K. Anglong	44.15	26.76	45.57	67.22	47.30	57.70	82.12	64.62	73.52
Karimganj	51.79	35.87	54.71	74.69	57.28	66.24	85.70	73.49	79.72
Lakhimpur	54.86	38.82	58.96	77.06	59.59	68.56	84.66	71.91	78.39
Morigaon	38.05	30.40	47.99	65.15	51.51	58.53	73.66	64.99	69.37
Nagaon	49.84	36.48	54.74	68.27	54.74	61.73	78.19	69.21	73.78
NC Hills	54.39	37.46	57.76	75.67	58.39	67.62	85.34	72.15	78.99
Sibsagar	60.19	46.30	64.46	81.53	66.81	74.47	86.75	75.69	81.36
*Sonitpur	46.16	30.90	48.14	67.54	49.73	59.00	76.98	62.53	69.96
Tinsukia	48.26	31.90	50.28	70.15	50.78	60.95	77.89	63.54	70.92
*Udalguri							73.79	59.17	66.60
State	**49.98**	**34.29**	**52.89**	**71.28**	**54.61**	**63.25**	**78.81**	**67.27**	**73.18**

Source: Census of India 1991, 2001 & 2011. * Note: Due to the creation of 4 new districts the rates for 2011 have been affected in 12 districts.

Annexure IV

Population Characteristics of the Bodos in the North Bank of Brahmaputra River

District	Total Population		Tribal population		% of Tribal to Total Population		Bodo Population		% of Bodo to Total population		% of Bodo to Total Tribal Population	
	Year		Year		Year		Year		Year		Year	
	1991	2001	1991	2001	1991	2001	1991	2001	1991	2001	1991	2001
Barpeta	1385658	1647201	110452	123266	7.97	7.48	90484	109953	6.53	6.68	81.92	89.20
Bongaigaon	807523	904835	141542	110696	17.53	12.23	79541	94435	9.85	10.44	56.20	85.31
Darrang	1298860	1504320	224957	249861	17.32	16.61	155863	188520	12.00	12.53	69.29	75.45
Kokrajhar	808730	905764	329461	304985	41.15	34.00	257079	290132	31.78	32.03	78.03	95.13
Nalbari	1016390	1148824	179641	202577	17.67	17.63	131623	159448	12.95	13.88	73.27	78.71
Dhemaji	478830	571944	210312	270496	43.92	47.29	42951	52095	8.97	9.11	20.42	19.26
Dhubri*	1324404	1637344	32260	32523	2.42	1.98	7080	8781	0.53	0.54	21.95	27.00
Kamrup*	2000071	2522324	214340	250393	10.72	9.93	42740	53008	2.14	2.10	19.94	21.17
Lakhimpur	751517	889010	177156	308864	23.57	23.49	117688	141305	15.66	15.89	66.43	45.75

Sonitpur	1424287	1681513	152498	195083	10.71	11.60	78336	94128	5.50	5.60	51.37	48.25
Demanded districts	11296270	13413079	1772619	2048744	15.69	15.27	1003385	1191805	8.88	8.89	56.64	58.17
State	22414322	26655528	2874421	3308570	12.82	12.41	1133235	1352771	5.05	5.08	41.12	40.89

Source: Census Report 1991, Govt. of India, The Bodos, Souvenir, Bodo Sahitya Sabha, 45th (2005) Issue Statistical Hand Book- 2007 Assam.

Note: Dhubri and Kamrup are located on both banks of the Brahmaputra River, so population of these two districts can't be divided.

Annexure V

Literacy Trends Among Scheduled Tribes in Assam (in Percentage)

Tribe	1991			2001			Improvement During 1990s Male Female Person Male Female Person (By Per Cent Points)
	Male	Female	Total	Male	Female	Total	
Bodo	49.77	32.53	41.15	59.81	43.00	51.48	10.33
Miri	48.46	28.98	38.72	58.42	39.43	49.12	10.4
Karbi	50.73	33.17	40.35	51.25	34.31	51.25	10.9
Rabha	55.95	32.01	44.98	64.33	48.20	56.37	11.39
Sonowal Kachari	62.60	50.62	56.11	76.22	64.66	70.52	14.41
Lalung	50.33	32.65	41.49	59.77	43.17	51.53	10.04
Dimasa	59.41	36.76	47.04	57.28	40.58	49.14	2.10
Deori	61.68	44.04	52.88	72.72	58.03	65.46	12.58
Others	53.43	45.51	49.47	58.27	42.20	50.54	1.07
State	61.24	46.32	53.78	72.30	52.40	62.52	8.74

Source: Census of India 1991 & 2001, The Bodos, Mouthpiece, Bodo Sahitya Sabha-40th (1993) & 45th (2005) *Issues.*

Annexure-VI

Union Government notification proscribing the Bodo terrorist outfit in Assam, the National Democratic Front of Bodoland (NDFB)

The Union Ministry of Home Affairs proscribed the Assam-based National Democratic Front of Bodoland on November 23, 2002. Following is text of the proscription.

MINISTRY OF HOME AFFAIRS

NOTIFICATION

NEW DELHI, THE 23RD NOVEMBER 2002

Whereas, the Bodo Security Force since rechristened at National Democratic Front of Bodoland (hereinafter referred to as the NDFB) has as its professed aim, the 'Liberation' of Bodoland resulting in bringing about the secession of the said areas from India, in alliance with other armed secessionist organisations of the North East Region and to carry on struggle for the National Liberation of the Indo-Burma region in alliance with like-minded organisations of that region and thereby, the secession of Bodoland from India;

And whereas, the Central Government is of the opinion that the NDFB has –

(i) Indulged in various illegal and violent activities intended to disrupt or which disrupt the sovereignty and territorial integrity of India in furtherance of its objective of achieving a separate Bodoland;

(ii) Aligned itself with other unlawful associations like the United Liberation Front of Asom (ULFA) and the National Council of Nagaland (NSCN) to create a separate Bodoland;

(iii) In pursuance of its aims and objectives, engaged in several unlawful and violent activities during the period when it had been declared as an unlawful association, thereby undermining the authority of the Government and spreading terror and panic among the people;

And whereas, the Central Government is further of the opinion that the violence activities include–

(i) Large scale violent and terrorist incidents including 275 killings attributed to the NDFB during the period from 23.11.2000 to 30.6.2002.

(ii) Indulging in extortions of money from businessmen, government officials and other civilians in addition to acts of kidnapping for ransom with a view to finance and execute plans for creation of a separate Bodoland;

(iii) Embarking on a systematic drive for recruitment of fresh cadres and revamping the district, anchalik and sakha committees, while continuing its terrorist and insurgency activities;

(iv) Publishing clandestine magazines highlighting the goal of the outfit and alleging exploitation by the Central Government and inciting the people to join the so-called liberation struggle thereby subverting their loyalties;

(v) Instructing its cadres to compile the list of police informers/ Government collaborators to identify targets for retaliatory action against them;

(vi) Carnage and ethnic violence resulting in killings, destruction of property and exodus of thousands of non-Bodos inhabiting in Bodo dominated areas in Assam from Bongaigaon and Barpeta districts with a view to spread panic and insecurity among non-Bodos and forcing them to migrate from Bodo areas;

(vii) Establishing camps and hideouts across the country's border to carry out its secessionist activities;

(viii) Obtaining assistance from anti-India forces in other countries to procure arms and other assistance in their struggle for creation of a separate Bodoland;

And whereas, the Central Government is also of the opinion that for the reasons aforesaid, the activities of the NDFB are detrimental to the sovereignty and integrity of India and that it is an unlawful association;

Now, therefore, in exercise of the powers conferred by sub-section 91) of Section 3 of the Unlawful Activities (Prevention) Act, 1967 (37 of 1967) the Central Government hereby declares the National Democratic Front of Bodoland (NDFB) to be in unlawful association;

And whereas, the Central Government is also of the opinion that unless the unlawful activities of the NDFB are kept under control, the organisation may re-group and re-arm itself, make fresh recruitments indulge in violent, terrorist and secessionist activities, collect funds and endanger the lives of innocent citizens and security forces personnel; and therefore, circumstances do exit which render it necessary to declare the NDFB as an unlawful association with immediate effect;

And whereas, the Central Government, having regard to the activities of the NDFB mentioned above and to meet the sustained and ever increasing violence committee by this outfit in the recent past against the police, the armed forces and the civilians, is of the firm opinion that it is necessary to declare the NDFB to be an unlawful association with immediate effect and accordingly, in exercise of the powers conferred by the proviso to sub-section (3) of Section 3, the Central Government hereby directs that this notification shall, subject to any order that may be made under section 4 of the said Act, have effect from the date of its publication in the Official Gazette.

(F. No. 11011/25/2002-NE-IV)

A.K. JAIN,

Joint Secretary, (N.E.)

Source: South Asian Terrorism Portal

Annexure VII

Chronology of ban on the NDFB

Date/Month/ Year	Authority	Provisions	Duration
23/11/1992	Union Government	Unlawful Activities (Prevention) Act, 1967	Indefinite period
21/12/2000	Union Government	Unlawful Activities (Prevention) Act, 1967	Indefinite period
31/03/2003	Assam Government	Unlawful Activities (Prevention) Act, 1967	Indefinite period
23/04/2008	Union Government	Unlawful Activities (Prevention) Act, 1967 Amendment Act, 2008.	2 Years
23/04/2010	Assam Government	Unlawful Activities (Prevention) Act, 1967, Amendment Act, 2008.	2 Years
15/12/2012	Union Government	Unlawful Activities (Prevention) Act, 1967 Amendment Act of 2008.	2 Years
22/12/2014	Union Government	Unlawful Activities (Prevention) Act, 1967, Amendment Act of 2012.	5Years

Source: Ministry of Home Affairs, Government of India

Bibliography

'1,549 civilians, 205 securitymen, 1,703 ultras killed during 2001-10'. (2010, July 13). *The Assam Tribune.*

'124 killed in Bhutan operation. (2010, September 21)'. *The Tribune.*

'16 gunned down in Bodo outfit's eye-for-an-eye attacks'. (2010, November 9). *The Telegraph.*

'32 NDFB rebels surrender'. (2011, December 4). *The Telegraph.*

'7 militant groups active in State'. (2010, March 30). *The Assam Tribune.*

'70 NDFB cadres still in B'desh'. (2011, October 2). *The Assam Tribune.*

'A father's plea to Daimary to return abducted boy'. (2010, May 6). *The Telegraph*

A Memorandum to the Honourable Chairman of the Union Public Service Commission, submitted by the Bodo Sahitya Sabha, New Delhi, January 23, 1996.

'Abduction-hit customs staff suspend work'. (2003, March 18). *The Telegraph.*

'ABSU vows to intensify Statehood movement'. (2011, February 11) *The Assam Tribune.*

ABSU, *Bodoland Movement (1986-2001): A Dream Reality*, Kokrajhar, Assam, 2001.

'AGP seeks Mohilary's arrest-Opp. Dares Dispur to book BPF chief for rebel 'link''. (2009, July 1). *The Telegraph.*

Anand, V.K. (1981). *Insurgency and Counter- Insurgency: A Study of Modern Guerrilla Warfare*. New Delhi: Deep and Deep Publications.

Annual Report, Ministry of Home Affairs, Government of India, 2002-03, 2003-04, 2004-05, 2005-06, 2006-07, 2007-08, 2008-09, 2009-10, 2010-11, 2011-12.

'Arrested'. (2008, November 20). *The Telegraph.*

'Assam moves court for Boro custody'. (2003, January 3). *The Telegraph.*

Asthana, N.C. & Nirmal, A. (2001). *Terrorism, Insurgencies and Counter-Insurgency Operations*. Jaipur: Pointer Publishers.

Azam, Kousan J., *Political Aspects of National Integration*, Meenakshi Prakashan, Meerut, 1981.

'Bandh Call'. (2009, August 4). *The Telegraph.*

Banerjee, A. C. & Roy, S. S. (2010). *Problems and prospects of Bodoland.* New Delhi: Mittal Publication.

Barbora, S. (2012, July 31). 'Identity of a recurring conflict'. *The Hindu.*

Bard, N. (1990). *Insurgency and Terrorism: Inside Modern Revolutionary Warfare.* Brassey's Virginia: Inc. Maxwell Pergamon Publishing Corporation.

Barkataki, S. (1969). *Tribes of Assam.* New Delhi: N.B.T.

Barpujari, H.K. (1990). *The Comprehensive History of Assam*, Voll-I, Guwahati: Publication Board Assam.

'Baruah trying to derail peace talks with ULFA: Gogoi'. (2010, February 13). *The Assam Tribune.*

Baruah, A. K. (1991). *Social Tensions in Assam: Middle Class Politics.* Guwahati: Purbanchal Prakashan.

Baruah, A.K. (2007). Communities and Democracy: A Northeast Indian Perspective. *North East India Studies*, Vol.1, No.1.

Baruah, S. (1999). *India Against Itself: Assam and Politics of Nationality.* New Delhi: Oxford University Press.

Baruah, S. (2005). *Durable Disorder: Understanding the Politics of North-East India.* New Delhi: Oxford University Press.

Basu, S. (1992). *Regional Movements: Politics of Language, Ethnic Identity*. Shimla: Indian Institute of Advanced Study.

Basumatary, B.K. (1992). *Plains Tribal before the Simon Commission*. Harisinga : Becon Publishers.

Basumatary, B.K. (1992). Political Aspiration of the Aboriginal Primitive Tribes vis-à-vis the United Tribal Nationalists Liberation Front. L.S. Gassah (ed.) *Regional Political Parties in North-East India* (pp 88-95). New Delhi: Omson Publication.

Basumatary, J. (2014). Quest for Peace in Assam: A Study of the Bodoland Movement. *Centre for Land Warfare Studies*, Manekshaw Paper No.44. New Delhi. Retrieved January 23, 2015, from www.claws.in/images/publication.../324891001_MP44Inside14.

Basumatary, J. K. (2007). *Sangram*. Kokrajhar: Bodo Sahitya Sabha.

'BDR assured action against NE insurgents: BSF'. (2010, March 12). *The Assam Tribune*.

'Bengal blast slur on NDFB-Bodo rebel provided RDX to KLO'. (2006, December 1). *The Telegraph*.

Bhattacharjee, C. (1993). *Ethnicity and Autonomy: Case of Bodo Kacharis of Assam*. New Delhi: Vikas Publications.

Bhattacharya, M. & Deka. D.N. (2010). Political Participation of Bodo Women in the Bodoland Movement of Assam. Sonowal, C.J. (ed). *Quest for Identity and Autonomy and Development*. Guwahati: Akansha Publication.

Bhushan, C. (2004). *Terrorism and Separatism in North- East India*. Delhi: Kalpaz Publications.

Bhuyan, A. (2005). *The Socio- Political Movement for Bodoland and Beyond: A Gendered Paradigm*. Guwahati: Peace Studies.

'Bike-owner surrenders'. (2008, November 20). *The Telegraph*.

BLTF, *Manifesto of Bodo Liberation Tigers Force*, 1996.

'BNC slams extortion bids'. (2012, January 7). *The Telegraph*.

'Bodo body meets CM for NDFB talks'. (2011, July 10). *The Assam Tribune*.

'Bodo forum slams police'. (2009, June 28). *The Telegraph*.

'Bodo group ready for talks with New Delhi'. (2002, April 2). *The Economic Times.*

'Bodo groups demand Daimary's release'. (2011, June 30). *The Telegraph.*

'Bodo groups warn NDFB-S against killings'. (2014, December 30). *The Telegraph.*

'Bodo rebel leaders held in Calcutta hotel'. (2003, May 1). *The Telegraph.*

'Bodo top gun held in Sikkim hideout swoop'. (2002, January 2). *The Telegraph.*

'Bodoland at the Cross Road'. (2012, March 13). *The Hindu.*

'Bodoland shuts down to protest fratricidal killings'. (2009, November 19). *The Hindu.*

'Bodoland to ensure security for all: NDFB-P'. (2010, June 30). *The Assam Tribune.*

'Bodos cry discrimination-Tribal organisations see bias in treatment meted out to Daimary; citizens decry trend'. (2010, May 7). *The Telegraph.*

'Bodos spew fire at rebels-Hundreds rally and shout slogans against militancy on highway'. (2009, November 9). *The Telegraph.*

'Bodos want Daimary freed'. (2010, May 6). *The Telegraph.*

'Boost for peace in release move-NDFB faction declares truce'. (2011, January 11). *The Telegraph.*

Borah, P. (2012, August). Cultural Reconstruction and Ethnic Movements in North-East India: An Analysis on the Bodo Movement. *International Journal of Social Science Tomorrow.* (pp.1-3). *Vol. 1 No. 6.*

Bordoloi, B.N. and others (1987). *Tribes of Assam (Part-I).* Guwahati: Tribal Research Institute.

Boro, A. (1994). The Rise of the Bodo Middle Class- Its Impact on Literature, Culture and Society of the Bodos. *The Bodo* (pp.11-18), 19th Issue, Guwahati.

Boro, S. (2011, November 5). 'NDFB call for Daimari's release for peace talks'. *The Assam Tribune.*

'Boycott cloud on Bodo Rally'. (2005, June 17). *The Telegraph.*

Brahma C.S. (1986). On Udayachal Movement. *Recent Trends in Political Development of the North-East.* A Monograph of the Department of Political Science, Diphu Govt. College, Diphu, Assam, Vol.1.

Brahma Choudhury, P. (2005, February 28). 'Delhi delay tests NDFB patience'. *The Telegraph.*

Brahma Choudhury, P. (2006, August 29). 'NDFB shoots with book-Outfit livid over continuous migration'. *The Telegraph.*

Brahma Choudhury, P. (2006, February 8). 'NDFB adopts new talks line-Outfit seeks facts on missing leaders before dialogue'. *The Telegraph.*

'Brahma frowns at Mohilary's trips'. (2008, June 12). *The Telegraph.*

Brahma, A. (1990). *The Emerging Role of All Bodo Students' Union in Assam Politics; A Historical Analysis, 1919-1990,* Unpublished Ph.D. Thesis, NEHU.

Brahma, K. (2012, December 12). History of the Recognition of Bodo Language as Medium of Instruction in Assam. *Language in India: Strength for Today and Bright Hope for Tomorrow.* (pp.55-64). Vol.12.

Brahma, K. (2013). *Politics of Identity: A Case Study of Bodos in Assam.* Unpublished Ph.D. Thesis, Department of Political Science, Assam University, Silchar.

Brass, P. R. (1991). *Ethnicity and Nationalism: Theory and Comparison.* New Delhi: Sage Publication.

'BTC chief wants probe-Hagrama accuses BPPF and NDFB of fratricidal killings'. (2008, June 10). *The Telegraph.*

'Cadre Killed'. (2010, January 2). *The Telegraph.*

'Ceasefire ends without alarm'. (2005, April 15). *The Telegraph.*

'Centre bans three more rebel outfits-ULFA abettors' penalised'. (2006, November 10). *The Telegraph.*

Chadha, Lt Col V. (2005). *Low Intensity Conflicts in India: An Analysis.* New Delhi: Sage Publications.

Chakladar, S. (2004). *Sub-Regional Movement in India: With reference to Bodoland and Gorkhaland.* Kolkata: K.P. Bagchi & Company Pvt. Ltd.

Chatterjee, S. K. (1974). *Kirata- Jana- Kriti.* Calcutta: Asiatic Society.

Chatterjee, S.S. (2011, August 1). Indian Militant Group Appeals to Leaders of Indian Parliament for Separate State. *News Blaze*. Retrieved from http://newsblaze.com on 28-06-2015 at 1:51.

Chaube, S.K. (1973). *Hill Politics in North-East India.* New Delhi: Orient Longman Publications.

'Chidambaram directs all-out operation against NDFB'. (2010, November 12). *The Telegraph.*

Choudhury, P.C. (1987). *The History of Civilization of the People of Assam of the Twelfth Century A.D.* Guwahati: Department of Historical and Antiquarian Studies.

'Citizenship Act amendments to be challenged in SC'. (2012, September 17). *The Assam Tribune.*

'Cops target NDFB headhunters'. (2009, December 26) *The Telegraph.*

'Custody for accused'. (2008, November 18). *The Telegraph.*

'Daimary arrest triggers hope of parleys'. (2010, May 3). *The Telegraph.*

'Daimary asserts authority'. (2008, December 28). *The Telegraph.*

'Daimary ready for talks-NDFB leader will rethink demand for sovereignty; panel pushes for unconditional dialogue'. (2010, May 5). *The Telegraph*

'Daimary signs truce with Delhi, Dispur'. (2013, November 30). *The Telegraph.*

Daimary, B. K. (1986). *Boro Politics in Assam since Independence.* Unpublished dissertation for M.Phil, NEHU.

Das,G. (1997). Understanding the Insurgency Phenomena in India's North-East. B. Pakem (ed.), *Insurgency in North- East India,* New Delhi: Omsons Publications.

Datta, P.S. (1992). Roots of Insurgency. B.C. Bhuyan (ed.), *Political Development of the North-East*, Vol.-II. New Delhi: Omsons Publications.

'Delhi rules out Bodo statehood'. (2009, July 31). *The Telegraph.*

'Delhi wants Nunisa to whittle demands'. (2009, December 2). *The Telegraph.*

'Delhi warned on Bodo talks'. (2008, May 3). *The Telegraph.*

'Demo, strike keep Bodo belt on boil'. (2009, July 29). *The Telegraph.*

Dholabhai, N. (2011, May 18). 'NDFB slams Govt 'softness for ULFA-Outfit questions preferential treatment, writes to Union Home ministry'. *The Telegraph.*

Dholabhai, N. (2013, February 2). 'NDFB-P impasse continues - Centre insists on resolution by Assam Assembly'. *The Telegraph.*

Dholabhai, N. (2014, December 23). 'NDFB accord on the horizon- Daimary group, Centre hold talks, to meet more often'. *The Telegraph*

'Dialogue link in NDFB extortion'. (2003, May 16). *The Telegraph.*

'Dispur rules out talks rush'. (2005, May 27). *The Telegraph.*

'Dispur sets pace for Bodo peace parleys'. (2004, October 26). *The Telegraph.*

Dutta Choudhury, R. (2010, March 29). 'Peace talks moving at slow pace'. *The Assam Tribune.*

Dutta Choudhury, R. (2010, May 4). 'Daimary arrest shot in the arm for Indian diplomacy'. *The Assam Tribune.*

Dutta Choudhury, R. (2011, December 4). 'Centre lines up series of talks beginning today'. *The Assam Tribune.*

Dutta Choudhury, R. (2013, September 13). 'Govt. deadline to NDFB-R to deposit arms.' *The Assam Tribune.*

Dutta Choudhury, R. (2015, February 15). 'Stress on full-scale operation against NDFB-S'. *The Assam Tribune.*

Endle, R.S. (1975). *The Kacharis.* New Delhi: Cosmos Publications & Low Price Publications.

'Ex-rebels seek leash on NDFB'. (2009, August 11) . *The Telegraph.*

'Flare-up fear in Bodo belt-Administration works on strategies to tackle violence'. (2010, April 12). *The Telegraph.*

'Forces arrest NDFB rebel'. (2011, May 12). *The Telegraph.*

'Fratricidal killings feared between NDFB-R, new faction'. (2012, November 24). *The Times of India.*

Gait, E.A. (1967). *A History of Assam*. Guwahati: Lawyer's Book Stall.

Galtung, J. (1964). A Structural Theory of Aggression. *Journal of Peace Research*. Vol. 1. Oslo: International Peace Research Institute.

George, S. J. (1994). The Bodoland Movement: Unrest to Accord. *Asian Survey*. Vol.34. No. 10, October, University of California Press. pp.878-892. Retrieved August 27, 2012, from http://www.jstor.org/stable/2644967.

Gill, K.P.S., (Ed.). (2001). *Terror and Containment Perspectives of India's Internal Security*. New Delhi: Gyan Publishing House.

'Gogoi opposes division of Assam as Centre forms panel on Bodoland'. (2014, March 1). *The North-East Times.*

'Gogoi warns of joint NDFB-ULFA attacks'. (2010, May 4). *The Telegraph.*

Goswami, A. (2003). *Combating Terrorism; The Legal Challenge*. New Delhi: Har-Anand Publications.

Goswami, S. (2003, January-June). Assam: Multiple Realignments and Fragmentation of Party System. *Journal of Indian School of Political Economy*. (pp.221-246). Vol. 15. Nos. 1&2.

'Govt begins talks with NDFB-P, DHD-N'. (2011, December 5). *The Assam Tribune.*

Grierson, G. A. (1967). *Linguistic Survey of India*, Vol.I, Part.I & Vol. I & Vol.III, Part.II, (Reprint).

Gunaratna, R. (2007). Ideology in Terrorism and Counter Terrorism: Lessons from Combating al Qaeda and al Jemaah Islamiyah in Southeast Asia. Anne Aldis & Graeme Herd (eds.), *The Ideological War on Terror: Worldwide Strategies for Counterterrorism*. New York: Routledge.

Gupta, B.N. (1989, June 24). Bodo Agitation- Problem and Prospects. *Mainstream*, Vol-7, No.39. New Delhi.

Gurr, T. R. (1968). A Casual Model of Civil Strife: A Comparative Analysis Using New Indices. *American Political Science Review*, Vol-62.

Gurr, T. R. (1974). *Why Men Rebel?* New Jersey: Princeton University Press.

Gurr, T. R. (1993). *Minorities at Risk: A Global View of Ethno-political Conflicts.*

New Jersey: Princeton University Press.

'Hagrama offer to mediate'. (2010, May 19). *The Telegraph.*

'Hagrama open to statehood'. (2008, October 1). *The Telegraph.*

Hazarika, S. (2011). *Strangers of the Mist.* New Delhi: Penguin Books.

'High alert in Guwahati following bomb explosion'. (2010, July 16). *The Assam Tribune.*

Hodgson, B. H. (n.d.). Essay the First on Koch, Boro and Dhimal Tribes. *Journal of Asiatic Society.* Calcutta. JL-1847-XVI.

Hoffman, B. (1998). *Inside Terrorism.* New York: Columbia University Press.

Huntington, S. P. (1962). Guerrilla Warfare in Theory and Policy. Franklin Mark Osanka (ed.). *Modern Guerrilla Warfare.* New York: The Free Press of Glencoe.

Huntington, S. P. (1965, April). Political Development and Political Decay. *World Politics.* The John Hopkins University Press, Vol.17., No.3.

Huntington, S. P. (1969). *Political Order in Changing Societies.* Yale: Yale University Press.

Huntington, S. P. (1996). *The Clash of Civilizations and the Remaking of World Order.* (n.d.): Simon and Schuster.

'Interpol issues Daimary alert-Red corner notice a fallout of Haldar-NDFB talks-Fratricidal clashes feared'. (2010, January 3). *The Telegraph.*

'Interpol notice against NDFB leader'. (2011, January 14). *The Assam Tribune.*

Joshi, S. (2013, July 15). '555 fake encounter cases registered across India in last four years; Rise in disturbed areas like Naxal-affected States and the north east'. *The Hindu* (New Delhi).

Juergensmeyer, M. (2000). *Terror in the Mind of God.* California: University of California Press.

Kashyap, A. (2011, February 20-26). 'Bodo Stir: The November'10 Carnage'. *Frontier.* Vol.43. No. 32.

Kashyap, S. G. (2011, Jun 21). 'NDFB pro-talk faction renews its demand for Bodoland state'. *Indian Express.* Retrieved from http://www.indianexpress.com/ on 16-09-13 at 19:49.

Kashyap, S.G. (2010, January 11), 'Bodoland badlands'. *The India Express.*

'KLO strikes coordination with NDFB faction'. (2013, September 7). *The Shillong Times.*

Kumar, B.B. (1993). *Tension and Conflict in North- East India.* New Delhi: Cosmos Publications.

Kumar, P. (2004, July-September), External Linkages and Internal Security: Assessing Bhutan's Operation All Clear. *Strategic Analysis.* (pp.390-410). Vol. 28. No. 3.

'Leaders wiser from mistakes'. (2003, February 11). *The Telegraph.*

Machahary, P. (2004). *Socio-Political Life of Boros in Karbi Anglong District of Assam.* Nagaon: Maulana Offset Press.

Maitra, K. (2001). *The Noxious Web: Insurgency in the North- East.* New Delhi: Kanishka Publishers.

Mishra, U. (2012, September 15). Bodoland: The Burden of History. *Economic and Political Weekly* (pp.36-42). Vol.XLVII. No.37.

Misra, U. (1993). *Nation Building and Development in North East India.* Guwahati: Purbanchal Prakash.

Misra, U. (1998). *North- East India: Quest for Identity.* Guwahati & New Delhi: Omsons Publications.

'Mohilary paid us Rs 50 lakh: NDFB'. (2009, July 7). *The Telegraph.*

'Mohilary withdraws truce offer'. (2008, April 1). *The Telegraph.*

Mosahari, R.N. (2002). Bodo Student Movement. A.K. Baruah (ed.). *Student Power in North-East India.* New Delhi: Regency Publications.

Mukhim, P. (2009, November 12). 'When Dreams turn sour'. *The Assam Tribune.*

'Myanmar Operation in sight'. (2004, January 3).*The Telegraph.*

'Myanmar's KIA helping Northeast rebels to create bases in China'. (2010, April 12). *The Assam Tribune.*

Nag, S. (1999). *Nationalism, Separatism and Secessionism.* Jaipur & New Delhi:

Rawat Publications.

Narzary, B. (2007). *Upendra Nath Brahma: Life and Philosophy*. Dhaligaon (BTAD): Chirang Publications Board.

Narzary, K. (1993). *Roman (English) Script and Bodo Sahitya Sabha*. Kokrajhar: (n.d.).

Narzary, P. K. (2006). Hidden Truth of Ethnic Clash between Boro Tribe and Santhals in Assam, India. *Studies on Tribes Tribal's* (pp.57-62). Vol. 4. No. 1.

Nath, M.K. (2003). Bodo Insurgency in Assam: New Accord and New Problem. *Strategic Analysis*, Vol-27 No.4.

'NDBF denies role in Bodoland clashes'. (2010, October 6). *The Telegraph.*

'NDFB appoints new chief'. (2008, December 16). *The Telegraph.*

'NDFB calls ceasefire'. (2011, July 27). *The Telegraph.*

'NDFB ceasefire on PC table-Union home minster arrives today to discuss serial blasts case, ULFA & truce'. (2008, January 1). *The Telegraph.*

'NDFB chief Ranjan Daimary held'. (2010, May 2). *The Assam Tribune.*

'NDFB declares unilateral truce'. (2011, July 27). *The Assam Tribune.*

'NDFB expels Daimary'. (2009, January 2). *The Telegraph.*

'NDFB extends ceasefire'. (2005, April 17). *The Hindu.*

'NDFB faction dares forces'. (2010, November 2). *The Telegraph.*

'NDFB formally appeals for ceasefire'. (2004, October 15) *The Assam Tribune.*

'NDFB helped Congress candidates: Mahilary'. (2009, April 27). *The Hindu.*

'NDFB hires tech-savvy youths - Outfit's publicity cell busted in Guwahati, three Bodo rebels held in Baksa'. (2010, July 31). *The Telegraph.*

'NDFB keen on sovereignty; National Democratic Front of Bodoland held a series of rallies to evolve a consensus on their demand for sovereignty'. (2005, September 16-30). *North East News Agency,* Major Events Vol. 2 Issue No. 1. Retrieved 11 November, 2013, from http://www.nenanews.com/.

'NDFB leader held in Mizoram'. (2010, December 12). *The Telegraph.*

'NDFB links with Pak come to light'. (2010, May 5). *The Assam Tribune.*

'NDFB peace process gains momentum'. (2005, June 20). *The Assam Tribune.*

'NDFB pushes for early result'. (2010, February 2). *The Telegraph.*

'NDFB reaffirms its fight for liberation of Bodoland'. (2013, October 4). *The Sentinel*

'NDFB reiterates 'war' option'. (2008, October 4). *The Telegraph.*

'NDFB rift'. (2008, December 29). *The Telegraph.*

'NDFB Screams truce 'murder'-Rebel dies in police firing during strike'. (2006, April 26). *The Telegraph.*

'NDFB Shuns charter Demand'. (2007, March 13). *The Telegraph.*

'NDFB targets migrants-Daimary faction guns down four of a family, Pro-talks group confident of ceasefire extension'. (2009, July 1). *The Telegraph.*

'NDFB truce'. (2006, May 28). *The Telegraph.*

'NDFB tussle behind blast: Police'. (2008, December 31). *The Telegraph.*

'NDFB ups 'sovereign' ante - Outfit not to settle for separate state or Union Territory'. (2005, June 28). *The Telegraph.*

'NDFB wants a Bodo state'. (2009, December 17). *The Telegraph.*

NDFB, *A Brief History of Bodo People*, Publicity Wing, 2nd Edition, 2002.

NDFB, *Manifesto of National democratic Front of Bodoland*, Publicity Wing, 2nd Edition, 2002.

'NDFB's extortion activities flayed in Karbi Anglong'. (2010, May 4). *The Assam Tribune.*

'NDFB-P blocks highway in Kokrajhar-12 hour bandh leaves goods-laden trucks to the region stranded'. (2011, January 11). *The Telegraph.*

'NDFB-P calls blockade'. (2011, February 12). *The Telegraph.*

'NDFB-P demands removal of P C Haldar'. (2012, February 18). *Times of Assam.* Retrieved from https://www.timesofassam.com/on 22-02-2014 at 22:15.

'NDFB-P demands separate Bodoland'. (2012, December 8). *The Assam Tribune.*

'NDFB-P favours China control than Indian autonomy'. (2013, July 16). *The Times of India.*

'NDFB-P links arms surrender to pact'. (2012, July 18). *The Telegraph.*

'NDFB-P meets governor - Team seeks Patnaik's help to expedite peace process'. (2011, July 15). *The Telegraph.*

'NDFB-P meets minister-Outfit submits memorandum on early solution to problem'. (2011, October 21). *The Telegraph.*

'NDFB-P outlines Bodoland area'. (2012, March 4). *The Telegraph.*

'NDFB-P pushes for statehood'. (2010, October 4). *The Telegraph.*

'NDFB-P renews demands'. (2012, July 17). *The Telegraph.*

'NDFB-P sticks to state demand Remark misread: Outfit chief'. (2013, August 19). *The Telegraph.*

'NDFB-P tables 'Bodoland' map'. (2011, June 21). *The Telegraph.*

'NDFB-P team to meet Chidambaram'. (2012, February 17). *The Telegraph.*

'NDFB-R stares at split'. (2012, November 21). *The Telegraph.*

'NDFB-R stresses statehood-Ranjan Faction says no alternative to Bodoland'. (2012, June 26).*The Telegraph.*

'New State govt. to resume peace talks: Chidambaram'. (2011, May 13). *The Telegraph.*

Nibedon, N. (1981). *North- East India: The Ethnic Explosion.* New Delhi: Lancer Publishers.

'No decision yet on NDFB truce offer: Gogoi'. (2004, October 13). *The Assam Tribune.*

'No good or bad militants'. (2010, May 7). *The Telegraph.*

'Non-Bodos oppose bifurcation of Assam'. (2012. August 16). *Times of India.*

'Old link in tea rebel payoff'. (2003, May 4). *The Telegraph*

'Panel to look into Bodoland-Pillai to submit report in nine months'. (2014, February 28). *The Telegraph.*

Pape, R. A. (2005). *Dying to Win: The Strategic Logic of Suicide Terrorism.* London: Random House.

'PC hints at softening of stand'. (2010, January 1). *The Telegraph.*

'Peace at a premium'. (2004, November 5). *The Hindu.*

'Peace rally'. (2003, April 22). *The Telegraph*

Pegu, J. (2004). *Reclaiming Identity: A Discourse on Bodo History.* Kokrajhar: Jwngsar Publications.

Phanjoubam, T. (1996). *Insurgency Movement in North- Eastern India.* New Delhi: Vikash Publishing House.

Phukan, G. (1996). *Politics of Regionalism in North-East India.* Guwahati: Spectrum Publications.

Poland, J. (1993). *Understanding Terrorism: Groups, Strategies, and Responses.* New Jersey: Prentice Hall.

Prakash, V. (2008). *Terrorism in India's North- East: A Gathering Storm,* Vol- I. New Delhi: Kalpaz Publications.

'Pro-talks Bodo leader's kin killed'. (2010, January 3). *The Telegraph.*

'Pro-Talks rebel held'. (2009, May 27). *The Telegraph.*

'Protests, relief for students in BTAD Bike rally over influx'. (2012, October 3). *The Telegraph.*

Pulloppilil, T. & Jacob A. (Ed.). (2001). *The Bodos: Children of Bhullumbutter.* Guwahati: Spectrum Publications.

'Pull-out threat after killings-NDFB alleges violation of truce rules'. (2006, August 3). *The Telegraph.*

Rajagopalan, S. (2008). *Peace Accords in North-East India: Journey over Milestones.* Washington: East-West Center.

'Rebel chief in flip-flop'. (2008, March 31). *The Telegraph.*

'Rebel death triggers NDFB ire'. (2004, November 7). *The Telegraph.*

'Rebel in police custody'. (2002, December 7). *The Telegraph.*

'Rebel reveals bomb plan-NDFB training Meghalaya militants on explosives'. (2011, February 18). *The Telegraph.*

'Rebels arrested'. (2012, March 13). *The Telegraph.*

'Rebels held'. (2009, September 15). *The Telegraph.*

Reich, W. (1990). *Origins of Terrorism: Psychologies, Ideologies, Theologies, States of Mind.* New York: Cambridge University Press.

'Remanded'. (2009, November 10). *The Telegraph.*

'Roadmap to Boroland'. (2012, February 8). *Bodosa.*

Roy Burman, J.J. (2010). The Bodoland Ethnic Conflict. C.J. Sonowal (ed.) *Quest for Identity, autonomy and development: The Contemporary trends of ethnic and tribal assertion in Assam*, Vol.2. New Delhi: Akansha Publishing House.

Roy, A. (1995). *The Boro Imbroglio.* Guwahati: Spectrum Publications.

Runciman, W.G. (1966). *Relative Deprivation and Social Justice.* London: Routledge and Kegan Paul.

Saikia, P. (2011). Political Opportunities, Constraints, and Mobilising Structures: An Integrated Approach to Different Levels of Ethno-Political Contention in Northeast India. *India Review (pp.1-39).*10:10.

Sanyal, C.C. (1973). *The Meches and the Totos of North Bengal.* (n.d.): The University of North Bengal.

Sarma, P. (2008, November 19). 'Key Conspirator named-An NDFB rebel, who was part of the blast plan, was in police custody just a week before the attacks'. *The Telegraph.*

Sarma, P. (2014, December 22). 'Rajiv fuelled Bodo unrest: Mahanta'. *The Telegraph.*

Scruton, R. (1982). *A Dictionary of Political Thought.* New York: Hill & Wang.

'Security Troops Continue Operations to Flush Indian Militants Out of Bhutan'. (2003, December 20). *The Kuensel.* Retrieved November 28, 2009, from http://kuenselonline.com.

Sengupta, S. (2010). Socio Political assertion of the Bodos: An Analysis. C.J. Sonowal (ed.), *Quest for Identity, autonomy and development: The Contemporary trends of ethnic and tribal assertion in Assam*, Vol.2. New Delhi: Akansha Publishing House.

Sengupta, S. (2014, August). Extremist Politics as an Instrument of Ethnic Assertions among the Bodos of Northeast India. *Journalism and Mass Communication.* (pp.527-534). Vol.4, No.8.

'Serial blasts key accused arrested'. (2010, December 12). *The Assam Tribune.*

Settlement of Bodo Accord- A Memorandum to the Honourable Chief Minister of Assam Shri Hiteswar Saikia and the Honourable Minister of State (Internal Security) Shri Rajesh Pilot, submitted by the All Bodo Students' Union and Bodo Peoples' Action Committee, Guwahati, March, 1993.

Sharma, C. K. (2000). The Bodo Movement: A Preliminary Enquiry into the role of the Middle Class and the State. Girin Phukan (ed.). *Political Dynamics of North-East India.* New Delhi: South Asian Publishers.

Singh, A. K. (2008). *Ethnicity and Security of India: A Case Study of North East.* Allahabad: Anubhav Publishing House.

Singh, B. (2002). *Autonomy Movements and Federal India.* Jaipur & New Delhi: Rawat Publications.

Singh, C. (2004). *North- East: Politics and Insurgency.* Omsons Publications: Manash Publications.

'Six more fall to NDFB vendetta- Outfit warns of killing spree'. (2010, November 10). *The Telegraph.*

'Sleuths smell NDFB role in abduction'. (2011, February 10). *The Telegraph.*

'Slow start to Bodo bandh'. (2011, August 27). *The Telegraph.*

'Some NDFB-R rebels joined outfit's hardline faction'. (2013, September 17). *The Times of India.*

Sondhi, M.L. (Ed.). (2000). *Terrorism and Political Violence: A Source Book.* New Delhi: Har-Anand Publications.

'Songbijit 'ousted' from NDFB'. (2015, June 27). *The Sentinel.*

Sonowal, K. (2013). *Why Bodo Movement?* Guwahati: EBH Publishers.

South Asian Terrorism Portal (SATP). Incidents Involving NDFB. Retrieved from http://www.satp.org/satporgtp/countries/india/states/assam/terrorist_outfits/ndfb.htm.

Souvenir of 1st Conference of BPF, Udalguri, BTC, 2007.

'SP warns of Bodo clashes'. (2009, August 12). *The Telegraph.*

Srikanth, H . (2000, November 18), Militancy and Identity Politics in Assam. *Economic and Political Weekly.* (pp. 4117- 4124).

Suykens, B. (2006, June). Internal Borders and Conflict: Lessons from Bodoland, Assam (India). *Conflict Research Group*, Working paper No. 5.

'Talks nod for Ulfa, NDFB'. (2010, February 2). *The Telegraph.*

Talukdar, S. (2007, April 4). 'Fears of Fratricide in Bodo Heartland'. *The Hindu.*

Talukdar, S. & Brahma Choudhury. P. (2003, February 17). 'ABSU woos last outfit standing'. *The Telegraph.*

Talukdar, S. (2005, June 18). 'Bodos hail Ceasefire agreement'. *The Hindu.*

Talukdar, S. (2010, June 4). 'Cautious hopes'. *The Hindu.*

Talukdar, S. (2010, November 13). 'Apprehend NDFB faction leaders, Chidambaram tells security forces'. *The Hindu.*

Talukdar, S. (2010, November 20). 'New Body of Bodos to work for Statehood'. *The Hindu.*

'Tea garden owner killed in Sootea'. (2012, November 14). *The Assam Tribune.*

'Telangana no justification for creating Bodoland: Non-Bodo forum'. (2013, August 8). *The Times of India.*

'Three more killed by NDFB militants, toll rises to 21'. (2010, November 10). *Deccan Herald.*

'Top Assam police officials interrogate NDFB chief'. (2010, May 1). *The Assam Tribune.*

'Top Boro leader held'. (2003, January 2). *The Hindu.*

'Train services hit after derailments'. (2011, August 2). *The Assam Tribune.*

'Trains stranded in blockade belt'. (2007, May 25). *The Telegraph.*

'Treat Daimary like arrested ULFA leaders'. (2010, May 5). *The Assam Tribune.*

'Truce call-off hint on NDFB agenda'. (2009, September 23). *The Telegraph.*

'Truce thrust to early talks - Gogoi to bring NDFB to table soon'. (2004, October 20). *The Telegraph.*

'Twin rallies decry illegal migration'. (2012, October 12). *The Telegraph.*

'Two forest officials abducted'. (2003, June 4). *The Telegraph.*

'Two NDFB-S cadres killed- Hostage rescued after gun battle in'. (2014, December 22). *The Telegraph.*

Udangsri, A Souvenir published by the Information and Publicity Wing NDFB on the Occasion of Celebrating 21st Anniversary of Foundation Day, National Democratic Front of Bodoland, 2007.

'ULFA Warns Bodo Militants'. (1997, February 10). *Business Standard.*

'UPDF Contesting in BTC Elections for NDFB'. (2010, April 5). *Bodosa.*

Varghese, B. G. (1996). *India's North-East Resurgent: Ethnicity, Insurgency, Governance, Development.* New Delhi: Konark Publishers Pvt. Ltd.

Verma, B. (1998). *Insurgency and Counter- Insurgency.* New Delhi: Uppal Publications.

Why Separate State? To the President of India, the Prime Minister of India and the Home Minister of India, New Delhi, a Memorandum submitted by All Bodo Students' Union, Kokrajhar, November 10, 1987.

Wilkinson, P. (1974). *Political Terrorism.* London: MacMillan.

'Will kill 20 Indians for one Bodo: NDFB'. (2010, November 2). *Hindustan Times.*

Acknowledgements

I express my profound gratitude to all those persons who have directly or indirectly helped me in the course of this work. First of all, I would like to express my heartfelt gratitude to Dr Susmita Sen Gupta, Associate Professor, North-Eastern Hill University, Shillong, who encouraged me to endevour for this work. I also owe my gratefulness to Dr. J.L. Narzary, Principal, Bodofa U.N. Brahma College, Dotma for his words of encouragement. I have no adjective to explain the amount of assistance provided by Dr Santosh Borah in analysing the data and interpreting the results. My special thanks are also due for Dr. Shasanka Shekhar Sharma, Kamal Kr. Brahma and Chilarai Mushahary, my sincere colleagues, who always help me to ignite my mind. I am equally thankful to them whose words of discouragement and consistent aggravation inspired me to complete this work.

It is a matter of cherished and lifelong commemoration for the generous aid that my wife Dipanjali has been offering. I am really grateful to my wife and daughter Adrita for their continuous endurance of my absence from home in connection with this work. It is a matter of great regret that I missed the nostalgic moment of Adrita's first walk. I acknowledge the tremendous efforts of my father Mr. Chandra Hakhrari, mother Mrs. Padmeswari Thakuria, brother Arun and his wife Madhavi, sister Karabi, brother-in-law Nijwm and my Mother-in-Law, each of who enabled me to reach this stage of my life.

Above all, I consider it my duty to express my deep sense of gratitude and sincere sense of indebtedness to those authors and publishers whom I missed to refer at the right place. I request them to accept those as unintentional error, and appeal to them to notify me about the same via the publishers of this book and provide opportunity to rectify in the next editions.

Last but not the least, I should also thank Avi Publishers, New Delhi, and their Editorial Team for their suggestions and bringing out this book on time.

January, 2017 Nabin Hakhrari

Index

B

C

D

E